Caregiving Without Losing Yourself

Caregiving Without Losing Yourself

Boundaries, Guilt, and Daily Stability

Kaia Solander

Mindful Pages

Published in 2026

ISBN: 9788169888714 (PB)
ISBN: 9788169888707 (eBook)

Published by

Mindful Pages
Imprint of Alpha Editions LLC
312 W. 2nd St #1834
Casper, WY 82601, USA

Content

Introduction

Caregiving often begins in a language too small for what it will become. You are "popping in". You are "checking on things". You are "helping out for a bit". At first, the work may seem manageable because it arrives disguised as ordinary kindness: a lift to an appointment, a few phone calls, a weekly shop, a reminder about tablets, a conversation with a doctor, a form completed late at night when everyone else has gone to bed.

Then, almost without ceremony, the centre of gravity shifts. The occasional favour becomes the expected arrangement. The small task becomes the system. You are no longer simply visiting; you are monitoring. You are no longer merely supporting; you are coordinating. You are no longer responding to one need; you are holding together a fragile network of medicines, meals, moods, appointments, paperwork, family opinions, professional advice, financial worries, emotional outbursts, practical risks, and the quiet terror of what might happen if you stop paying attention.

This is one of the most confusing truths about caregiving: it can make you feel both indispensable and invisible. Everyone relies on you, yet few people see the cost. They may notice when something goes wrong, but not the hours of prevention that kept a dozen other things from going wrong. They may praise your patience, but not notice how often patience has become exhaustion in formal clothing. They may assume you are coping because you are still functioning, still answering messages, still turning up, still remembering, still smoothing over, still saying, "It's fine," when what you mean is, "I do not know how much longer I can do this in the same way."

This book is for the family caregiver, close supporter, adult child, spouse, sibling, friend, neighbour, or informal organiser who has become the reliable person in someone else's life while slowly becoming unreliable to themselves. It is for the person who feels guilty when they rest, resentful when they are needed, ashamed of their resentment, and afraid that setting limits will make them look cold, selfish, or ungrateful. It is for the person who loves someone deeply and still needs the current arrangement to change.

Caregiving Without Losing Yourself is built on a firm conviction: care that destroys the carer is not sustainable care. It may look noble from the outside for a while. It may be praised by people who do not have to live inside it. It may even appear efficient because one person is carrying what should have been shared, planned, funded, discussed, or redesigned. But eventually, an overloaded caregiver becomes part of the crisis. Exhaustion changes judgement. Sleeplessness shrinks patience. Constant pressure corrodes relationships. Unclear roles breed conflict. Unspoken expectations turn love into obligation and obligation into bitterness.

The answer is not to care less. The answer is to care with structure, limits, honesty, and a daily rhythm that a real human being can survive.

Many caregivers are told, directly or indirectly, that the solution is to become more selfless. This advice is not only inadequate; it is dangerous. The problem is rarely that caregivers lack devotion. More often, the problem is that devotion has been allowed to operate without boundaries, without support, without recovery, and without a truthful account of the load being carried. You cannot solve structural strain with private guilt. You cannot organise a complex care situation by simply trying harder. You cannot build stability out of endless emergency.

The work begins by telling the truth.

The truth is that caregiving is work, even when it is done with love. Emotional labour is work. Remembering is work. Anticipating is work. Being available is work. Sitting in waiting rooms is work. Managing another person's fear, confusion, frustration, or disappointment is work. Explaining the same thing to different relatives is work. Chasing prescriptions, checking supplies, arranging transport, listening for changes in mood, noticing whether food has been eaten, watching for signs of decline, and absorbing other people's opinions are all forms of work.

Because much of this work is invisible, caregivers often underestimate their own burden. They measure only the obvious hours and ignore the mental tabs left open all day. They count the visit, but not the worry before it or the recovery afterwards. They count the appointment, but not the scheduling, persuading, travelling, waiting, explaining, updating, and rearranging that surround it. They count the crisis, but not the weeks of quiet vigilance that made the crisis less severe than it could have been.

This invisibility matters because what is not named cannot be negotiated. A care load that remains vague will always expand. A responsibility that is not defined will always drift towards the most conscientious person. A family system that runs on assumptions will usually reward the person who complains least by giving them the most to carry.

One of the central tasks of this book is to make the invisible visible. Not for blame. Not to build a case against the person receiving care. Not to create a courtroom in which every relative must be found guilty or innocent. The purpose is practical accuracy. You cannot set a fair boundary around a workload you have not measured. You cannot ask for meaningful help when you cannot describe what needs doing. You cannot decide what must change first if everything is felt as one large, unbearable fog.

Once the real care load is visible, the next task is to separate responsibility from over-functioning. These two are often confused. Responsibility says, "This matters, and I will take my proper part." Over-functioning says, "Because this matters, I must absorb every gap, prevent every discomfort, compensate for every absent person, and override my own limits indefinitely." Responsibility is ethical. Over-functioning is a slow disappearance.

This distinction is essential because many caregivers are trapped by a cruelly narrow idea of duty. They believe that being loving means being constantly available. They believe that being dependable means never disappointing anyone. They believe that saying no to a request means saying no to the person. They believe that if something needs doing and they can physically do it, then they must do it, regardless of the cost.

A more mature definition of duty is needed. Duty is not the abandonment of the self. Duty is a commitment to act wisely within reality. It includes the recipient's needs, the caregiver's capacity, the available resources, the likely consequences, and the long-term viability of the arrangement. A duty that ignores your sleep, health, work, parenting, marriage, finances, friendships, and emotional stability is not a higher form of love. It is an unstable contract with eventual collapse.

Boundaries are the practical expression of that mature duty.

There is a great deal of misunderstanding around boundaries, especially in families. Boundaries are often treated as rejection, punishment, selfishness, or emotional distance. In truth, a boundary is not an attempt to control another person. It is a clear limit around what you will do, when you are available, what you can carry, and what conditions are necessary for you to continue providing care without becoming harmed by the arrangement.

A boundary does not say, "You are not allowed to need me." It says, "This is how I can help without breaking." It does not say, "Your feelings do not matter." It says, "Your feelings cannot be the only factor in every decision." It does not say, "I no longer care." It says, "Care must now become more honest, more shared, and more sustainable."

This is why boundaries must be concrete. Vague boundaries collapse under pressure. "I need more time for myself" is true, but it is too easy for others to ignore, debate, or sentimentalise. "I do not take non-urgent calls after 9 p.m." is harder to distort. "I can coordinate appointments, but I cannot provide transport every week" gives the care system something to work with. "I will visit on Wednesdays and Sundays, and emergencies need to go through the agreed contact plan" turns exhaustion into policy. Good boundaries reduce the need for repeated emotional negotiation because they make the terms visible before the next crisis arrives.

Of course, boundaries do not remove guilt. In fact, the moment a caregiver begins to set limits, guilt often becomes louder. This does not mean the boundary is wrong. It means the old system is being challenged.

Guilt is one of the most powerful forces in caregiving because it often masquerades as morality. It tells you that discomfort is evidence of wrongdoing. It tells you that someone else's disappointment is proof that you have failed. It tells you that a good daughter, son, spouse, sibling, or friend would do more, stay longer, answer faster, feel kinder, need less, and somehow manage without complaint.

But guilt is not a ruler. It is not qualified to govern your life. At times, guilt is useful; it may signal that you need to repair, reconsider, apologise, or act. At other times, it is simply the emotional echo of old expectations, family pressure, cultural scripts, grief, fear, or comparison. The task is not to eliminate guilt entirely. The task is to interpret it intelligently.

A central question throughout this book is: "Is this truly mine to carry?" That question is not an escape route from responsibility. It is a safeguard against false responsibility. You may be responsible for making a reasonable plan. You are not responsible for being the entire plan. You may be responsible for speaking honestly. You are not responsible for ensuring no one ever feels upset by the truth. You may be responsible for helping with essential needs. You are not responsible for curing loneliness, reversing ageing, healing family history, or filling every gap left by unavailable people and imperfect systems.

This distinction changes the emotional architecture of caregiving. It allows you to respond to guilt without surrendering to it. It allows you to make deliberate decisions instead of reflexive sacrifices. It allows you to say, "I feel guilty, and I am still choosing the sustainable option." That sentence may feel uncomfortable at first, but it is often the beginning of genuine stability.

Stability also requires conversation. Not dramatic confrontation. Not a speech delivered after months of silent suffering. Not a desperate explosion when one more request becomes one too many. Sustainable care depends on clear, repeated, practical conversations about needs, limits, roles, and next steps.

Many caregivers avoid these conversations because they fear anger, tears, accusation, or manipulation. They worry that if they speak plainly, they will be seen as cruel. Yet silence has its own cruelty. When expectations remain unspoken, resentment grows. When agreements are vague, people disappoint one another without always knowing how. When one caregiver keeps absorbing the strain, others may genuinely fail to understand how serious the situation has become.

Clear requests are an act of respect. They give other people the chance to respond to reality rather than guess at it. "I need more help" is emotionally honest, but it rarely produces change. "Can you take Dad to his Tuesday appointment once a month?" is far more useful. "Everyone needs to step up" may be understandable, but it can invite defensiveness. "I am no longer able to handle all medication refills. I need one person to take over ordering and collecting them by Friday" creates a path.

This book will help you prepare for those conversations, stay steady during them, and document what has been agreed afterwards. That final step matters more than many families realise. Caregiving systems often fall apart not because people are malicious, but because memory, stress, and assumption make poor administrators. A shared calendar, a written summary, a checklist, or a clear message confirming who is doing what can prevent entire cycles of conflict. Documentation is not cold. It is relational protection. It reduces the number of arguments built on "I thought you meant" and "No one told me."

The work of care also needs a wider circle. One person may be central, but one person should not be the entire infrastructure. Support networks can include relatives, friends, neighbours, faith communities, voluntary organisations, local services, professionals, and paid help where available. The goal is not perfect fairness. Perfect fairness is often impossible and can become its own trap. The goal is workable distribution.

Some people can give time. Some can give money. Some can drive. Some can sit and listen. Some can manage forms. Some can cook. Some can make phone calls. Some can provide respite for one hour a week. Some cannot be trusted with sensitive tasks but can still collect groceries. A sustainable system matches tasks to capacity rather than chasing an idealised version of equality.

This requires caregivers to stop making vague appeals and start making bounded requests. People are more likely to help when they understand exactly what is needed, how long it will take, when it must happen, and what standard is required. "Could you help more?" often leaves people uncertain. "Could you visit for ninety minutes every second Saturday so I can have a fixed break?" is harder to misunderstand. Good requests reduce emotional labour because they prevent the caregiver from having to explain the entire situation afresh each time.

Yet help can create chaos if it is not designed well. Many caregivers know the frustration of finally getting assistance, only to spend more energy correcting mistakes, answering constant questions, or repairing the consequences of a poorly handled task. This is where handoffs, checklists, backups, and simple standards matter. A care system should not rely on one person's memory as its operating manual. The more information lives only in your head, the more trapped you become.

Daily routines are another form of liberation. This may sound modest, even dull, but routine is one of the most powerful tools in caregiving. Crisis care is exhausting because every problem demands a fresh decision. Stable routines reduce the number of decisions required. They create predictability. They prevent small problems from becoming large ones. They make it easier for other people to step in. They calm the nervous system because not everything has to be invented anew each day.

The best routines are not elaborate. They are repeatable. A morning check-in. A medication cue. A default meal plan. A weekly supply review. A fixed time for family updates. A folder with essential information. A regular rest block after a difficult visit. These small structures do not remove the emotional complexity of caregiving, but they reduce the avoidable chaos around it. A routine that works on a bad day is worth more than a beautiful schedule that collapses the first time reality interferes.

This book is deliberately practical because caregivers do not need more abstract admiration. They need usable ways to reduce the daily load. They need language for difficult conversations. They need decision rules when guilt is loud. They need a method for seeing what is actually happening. They need systems that survive tiredness. They need permission, yes, but permission alone is not enough. They need structure.

Burnout is the warning sign that structure, support, and recovery are insufficient for the load being carried. It is not always dramatic. It may appear as numbness, irritability, forgetfulness, dread, impatience, resentment, cynicism, or the sense that you have become a harsher version of yourself. Many caregivers ignore these signs because they believe collapse is the only legitimate proof that something is wrong. This is a serious mistake. By the time collapse arrives, options have narrowed.

Burnout signals should be treated as operational data. They tell you that the current system is exceeding capacity. They are not evidence that you are weak, unloving, or unsuited to care. They are evidence that a human being is being asked to function beyond sustainable limits. When those signals appear, the question is not, "How do I shame myself into carrying on?" The question is, "What must change in the system before the system damages everyone inside it?"

Recovery must therefore be built into the care plan, not left as a reward for when everything else is finished. Everything else is never finished. Caregiving produces an endless queue of possible tasks, and if rest must wait until the queue is empty, rest will never come. Recovery may begin in small forms: ten minutes outside, a protected cup of tea, an evening without care calls, a short walk after a hard conversation, one morning a week that belongs to your own life. It may also require larger forms: respite, paid support, rotating duties, professional guidance, or a change in living arrangements. The scale will vary, but the principle remains the same. A caregiver without recovery is not being efficient. They are being depleted.

Resentment deserves particular honesty. It is one of the emotions caregivers most often hide because it feels incompatible with love. Yet resentment is not proof that love has disappeared. More often, it is proof that something has become unjust, unseen, coerced, or repeatedly violated. It may point to workload. It may point to disrespect. It may point to grief. It may point to the pain of watching life narrow around someone else's needs. It may point to the absence of choice.

The goal is not to pretend resentment away. The goal is to understand what it is trying to reveal and then act before it hardens into contempt. Sometimes repair begins with an apology: "I snapped yesterday." But repair must not become self-erasure. A mature repair might continue: "I am sorry for how I spoke. I am still not available after 9 p.m., and we need a different plan for evenings." This is how relationships are protected without returning to the old pattern.

Caregiving also threatens identity. The danger is not only that you become tired. It is that you become reduced. Friendships fade because you keep cancelling. Hobbies disappear because they seem indulgent. Ambitions shrink because there is no room to think. The future becomes a luxury you cannot afford. Eventually, you may feel less like a person than a function: the driver, the caller, the organiser, the fixer, the one who knows.

This book argues that keeping your identity intact is not a sentimental extra. It is part of mental stability. You need parts of life that are not organised around care. One relationship that knows you beyond your usefulness. One activity that returns you to yourself. One goal that points beyond the current demands. These anchors may be small, but they resist the totalising force of caregiving. They remind you that devotion to another person does not require disappearance from your own life.

Finally, sustainable caregiving must adapt. Needs change. Illness changes. Mobility changes. Memory changes. Services change. Family availability changes. Your own capacity changes. A care plan that once worked may become unsafe or unrealistic later. This is not failure. It is maintenance.

A strong long-term care plan is not a rigid document pretending to control the future. It is a living overview of roles, routines, risks, contacts, thresholds, and next steps. It answers the questions that cause panic when left unanswered: Who does what? What happens if the main caregiver is unavailable? Which changes mean more help is needed? Where is the medication list? Who should be contacted in an emergency? What decisions are likely to arise next? What will we do if this arrangement stops working?

Planning cannot remove uncertainty, but it can reduce chaos. It can turn fear into preparation. It can prevent every transition from arriving as a shock. It can also make review normal. A monthly reset — what is working, what is breaking, what must be renegotiated — keeps care humane. It prevents the dangerous fantasy that the only acceptable path is to endure silently until endurance is no longer possible.

The deepest promise of this book is not that caregiving will become easy. Some seasons of care are genuinely hard. Some decisions are painful. Some family systems are unfair. Some services are difficult to access. Some losses cannot be organised into comfort. A practical book should never insult caregivers by pretending that a checklist can remove grief, fear, or complexity.

The promise is different: caregiving can become less chaotic, less lonely, less guilt-driven, and less destructive to the person providing it. You can learn to see the load clearly. You can set limits without cruelty. You can respond to guilt without obeying it. You can ask for help in ways people can understand. You can build routines that reduce avoidable crises. You can recognise burnout before it governs you. You can repair resentment without surrendering your boundaries. You can remain a person while being a caregiver.

This is not a book about doing less because you care less. It is a book about caring in a way that can last.

The central question is not, "How much can I force myself to carry?" It is, "What kind of care can remain humane for everyone involved, including me?"

That question is where sustainable caregiving begins.

Chapter 1
What Sustainable Care Requires

How can care be given with devotion and still become unsustainable? The question sounds almost disloyal when spoken aloud, especially by someone who loves the person receiving care. Care is supposed to be the proof of commitment, the visible shape of loyalty. Yet many caregivers discover that devotion alone does not decide what a human body can endure, what a household can absorb, or what a life can keep giving without beginning to fray.

The confusion often starts at the kitchen table, with a calendar open, a phone nearby, and a small list of tasks that look harmless in isolation. A prescription to collect. A form to complete. A call to return. A visit to arrange. None of these appears large enough to justify distress. But the list keeps renewing itself, and behind each task sits another layer of vigilance: remembering, anticipating, checking, soothing, explaining, correcting, preventing. The caregiver may still describe the whole arrangement as "just helping", even when help has quietly become a second life.

This is the paradox at the heart of sustainable care: the more reliable you become, the easier it is for the system around you to stop noticing the cost of your reliability. Your competence becomes the reason more is handed to you. Your kindness becomes the argument for asking again. Your silence becomes evidence that the current arrangement is acceptable. Before long, the question is no longer whether you care enough, but whether care has been allowed to expand beyond the boundaries of a liveable human life.

The central tension is not between love and limits. That is the false choice that traps so many caregivers. The real tension is between care that is emotionally sincere and care that is structurally possible. A person can be deeply committed and still unable to provide daily transport, constant availability, emotional containment, household management, medical coordination, and family diplomacy without serious consequences. Love may explain why you began, but it cannot by itself design a sustainable load.

This matters because caregiving arrangements rarely collapse in one dramatic moment. They usually erode. Sleep shortens. Patience thins. Work becomes harder to manage. Friendships are postponed until they stop expecting you. Your own appointments are delayed because someone else's needs feel more urgent. You become sharper in conversations, then guilty for being sharp, then more determined to compensate by doing even more. The decline is subtle enough to be denied and serious enough to change the quality of care itself.

A caregiver who is constantly stretched does not simply suffer privately. Their depletion enters the care system. Decisions become more reactive. Small problems feel intolerable. Requests sound like accusations. Family discussions become loaded with old resentments because there is no spare capacity left for generosity. The person receiving care may sense the strain and feel like a burden, which can create more distress, more reassurance, and more emotional labour. No one benefits when endurance is mistaken for stability.

The deeper issue is that many caregivers have inherited a definition of duty that is too blunt for the realities they face. Duty is treated as a moral demand to keep saying yes, especially when the need is real and the person is vulnerable. But a serious duty must include the conditions required for that duty to be carried out over time. It must ask what is possible across months, not merely what can be forced through today. It must recognise that a care load does not become sustainable because it is important; it becomes sustainable only when it fits within an actual life.

From there, the focus widens. Commitment has to be separated from over-functioning, so that being present does not become being endlessly available. The caregiver's wellbeing has to be placed inside the care equation, not outside it as an optional preference. The pattern of short-term rescue has to be examined with clear eyes, because every "just this once" has the power to become the arrangement everyone later treats as normal. The movement is from impulse to awareness, from strain to design, from private coping to a more honest account of what care truly requires.

This does not mean becoming cold, calculating, or detached. It means refusing to build care on denial. Sustainable care asks for a different kind of courage from the dramatic courage of emergency response. It asks for the courage to name limits before resentment speaks for you. It asks for the courage to include yourself before your body forces the issue. It asks for the courage to disappoint someone in a small, truthful way rather than preserve an arrangement that will eventually disappoint everyone more deeply.

The kitchen table will still hold its calendar, its messages, its reminders, its unfinished calls. The work will not vanish because you decide to see it clearly. But clarity changes the question. Instead of asking, "How do I keep carrying all of this without complaint?" the more honest question begins to press forward: "Which parts of this load are truly mine, and which parts have I accepted simply because no one has been made to face the limit yet?"

Redefining Duty and Limits

Duty is one of the most powerful words in caregiving, and one of the most easily misused. It can hold a family together when circumstances become difficult. It can keep a promise alive when illness, ageing, disability, grief, or frailty changes the shape of everyday life. It can remind a tired person that love is not only a feeling, but a series of practical acts performed when convenience has disappeared.

But duty can also become a trap when it is left undefined.

Many caregivers begin with a decent instinct: someone needs help, and they are able to provide it. There is nothing wrong with that instinct. In fact, much of the best care in families and communities begins there, in the quiet willingness to notice a need and respond. The difficulty comes when every need is treated as a command, every gap as your responsibility, and every moment of hesitation as moral failure. At that point, duty has stopped being a guide. It has become a pressure system.

A sustainable caregiving life requires a sharper definition. Duty does not mean doing everything that could possibly be done. Duty does not mean becoming the only reliable person in the room. Duty does not mean allowing your health, work, marriage, parenting, friendships, finances, and emotional stability to be slowly consumed because the need is real. A need can be real and still not be wholly yours to meet.

This distinction can feel uncomfortable because caregivers are often surrounded by urgent emotion. The person receiving care may be frightened, frustrated, lonely, confused, ashamed, or resistant. Other relatives may be absent, critical, impractical, or full of advice they do not intend to carry out. Professionals may offer recommendations that sound simple on paper but demand hours of unpaid labour in practice. Friends may say, "You must look after yourself," then disappear when actual help is needed. In that environment, the caregiver can begin to believe that the only honourable response is to absorb whatever lands in front of them.

That belief is not compassion. It is over-functioning dressed as virtue.

Commitment and over-functioning are not the same thing. Commitment says, "I will take this seriously." Over-functioning says, "I will take this all on myself." Commitment stays connected to reality. Over-functioning tries to defeat reality through effort. Commitment can be honest about fatigue, competing responsibilities, and practical limits. Over-functioning treats limits as evidence of personal failure. Commitment strengthens care over time. Over-functioning often makes care more fragile because it depends on one person remaining indefinitely available, capable, patient, and well.

The caregiver who over-functions often looks admirable from the outside. They know the appointment schedule. They remember the medication changes. They speak to the professionals. They manage the shopping, the forms, the transport, the phone calls, the emotional reassurance, the family updates, and the sudden crises. Others may describe them as wonderful, devoted, saintly, tireless. These words can sound like praise, but sometimes they are also a way of keeping the arrangement unchanged. If you are "the strong one", everyone else has permission to remain less strong. If you are "amazing", fewer people have to ask whether the current system is fair.

The danger is that admiration can become a polite form of abandonment.

A healthier definition of duty begins with a simple truth: a care load must fit a human life. Not an ideal life. Not a fantasy version of you who never gets ill, tired, resentful, distracted, or overwhelmed. Not a version of you who has no job, no children, no partner, no body, no bills, no private grief, no future. A real life. A life with finite hours, finite emotional energy, and finite capacity for disruption.

To say that a care load must fit a human life is not to reduce care to convenience. It is to respect the conditions under which care can continue. A bridge is not stronger because more weight is placed upon it. A caregiver is not more loving because every limit has been ignored. Stability depends on load-bearing truth. When the weight exceeds the structure, something will give, and it will rarely give in a graceful or planned way.

The first practical shift is to stop asking, "Can I do this today?" and begin asking, "Can I keep doing this over time?" These are very different questions. Many caregivers can manage almost anything once. They can cancel plans, miss sleep, rearrange work, drive across town, absorb a difficult conversation, stay late, answer at midnight, or solve a last-minute problem. The fact that something can be done once does not mean it can become the standing arrangement.

This is where caregiving systems quietly become dangerous. A one-off rescue becomes a pattern. A pattern becomes an expectation. An expectation becomes a duty. No one may formally announce this transition, but everyone begins to behave as though it has occurred. You drove to the appointment once, so now transport is yours. You answered the late call once, so now late calls are normal. You handled the paperwork once, so now every form finds its way to you. You calmed the argument once, so now you are the family regulator.

The question is not whether you should ever make exceptions. Real care sometimes requires flexibility. The question is whether you are noticing when exceptions are hardening into obligations. "Just this once" is one of the most expensive phrases in caregiving when it is used without reflection. It can purchase short-term peace at the cost of long-term stability.

Redefining duty therefore requires a more precise relationship with the word "yes". A guilt-driven yes is often immediate, tense, and full of hidden resentment. It is given to avoid discomfort, criticism, disappointment, or fear. It may solve the visible problem while creating a private debt in the caregiver's body and mind. A deliberate yes is different. It is chosen after considering capacity, timing, consequences, and alternatives. It does not require you to pretend the cost is nothing. It allows you to say, "I can do this," without silently adding, "and I must never admit what it takes from me."

The same precision is needed with "no". In caregiving, no is often treated as a moral insult, as though refusing a task means refusing the person. This is one of the most damaging confusions in family care. You can refuse a task and still love the person. You can decline a request and still remain committed. You can say no to daily transport while saying yes to appointment coordination. You can say no to unscheduled evening calls while saying yes to a planned conversation the next morning. You can say no to being the only person responsible while saying yes to helping build a wider support system.

A boundary is not the end of care. It is a condition for care to remain possible.

The most useful boundaries are not dramatic declarations. They are clear descriptions of what you can and cannot reliably provide. They do not need to be wrapped in a courtroom defence. They do not need to persuade everyone that you are a good person. They work best when they are concrete, repeatable, and attached to behaviour rather than emotion.

For example, "I cannot keep doing everything" may be true, but it is too broad to guide action. "I can organise medical appointments, but

I cannot provide transport more than once a month" is more useful. "I need people to respect my time" may be justified, but it will mean different things to different people. "I do not answer non-urgent calls after 8 p.m." gives the care system a clear edge. "I am exhausted" may invite sympathy, debate, or minimisation. "I need someone else to take over the pharmacy collection by Friday" creates a practical handover.

This is not coldness. It is clarity.

Caregivers often resist this level of clarity because it feels too firm, too formal, or too unlike the way families are "supposed" to work. But vague care arrangements are rarely kinder. Vagueness allows everyone to imagine a different agreement. It leaves the most responsible person filling the gaps. It turns every request into a fresh emotional negotiation. It makes refusal feel personal because no shared structure exists to point towards. Clarity, by contrast, gives relationships something sturdier than mood, memory, or guilt.

It is also important to distinguish limits from preferences. A preference is something you would like. A limit is something necessary to protect your functioning. You may prefer not to drive in heavy traffic. You may have a limit around driving when exhausted. You may prefer a quiet evening. You may have a limit around taking distressing calls late at night because you cannot sleep afterwards and still work the next day. You may prefer not to manage family conflict. You may have a limit around being used as the messenger between adults who refuse to speak directly.

When caregivers treat true limits as mere preferences, they become too easy to bargain away. The result is not generosity; it is erosion. A sustainable care plan must identify what protects the caregiver's basic stability. Sleep is not a decorative extra. Paid work is not selfish. Parenting responsibilities are not secondary because an older relative is in distress. Medical needs are not optional. A marriage or partnership cannot survive indefinitely on leftovers. A person who never has recovery time does not become more devoted; they become depleted.

This is why redefining duty also means rejecting the fantasy of unlimited availability. Being reachable all the time may seem comforting to others, but it can create a constant state of alert in the caregiver. The phone becomes a small alarm system. Even when it is silent, part of the mind remains braced. Over time, this changes the texture of ordinary life. Meals are interrupted. Rest is shallow. Conversations are half-attended. The caregiver is physically present in one place but mentally stationed beside the next possible demand.

Availability must therefore be designed, not assumed. This might mean fixed check-in times, agreed emergency criteria, shared responsibility for calls, or a clear distinction between urgent and non-urgent contact. The exact arrangement will differ from one care situation to another, but the principle is consistent: if every channel is always open, the caregiver eventually has no protected space in which to recover.

A common objection rises here: "But what if something happens?" This fear is understandable. Caregiving involves vulnerability, and vulnerability invites imagination. The mind can always produce a frightening possibility. Yet a life governed entirely by "what if" becomes unliveable. Sustainable care does not deny risk; it sorts risk. It asks what is genuinely urgent, what is likely, what can be planned for, who else can respond, and what systems reduce danger without requiring one person to remain permanently on call.

The more honest question is not, "Can I prevent every bad thing?" You cannot. No caregiver can. The more useful question is, "What reasonable safeguards can exist without destroying the caregiver's life?" This is the ground on which mature duty stands. It recognises danger without making one person responsible for eliminating uncertainty itself.

There is also a relational reason to define limits early. When caregivers wait until they are depleted, boundaries often arrive with anger attached. A request that might once have been answered calmly now feels like an attack. A minor inconvenience triggers a disproportionate response because it lands on months or years of unspoken strain. The caregiver then feels guilty for snapping and may overcorrect by withdrawing the boundary or doing even more.

The cycle continues: silence, overload, resentment, eruption, guilt, renewed over-functioning.

Clear limits interrupt that cycle. They allow truth to appear before it becomes bitterness. They make it possible to say, "I want to help, and this is what I can reliably do," instead of waiting until the only honest sentence left is, "I cannot take this anymore." The earlier version is easier for others to hear and easier for the caregiver to maintain. It is not always welcomed, but it is less likely to arrive as an explosion.

Some caregivers fear that if they stop over-functioning, everything will fall apart. Sometimes, in the short term, parts of the arrangement may indeed wobble. People who have benefited from your constant availability may resist the change. Tasks that were silently absorbed may become visible because they are no longer automatically completed. Other relatives may complain, delay, or claim they do not know what to do. The person receiving care may feel anxious or abandoned when familiar patterns shift.

This discomfort does not prove that the boundary is wrong. It proves that the old system depended too heavily on you.

There is a period in sustainable caregiving where things feel less smooth precisely because the hidden labour is being revealed. This is not failure. It is exposure. A family may discover that transport was not "handled"; it was handled by you. Medication refills were not "sorted"; you sorted them. Emotional reassurance was not naturally available; you supplied it. When the automatic mechanism stops, the system must face what it has been using.

That moment requires steadiness. Not harshness. Not apology for existing. Steadiness. The caregiver has to resist the urge to rescue everyone from the discomfort of adjustment. Otherwise, the old pattern reasserts itself. The point of a limit is not to make others feel punished, but neither is it to guarantee that no one feels inconvenienced. All meaningful change inconveniences a system that has adapted to your self-sacrifice.

Redefining duty also requires moral humility. Caregivers are not always right simply because they are tired. Families can be complicated. The person receiving care may have legitimate fears. Other relatives may have constraints that are not immediately visible. Professional systems may be under strain. There may be cultural, financial, emotional, or historical reasons why decisions feel loaded. Sustainable care is not built by declaring the caregiver the only injured party.

But humility is not the same as self-erasure. You can consider other people's realities without denying your own. You can listen without surrendering. You can accept that others are distressed without making distress the final authority. You can recognise that someone needs more than you can give and still refuse to pretend that your refusal is the cause of the need.

One of the hardest parts of caregiving is accepting the gap between what someone deserves and what you can provide. A parent may deserve tenderness, safety, company, dignity, and patience. A spouse may deserve loyalty and comfort. A sibling may deserve advocacy. A friend may deserve not to be abandoned. But no single caregiver can personally supply every good thing another person deserves. To confuse deserving with capacity is to create impossible guilt.

The question "What do they deserve?" must be paired with "What can I realistically provide, and what else must be arranged?" Without the second question, the first becomes a moral weight with no practical floor. It turns love into a bottomless obligation. It also prevents more appropriate solutions from being considered because the caregiver keeps trying to stretch themselves rather than redesign the arrangement.

This is why a care load has to be named in plain terms. Not as an emotional cloud, but as actual responsibilities. Appointment coordination. Transport. Medication management. Meal preparation. Personal care. Household tasks. Financial administration. Emotional support. Night-time availability. Family communication. Crisis response. Advocacy. Companionship. Monitoring. Each category has a cost. Each cost must land somewhere. If it all lands on one person, the problem is not that the person lacks devotion. The problem is that the system is badly designed.

A useful exercise is to imagine the care arrangement as if it had to be explained to an outsider. What exactly are you responsible for? How often? At what times? With what backup? What happens if you are ill? What happens if you are at work? What happens if you need sleep? What happens if two needs collide? Where are the instructions written? Who else knows them? Which tasks require you specifically, and which tasks have simply drifted towards you because you are dependable?

These questions are uncomfortable because they expose the difference between a loving impulse and an operational plan. Many care arrangements run for months or years on impulse. Someone notices, someone responds, someone adapts, someone absorbs. But long-term care cannot depend on improvisation alone. Improvisation is useful in a crisis. It is exhausting as a lifestyle.

Limits are therefore not merely personal boundaries; they are design information. They tell the care system what is possible. If you cannot provide daily transport, that fact must become part of the plan. If you cannot take calls during work hours, that fact must shape communication. If you cannot be the only person managing appointments, that fact must trigger redistribution. If you need one evening each week without care responsibilities, that fact is not an indulgence. It is a maintenance requirement.

The caregiver who names limits is not creating the problem. They are revealing the problem early enough for others to respond.

The alternative is far more damaging. When limits are denied, the care system continues as though capacity is infinite. The caregiver becomes increasingly tired, then increasingly resentful, then increasingly unreliable in ways they may not recognise at first. Mistakes creep in. Details are missed. Tone hardens. The relationship becomes contaminated by obligation. The person receiving care may still be getting tasks completed, but the emotional climate around those tasks becomes strained and brittle.

This is why sustainable care must be judged not only by whether needs are being met today, but by what meeting those needs is doing to the people involved. A plan that depends on one person's exhaustion is not a good plan merely because it has not yet collapsed. A plan that preserves appearances while damaging the caregiver is not compassionate. A plan that avoids difficult conversations by overusing the most responsible person is not family harmony. It is deferred conflict.

Redefining duty is an act of moral seriousness. It asks more from the caregiver than blind sacrifice. It asks for discernment. It asks the caregiver to distinguish love from fear, responsibility from guilt, flexibility from self-abandonment, and temporary crisis response from permanent role assignment. It asks them to stop treating their own depletion as a private inconvenience and start treating it as relevant information.

The new definition is not softer. It is stronger.

Duty means taking the situation seriously enough to tell the truth about what it requires. Duty means refusing to build care on fantasy. Duty means recognising that the caregiver is not a limitless resource. Duty means choosing commitments that can be sustained over time rather than making promises under emotional pressure that later turn into resentment. Duty means asking not only, "What does this person need?" but also, "What structure will allow care to continue without destroying the carer?"

That question changes everything. It does not remove pain, conflict, grief, or uncertainty. It does not guarantee that others will respond well. It does not make every limit easy to state or every request easy to refuse. But it moves caregiving out of the fog of unspoken obligation and into the clearer, more adult territory of reality.

A caregiver can be loving without being endlessly available.

A caregiver can be committed without being consumed.

A caregiver can say, "I will help," and still say, "This is where my part ends."

The difficult work is learning to believe all three at the same time.

The Caregiver as Part of Care

Caregiving is often spoken about as though there is only one person whose wellbeing matters: the person receiving care. Their pain, safety, appointments, medicines, meals, comfort, dignity, and mood become the centre of attention. Their needs are visible, urgent, and emotionally compelling. Everyone can understand why they matter.

The caregiver's needs, by contrast, are often treated as background conditions. They are acknowledged politely, then pushed aside. A tired caregiver is told to "take care of yourself", but the care plan rarely changes to make that possible. A stressed caregiver is praised for being strong, but not relieved of enough responsibility to recover. A lonely caregiver is admired for loyalty, while their own life becomes thinner, quieter, and more difficult to protect.

This is one of the great errors in family care: the caregiver is treated as the delivery mechanism, not as a person inside the system.

That error has consequences. Care does not come from nowhere. It comes through a human body, a human mind, a human nervous system, a human life. It is shaped by sleep, patience, money, time, work, grief, fear, health, relationships, and practical capacity. A caregiver who is exhausted does not provide care in the same way as a caregiver who has slept. A caregiver who feels trapped does not speak with the same steadiness as a caregiver who has room to breathe. A caregiver whose own medical needs are ignored does not remain an endlessly reliable support simply because the person they care for has greater needs.

The care recipient and the caregiver are not separate planets. They are part of one care ecology. What happens to one affects the other.

This does not mean their needs are identical. The person receiving care may be living with illness, frailty, disability, confusion, pain, fear, or loss of independence. Their vulnerability may be immediate and profound. It would be wrong to flatten that reality or pretend that the caregiver's discomfort is always equivalent. But it is equally wrong to build the arrangement as if the caregiver's wellbeing has no bearing on the quality, safety, and emotional climate of care.

A care system has at least two outcomes to protect: the condition of the person receiving care and the condition of the person providing it. When only one outcome is measured, the system gives a false picture of success. The meals may be delivered. The medicines may be organised. The appointments may be attended. The house may be kept functioning. From the outside, everything may appear to be working. Yet if the caregiver is losing sleep, snapping at their children, neglecting their own health, falling behind at work, withdrawing from friends, and waking each morning with dread, the system is not truly working. It is borrowing stability from the caregiver's decline.

That borrowing can continue for a surprisingly long time. Many caregivers are capable, conscientious people. They know how to push through. They are accustomed to being needed. They may have spent years being the responsible one in the family, the person who notices what others miss, the person who can be counted on when plans fall apart. These qualities are valuable. They are also dangerous when no one asks what they cost.

The most dependable caregivers are often the least protected.

They know how to minimise their own strain because doing so keeps the peace. They say, "It is fine," because explaining the whole truth would take too much energy. They refuse help before it is offered because they assume it will be unreliable, awkward, or more work to organise than to do the task themselves. They become experts in carrying distress discreetly. Their competence becomes camouflage.

Over time, this camouflage can fool even the caregiver. When pressure becomes normal, they stop recognising it as pressure. They treat exhaustion as the price of love, irritability as a private flaw, forgetfulness as carelessness, and resentment as shameful evidence that they are not kind enough. They may not think, "This load is too heavy." They think, "I should be coping better."

That sentence is one of the most damaging thoughts in caregiving.

It individualises what is often a system problem. It turns overload into character failure. It asks the caregiver to become more patient, more organised, more generous, more emotionally controlled, and more available, when the real issue may be that the role has expanded beyond any reasonable human capacity. There is a profound difference between needing a better attitude and needing a better arrangement. Many caregivers are not failing morally. They are operating without enough structure, support, recovery, and honest limits.

To see the caregiver as part of care is to stop treating their exhaustion as unfortunate but irrelevant. It is relevant. It is information. It tells the truth about the arrangement. If a particular pattern of care repeatedly destroys the caregiver's sleep, damages their work, isolates them socially, or leaves them emotionally raw, that pattern is not neutral. It is a risk factor within the care system.

Sleep is a useful place to begin because it exposes the illusion that the caregiver's needs are optional. A caregiver who is regularly interrupted at night, kept alert by late calls, or lying awake replaying worries is not simply "a bit tired". Their capacity to plan, regulate emotion, remember details, drive safely, communicate clearly, and respond with patience is affected. No serious care arrangement can ignore this and still call itself stable. The body keeps accounts even when the family does not.

Time matters in the same way. Caregiving often consumes time not only through obvious tasks, but through interruption. A call in the middle of work. A message that needs a decision. A prescription problem that becomes a two-hour detour. A relative's complaint that turns into emotional arbitration. These interruptions fragment the caregiver's life. They make rest less restful and work less focused. They make ordinary commitments feel fragile because anything can be displaced by the next demand.

Relationships also belong inside the care equation. A caregiver's marriage, partnership, parenting, friendships, and wider family connections are not decorative. They are part of the caregiver's resilience. When care repeatedly takes priority over every other relationship, the caregiver's support base weakens. Friends stop asking. Partners become resentful. Children learn that the caregiver is physically present but emotionally unavailable. The caregiver becomes more isolated, and then the care role feels even harder to question because there are fewer places left where they are known as anything other than useful.

This is how a person becomes absorbed by care.

Absorption is not the same as commitment. Commitment is chosen and shaped. Absorption is what happens when the care role spreads into every unprotected space. There is no clear start or stop. No reliable recovery. No agreement about what counts as urgent. No distinction between the caregiver's life and the needs of the person receiving care. The caregiver may still be technically free, but their mind is never fully released.

A sustainable arrangement must therefore ask a more disciplined question: what conditions does this caregiver need in order to keep providing good care without being damaged by it?

That question is sometimes dismissed as selfish, especially in families where sacrifice is treated as proof of love. But prevention is not selfish. It is wise. Protecting the caregiver's sleep is prevention. Protecting time away from care is prevention. Protecting income and work stability is prevention. Protecting essential relationships is prevention. Protecting the caregiver's medical appointments, movement, nourishment, and emotional recovery is prevention. These things do not compete with care; they make care more durable.

A useful comparison is maintenance. No one expects a car to run indefinitely without fuel, servicing, repairs, or rest from constant use. Yet caregivers often expect themselves to function under precisely those conditions. They become the vehicle for everyone else's needs, while their own maintenance is delayed until a breakdown occurs.

The absurdity is obvious when applied to machinery. It becomes strangely invisible when applied to a loyal human being.

The point is not that people are machines. The point is that even machines are granted limits.

The caregiver's limits are not obstacles to care. They are design requirements. If a caregiver needs seven uninterrupted hours in bed to function safely the next day, the care system must take that seriously. If they cannot answer calls during paid work, communication must be organised around that fact. If they become emotionally flooded after conflict-heavy visits, recovery time must be built into the week. If they are neglecting their own health appointments because the care schedule is too full, the schedule is not sustainable.

Caregivers often wait for permission to include themselves. They wait for the person receiving care to understand. They wait for siblings to notice. They wait for professionals to ask. They wait for a crisis serious enough to justify change. This waiting is understandable, but it is risky. People who benefit from an arrangement may not recognise its cost until the cost becomes visible in a painful way. By then, the caregiver may already be depleted, resentful, or unwell.

Including the caregiver in the care plan has to begin earlier than that.

One practical starting point is capacity awareness. Every caregiver has signs that their capacity is shrinking. These signs may be physical: headaches, disturbed sleep, tightness in the chest, recurring illness, constant fatigue. They may be emotional: irritability, numbness, tearfulness, dread, resentment, a sense of being trapped. They may be cognitive: forgetfulness, indecision, difficulty concentrating, making avoidable mistakes. They may be relational: withdrawing from friends, snapping at family, avoiding calls, feeling anger at small requests.

These signs should not be treated as embarrassing personal weaknesses. They are early warning signals. They say, "The load is exceeding the structure." They ask for adjustment before the situation becomes more difficult to repair. A caregiver who learns to notice these signals gains vital information for boundary-setting. Without that information, boundaries tend to arrive late, when the caregiver is already in survival mode.

Survival mode is a poor architect.

It can handle immediate danger, but it does not design humane routines. It narrows imagination. It makes every request feel threatening and every conversation feel urgent. It pushes the caregiver towards blunt refusals, emotional withdrawal, or exhausted compliance. It can make a person behave in ways that later fill them with guilt. This is why early recognition matters. The earlier a caregiver notices the signs of overload, the more choices remain available.

Capacity awareness also helps to challenge the habit of comparing suffering. Many caregivers silence themselves because the person receiving care has it worse. They say, "I am not the one who is ill," or "I should not complain when they are the one losing independence." There is compassion in that thought, but also a trap. Someone else's greater suffering does not make your strain unreal. Pain is not a competition in which only the person with the most visible hardship is allowed to need support.

The caregiver's suffering may be different, but it still matters.

It matters because it affects the caregiver's health. It matters because it affects the relationship. It matters because it affects the tone of care. It matters because unacknowledged strain often leaks out indirectly, through impatience, avoidance, martyrdom, sarcasm, or quiet despair. When caregivers are not allowed to speak honestly about their burden, the burden does not disappear. It goes underground and changes shape.

A mature care system can hold more than one truth at the same time. The care recipient may need help. The caregiver may need rest. The situation may be unfair to both. The caregiver may love the person deeply and still be angry about the demands. The person receiving care may not be to blame for needing help and still be affected by how their needs are managed. These truths do not cancel one another. They create the actual landscape in which sustainable care must be built.

This is where many families struggle. They prefer simple moral roles: the vulnerable person, the devoted helper, the difficult relative, the absent sibling, the selfish one, the strong one. These roles may contain fragments of truth, but they also freeze people in place. The "strong one" is not allowed to weaken. The "vulnerable one" is not expected to consider the caregiver's limits. The "absent one" is criticised but not effectively recruited. The "difficult one" becomes an excuse to avoid direct conversation. Everyone repeats the pattern because the pattern is familiar.

Seeing the caregiver as part of care interrupts those roles. It requires the family, or at least the caregiver, to stop asking only, "What does the cared-for person need?" and begin asking, "What does this whole arrangement require in order to remain safe, decent, and liveable?" That wider question does not diminish the person receiving care. It protects them from becoming dependent on a caregiver who is silently deteriorating.

It also protects the relationship from becoming purely functional. When every interaction is organised around tasks, the emotional bond can shrink. The caregiver becomes the one who manages, corrects, reminds, transports, monitors, and solves. The person receiving care becomes the one who needs, resists, forgets, asks, or complains. The relationship loses its wider identity. Parent and child become administrator and case. Spouses become patient and nurse. Siblings become manager and responsibility. Friends become helper and helped.

This narrowing can be painful for both people. The care recipient may feel watched rather than loved. The caregiver may feel useful but unseen. Both may miss the relationship they had before care took over the room. Protecting the caregiver's time and emotional energy is one way to preserve some space for the relationship to remain human, not merely operational.

There is a moral discipline in saying, "I am part of this too." For many caregivers, that sentence feels almost forbidden. They worry it sounds self-centred. They fear it will be misunderstood. They may have been trained by family history, culture, religion, gender expectations, or personal temperament to associate goodness with self-denial. Yet self-denial without limit does not produce endless goodness. It often produces exhaustion followed by resentment.

A caregiver who includes themselves is not asking to be placed above the person receiving care. They are refusing to be placed outside the frame.

That distinction matters. Caregiving does require sacrifice. It would be dishonest to pretend otherwise. There will be inconveniences, emotional demands, missed opportunities, difficult conversations, and moments when the caregiver chooses another person's need over their own preference. But sacrifice must be conscious and bounded if it is to remain humane. When sacrifice becomes the permanent operating system, the caregiver's life is gradually treated as raw material for someone else's stability.

No relationship should require one person to disappear so another can function.

This principle becomes especially important when the person receiving care resists boundaries. They may not understand the caregiver's exhaustion. They may interpret limits as rejection. They may be frightened that any reduction in availability means abandonment. They may be accustomed to a previous level of support and experience change as a loss. Their reaction may be sincere and painful. It still cannot be the only factor in deciding what is sustainable.

Emotional distress deserves compassion, not automatic control over the caregiver's choices. A person can be upset by a boundary without the boundary being wrong. A caregiver can comfort, explain, and remain kind without reversing a necessary limit. This is one of the hardest skills in caregiving: staying connected without surrendering the conditions that keep care possible.

The caregiver's wellbeing must also be protected from the judgement of outsiders who see only fragments. Someone who visits occasionally may think you are not doing enough because they witness a single unmet preference. A relative who is not involved in daily tasks may offer criticism without understanding the volume of hidden labour. A professional may recommend a plan that assumes more time and capacity than actually exist. Even the person receiving care may describe the situation in a way that leaves out what you are already carrying.

This is why the caregiver needs an internal measure of reality. Not defensiveness. Not hardness. A grounded understanding of the actual load, the actual limits, and the actual consequences of ignoring them. Without that internal measure, every complaint can become a verdict. Every disappointed face can rewrite the plan. Every suggestion can feel like an obligation. The caregiver becomes governed by the loudest emotion in the room.

Including yourself in care means building decisions on more than emotional volume. It means asking what is needed, what is possible, what is safe, what is fair, what is repeatable, and what support must be added. It means accepting that care decisions often involve trade-offs, not perfect answers. It means letting go of the fantasy that a sufficiently loving caregiver can prevent all distress.

This is a crucial point: some distress belongs to the situation itself. Ageing can be distressing. Illness can be distressing. Dependency can be distressing. Loss of control can be distressing. Family change can be distressing. The caregiver may be able to reduce distress, accompany it, soften it, or respond to it, but they cannot always remove it. When caregivers believe they are responsible for eliminating all discomfort, they become vulnerable to impossible demands.

The aim is not a care arrangement in which no one is ever upset. The aim is a care arrangement in which needs are addressed as honestly as possible without requiring the caregiver to live in permanent depletion.

This requires a change in language. Instead of saying, "I cannot cope," as though coping were a private test of character, the caregiver can begin to say, "This arrangement is no longer sustainable." Instead of saying, "I feel terrible for needing time," they can say, "Recovery time has to be part of the plan." Instead of saying, "I am letting them down," they can say, "One person cannot safely carry all of this." Language does not solve the problem by itself, but it changes the terms on which the problem is understood.

The shift is subtle but powerful. It moves the caregiver from confession to assessment. Confession says, "I am failing." Assessment says, "The current design is failing." Confession invites shame. Assessment invites adjustment. Confession isolates the caregiver. Assessment places the caregiver back inside the system where they belonged all along.

Once the caregiver is recognised as part of care, boundaries become less like acts of defiance and more like acts of maintenance. A boundary around sleep protects the next day's patience. A boundary around work hours protects income and stability. A boundary around emotional availability protects the caregiver from becoming a dumping ground for every fear, complaint, and conflict. A boundary around personal time protects identity. A boundary around shared tasks protects the care system from becoming dangerously dependent on one person.

These boundaries are not punishments. They are load-bearing supports.

The caregiver who understands this is better equipped to resist the false drama that surrounds limits. They do not need to prove that they are at breaking point before asking for change. They do not need to present collapse as evidence. They do not need to wait until they are resentful enough to sound convincing. They can act earlier, while their voice is still steady and their relationship still has room for respect.

This is not always easy. Some families respond poorly to early boundaries because they are accustomed to crisis as the only legitimate reason for adjustment. They may ignore a calm statement and respond only to an explosion. They may take steadiness as evidence that the need is not serious. This is why caregivers sometimes feel forced to dramatise their suffering before anyone listens. It is a destructive pattern. A sustainable care system should not require a caregiver to break down in order to be believed.

The responsibility, then, is partly internal and partly relational. Internally, the caregiver must learn to trust their own capacity signals before others validate them. Relationally, the care arrangement must be shaped so that those signals lead to practical change. The caregiver should not be the hidden shock absorber of the entire system.

A good care plan asks, "How is the person receiving care doing?" It also asks, "How is the caregiver doing?" Not as a courtesy. Not as small talk. As essential information.

If the caregiver is sleeping poorly, the plan needs attention. If the caregiver is becoming isolated, the plan needs attention. If the caregiver is constantly anxious, the plan needs attention. If the caregiver is neglecting their own health, the plan needs attention. If the caregiver is becoming resentful, the plan needs attention. These are not side issues. They are evidence about whether the care arrangement can continue without harm.

The caregiver's wellbeing is not the opposite of good care. It is one of its foundations.

This truth can feel almost radical in families where need has always outranked capacity. Yet it is a deeply practical truth. A caregiver who is supported, rested, and bounded is more likely to be patient, accurate, generous, and consistent. A caregiver who has room for their own life is less likely to experience the person receiving care as the thief of that life. A caregiver who is not forced into martyrdom is more able to offer care freely rather than resentfully.

The care recipient benefits from this too. They receive care from someone who is less brittle, less trapped, and less likely to vanish emotionally while continuing to perform tasks. They are not made the unconscious centre of another person's collapse. They are part of a more truthful arrangement, one that does not pretend love can thrive on exhaustion forever.

To place the caregiver inside the care system is to make care more honest. It means the plan must account for both vulnerability and capacity, both need and recovery, both duty and the limits of the person performing that duty. It rejects the sentimental image of the endlessly giving caregiver and replaces it with something sturdier: a human being whose wellbeing is inseparable from the care they provide.

From that position, every later boundary becomes clearer. The question is no longer, "Am I allowed to matter?" The caregiver already does. The sharper question is, "What has to change because my condition is part of the condition of care?"

Short-Term Heroics vs Long-Term Stability

Short-term heroics have a powerful emotional appeal. They look decisive. They produce visible results. They allow a caregiver to move quickly, solve the immediate problem, and feel, for a moment, that things are back under control. A missed prescription is collected late in the evening. A sudden transport problem is solved by cancelling work. A distressed phone call becomes a two-hour rescue mission. A family disagreement is quietened because the caregiver absorbs the tension and says, once again, "I will handle it."

There are moments when this kind of response is necessary. Caregiving sometimes involves genuine urgency. Someone falls. A symptom changes. A medication error needs attention. A frightening piece of news lands without warning. A person who is vulnerable may need immediate help, and a caregiver may have to act before the ideal plan exists. To pretend otherwise would be naive. Care cannot always be tidy, scheduled, or emotionally convenient.

The danger begins when emergency behaviour becomes the ordinary method of care.

Many caregiving arrangements slowly drift into this pattern. Nothing is planned until it becomes pressing. No role is clarified until someone is angry. No backup exists until the usual person is unavailable. No routine is created because the caregiver has become skilled at improvising. Each crisis is treated as separate, when in fact many are symptoms of the same design problem: care is being run on reaction rather than structure.

Reaction can feel caring because it is immediate. Structure can feel colder because it asks people to pause, define, schedule, and agree. Yet long-term stability is almost always kinder than repeated rescue. The person receiving care benefits from predictability. The caregiver benefits from reduced vigilance. Other supporters benefit from knowing what is expected. Relationships benefit because fewer conversations happen in the heat of panic.

Short-term heroics are expensive because they spend the caregiver's reserves quickly. They demand time, attention, emotional regulation, decision-making, and often physical energy at exactly the moment when the caregiver may already be stretched. The cost may be hidden at first. The task gets done. The appointment is attended. The argument is contained. The person is reassured. From the outside, it looks like success. Inside the caregiver, however, another layer of depletion has been added.

This is how caregiving burnout is often built: not only through large sacrifices, but through hundreds of small interruptions that never become visible enough to be counted. A late call here. A cancelled plan there. A lunch break lost to paperwork. A weekend rearranged because no one confirmed transport. A night of poor sleep after an avoidable family argument. Each incident may be survivable. Together, they create a life in which the caregiver is always braced for the next disruption.

The phrase "just this once" deserves particular attention. It is often spoken with tenderness, guilt, urgency, or fear. Just this once, take the call. Just this once, drive across town. Just this once, stay late. Just this once, cover for the person who forgot. The trouble is that caregiving systems remember behaviour more clearly than intention. What you do repeatedly, others begin to treat as available. What you rescue once without discussion may become the new expectation. What you absorb silently may be assumed to have no real cost.

Not every exception is a mistake. The issue is whether the exception is named as an exception. A caregiver can say, "I can do this today because it is urgent, but I cannot become the regular transport." That sentence protects the future while responding to the present. Without that clarity, the present keeps stealing from the future. Today's rescue quietly writes tomorrow's job description.

Long-term stability begins with a different question. Instead of asking, "How do I fix this right now?" the caregiver learns to ask, "Why did this become a crisis?" That question is not about blame. It is about pattern recognition. Did the problem arise because no one checked the supplies? Because the appointment was not confirmed? Because the person receiving care does not understand the routine? Because family members are using vague promises instead of assigned tasks? Because the caregiver is the only one who knows the necessary information? Because everyone waits until distress becomes loud before acting?

The answer matters because the same kind of crisis will often return until its source is redesigned.

For example, if medication refills repeatedly become urgent, the problem may not be the pharmacy, the doctor, or the person receiving care. The problem may be that no one has created a weekly supply check or assigned responsibility for ordering. If mealtimes repeatedly become stressful, the problem may not be a lack of goodwill. It may be that decisions are being made too late, preferences are unclear, or no default meals have been agreed. If family conflict erupts every time care needs change, the problem may not be one difficult conversation. It may be the absence of a regular communication rhythm.

Caregivers often underestimate the power of small structures because these structures do not feel dramatic. A fixed check-in time. A written medication list. A shared calendar. A weekly planning call. A backup driver. A visible note about emergency criteria. A simple folder with key contacts. These tools lack the emotional intensity of rescue, but that is precisely their value. They reduce the need for rescue in the first place.

Stability is not created by controlling every variable. That is impossible. People become unwell. Appointments change. Services are delayed. Relatives disappoint. Moods shift. Bodies are unpredictable. Long-term stability is created by reducing avoidable uncertainty. It does not promise that nothing difficult will happen. It ensures that predictable difficulties do not have to be reinvented each time they appear.

A sustainable care arrangement must therefore distinguish between true emergencies and recurring preventable problems. A true emergency demands immediate attention. A recurring preventable problem demands redesign. If everything is labelled urgent, nothing can be managed wisely. The caregiver becomes permanently available to the loudest demand, and the care system never learns. Urgency should be a signal, not a lifestyle.

This distinction is especially important because some families develop a crisis-based culture. People respond only when the situation becomes dramatic. Calm requests are ignored, while emotional explosions get action. The caregiver learns, often unconsciously, that they must sound desperate to be believed. The person receiving care may learn that distress is the fastest way to secure attention. Other relatives may avoid involvement until the problem becomes too visible to deny. Over time, crisis becomes the organising language of the whole system.

A crisis-based culture is exhausting because it teaches everyone to wait too long.

Long-term stability asks for earlier, quieter, less glamorous intervention. It asks the caregiver to notice pressure before it becomes rupture. It asks supporters to accept responsibility before they are shamed into it. It asks the person receiving care, where possible, to participate in routines rather than rely only on last-minute rescue. It asks the whole arrangement to respect the fact that repeated emergencies are often not evidence of unpredictable life, but evidence of missing structure.

This does not mean turning care into a rigid machine. Human beings do not flourish under systems that leave no room for mood, dignity, preference, grief, or change. A good routine must be firm enough to reduce chaos and flexible enough to survive reality. The aim is not perfection. The aim is repeatability. A routine that works reasonably well on a hard day is worth more than an ideal plan that depends on everyone being rested, cooperative, and clear-headed.

The caregiver also has to examine the emotional reward of heroics. This is delicate territory, but it matters. Being the rescuer can provide a sense of purpose, identity, and moral certainty. In a confusing care situation, action feels better than helplessness. Solving the immediate problem can temporarily relieve guilt. Others may praise the caregiver's dedication, which makes it even harder to step back and ask whether the pattern is healthy.

There is no shame in finding meaning in being useful. Caregiving would be poorer without capable people willing to act. The problem comes when usefulness becomes the caregiver's only recognised value. If you are loved mainly for what you fix, you may begin to fear that boundaries will make you less needed and therefore less secure. If praise arrives only after sacrifice, you may begin to confuse exhaustion with worth.

Long-term stability requires the caregiver to tolerate a different emotional atmosphere. It may feel less heroic. It may produce fewer dramatic expressions of gratitude. It may even make some people irritated because a structured system asks them to carry what you previously absorbed. Stability can feel strangely unrewarding at first because it prevents problems quietly. No one applauds the appointment that was not missed, the argument that did not escalate, the prescription that did not run out, or the caregiver who did not collapse because recovery time was protected.

Yet this quiet prevention is the real work of sustainable care.

To move from short-term heroics to long-term stability, the caregiver must become a pattern-reader. Where do problems repeat? Which tasks regularly become last-minute? Which people make vague promises? Which times of day produce distress? Which conversations spiral? Which needs are predictable but unmanaged? Which responsibilities live only in your memory? Which "temporary" arrangements have become permanent without consent?

These questions reveal the hidden architecture of the care situation. They show where the load is leaking. They make it possible to stop treating every difficulty as a fresh moral emergency. The caregiver begins to see that many crises are not proof that they must do more; they are proof that the current design is asking the wrong person to do too much, too late, with too little support.

One common pattern is unclear ownership. A task belongs to "everyone", which usually means it belongs to the person most likely to notice it. Someone should book the appointment. Someone should check the fridge. Someone should update the relatives. Someone should organise the paperwork. In practice, "someone" becomes the caregiver who cannot bear the consequences of leaving it undone.

A stable arrangement replaces vague ownership with named responsibility. Not because family life should become bureaucratic for its own sake, but because ambiguity creates work. Every unclear task generates monitoring. The caregiver has to wonder whether it has been done, check whether it has been done, remind someone to do it, and often complete it anyway. At that point, even delegated work has returned to the caregiver in another form.

Another pattern is the absence of recovery time. When care is run through repeated rescue, the caregiver is expected to return immediately to normal life after each disruption. But the body does not reset on command. A difficult visit may leave emotional residue. A frightening call may keep the mind alert for hours. A family argument may make sleep difficult. A long appointment may consume not only the appointment time, but the rest of the day's capacity.

Long-term stability recognises recovery as part of the schedule, not as a luxury added after everything else. A system that repeatedly uses the caregiver for crisis response must also protect time for that caregiver to return to steadiness. Without recovery, yesterday's emergency becomes the emotional weather of today. Care then becomes harsher, not because the caregiver lacks love, but because the nervous system is never allowed to stand down.

A further pattern is poor information flow. When one person holds all the details, every disruption has to pass through them. They become the living archive: the medication history, the appointment tracker, the preference list, the family messenger, the keeper of passwords, the interpreter of professional advice, the one who knows which symptoms are new and which are familiar. This may feel efficient until that person is unavailable, ill, exhausted, or simply unable to answer one more question.

Stability requires information to be shareable. Not perfect. Not elaborate. Shareable. The essential details must be written somewhere accessible to the right people. The goal is to reduce dependence on one person's memory. When information is distributed sensibly, help becomes easier to accept because helpers do not have to extract every instruction from the caregiver. The caregiver can step away without the whole arrangement immediately becoming confused.

There is also the pattern of emotional immediacy. Some care situations are driven less by practical urgency than by emotional urgency. A person feels anxious, lonely, angry, or abandoned, and the caregiver is expected to respond at once. Again, compassion matters. Emotional distress is real. But if every feeling becomes an emergency, the caregiver's life will be repeatedly interrupted by states that cannot always be solved through immediate availability.

Long-term stability creates containers for emotional support. A regular call may be more sustainable than unpredictable calls throughout the day. A planned visit may be more reassuring than a cycle of crisis-driven appearances. A clear statement of when the caregiver is available may feel less satisfying in the moment, but it helps both people live with less uncertainty. Emotional care does not have to mean emotional on-demand access.

This is where some caregivers struggle most. Practical routines may feel acceptable, but emotional limits feel cruel. Yet emotional over-availability is often where resentment grows fastest. When the caregiver becomes the primary outlet for fear, complaint, anger, loneliness, and family tension, they may begin to dread contact even with someone they love. That dread is not a sign that the relationship is lost. It is a sign that emotional care needs boundaries strong enough to preserve affection.

The shift from heroics to stability is rarely welcomed by everyone at once. A system accustomed to rescue may experience structure as withdrawal. People may say, "You never used to mind," or "Why is this suddenly a problem?" The honest answer is that it was always a cost; it simply went unnamed. The caregiver has to hold steady through the discomfort of making the hidden cost visible. This is not punishment. It is reality entering the conversation.

There may be a temporary increase in tension when old patterns are interrupted. A person who used to rely on last-minute help may feel exposed. A relative who used to offer opinions without tasks may feel pressured. The caregiver may feel guilty for not stepping in quickly. This transitional discomfort can be mistaken for failure, but it is often the sound of a care system learning new terms.

The key is not to replace one extreme with another. The aim is not to become rigid, unavailable, or indifferent. The aim is to reserve emergency energy for true emergencies and build ordinary care on ordinary structure. The caregiver should not have to live in a state of permanent readiness because no one has taken the time to design a better rhythm.

A fixed check-in time is a modest example, but it captures the larger principle. When contact is predictable, the person receiving care may feel less need to create urgency in order to be noticed. The caregiver can prepare emotionally and practically. Other tasks can be organised around the rhythm. Small concerns can be gathered and addressed together rather than scattered across the day. This is not a perfect solution, but it shifts care from constant interruption to intentional contact.

The same principle applies to weekly planning. A short, regular review of appointments, supplies, transport, and concerns can prevent a surprising amount of firefighting. It does not need to be elaborate. It simply asks, "What is coming? What is missing? Who is responsible? What could go wrong, and what is the backup?" These questions are not dramatic, but they are protective. They keep the caregiver from being ambushed by predictable needs.

Long-term stability also requires a more honest relationship with failure. A heroic system often hides failure until it becomes undeniable because the caregiver keeps compensating. A stable system allows small failures to be seen early. If a helper forgets a task, the issue is addressed. If a routine is too complicated, it is simplified. If a plan depends on unrealistic cooperation, it is redesigned. If the caregiver is still carrying too much, the load is renegotiated. The goal is not to avoid all error, but to learn before exhaustion becomes the teacher.

This kind of care asks for patience with unglamorous progress. The caregiver may not feel immediate relief. It takes time for routines to settle, for others to understand expectations, for the person receiving care to trust the new rhythm, and for the caregiver's own nervous system to believe that not every gap must be filled instantly. The body may continue to brace even after the schedule improves. Stability has to be practised before it feels natural.

It is important to say that some care situations are genuinely unstable because the needs are changing quickly, the risks are high, or the available support is too thin. In such cases, routines alone are not enough. More help, different arrangements, professional input, or a higher level of care may be necessary. Long-term stability is not achieved by decorating an unsafe setup with a calendar. A plan that cannot protect either person must be reconsidered at a deeper level.

Still, even in complex situations, the principle remains: repeated crisis should not be accepted as the default without examination. The caregiver is allowed to ask whether the current arrangement is being held together by courage or by denial. Courage acts when necessary. Denial keeps acting because it cannot bear to admit the structure is failing.

Short-term heroics ask, "What can I do right now to make this stop?"

Long-term stability asks, "What has to change so this does not keep returning in the same form?"

That second question is less dramatic, but it is far more powerful. It moves care away from the exhausting theatre of constant rescue and towards something quieter, sturdier, and more humane. It honours the real emergencies by not allowing preventable chaos to consume all the caregiver's strength before the true emergency arrives.

The caregiver who learns this distinction begins to protect both the care recipient and themselves. They stop using their own depletion as the main tool of problem-solving. They stop confusing speed with wisdom. They stop accepting every last-minute demand as proof of unavoidable need. They begin to see that sustainable care is not built by becoming endlessly heroic.

It is built by designing a life in which heroics are needed less often.

Chapter 2
Mapping the Real Care Load

How can a person be working all day and still feel unable to prove what they have done? This is one of the quiet humiliations of caregiving. The visible tasks may be few enough to sound manageable when described aloud: a visit, a phone call, a prescription, a meal, a form, a reminder. Yet the caregiver knows that the real work is not contained in the task itself. It is in the noticing before the task, the planning around it, the emotional weather during it, and the mental residue that remains afterwards.

A care load rarely announces itself as a single weight. It gathers as fragments. Remember whether the tablets were taken. Watch whether the milk is being used. Notice the change in tone on the phone. Check the appointment letter. Calm the panic about a bill. Explain the same arrangement to another relative. Think ahead to the weekend. Hold back irritation. Smile when you are tired. Carry the worry home. None of these actions looks dramatic enough to count as a burden on its own, but together they occupy the mind like a room with every surface covered.

This is why many caregivers underestimate themselves. They do not lie about what they do; they simply lack a full record of it. The work is scattered across ordinary moments, tucked between jobs, meals, school runs, sleep, errands, and conversations. It is too small to schedule and too constant to ignore. By the time someone asks, "What exactly is taking so much out of you?" the caregiver may struggle to answer without sounding defensive, because the evidence has been spread thinly across the week.

The central tension is between the care that can be seen and the care that is actually being carried. Families often negotiate from the visible version. Professionals may also see only the part that appears during appointments, calls, or crises. Even the caregiver may make decisions based on the obvious tasks while missing the hidden labour that makes those tasks possible. The result is a distorted picture: the load appears lighter than it is, so the expectations placed upon the caregiver become heavier than they should be.

This matters because vague strain cannot be managed well. When the workload remains blurred, every request feels personal, every refusal feels guilty, and every discussion about help turns into a fog of emotion. Without a clear map, the caregiver may keep trying to fix the wrong thing. They may tidy a kitchen because it is visible while ignoring the medication routine that prevents a more serious problem. They may respond to the loudest complaint while postponing the quieter task that would reduce future risk. They may treat all demands as equal simply because they all arrive with pressure attached.

The consequences build slowly. A caregiver who cannot see the full pattern cannot choose wisely where to place their limited energy. They may spend themselves on low-value tasks because those tasks are immediate, familiar, or emotionally charged. They may miss the predictable moments when the whole arrangement begins to wobble: mornings, mealtimes, transport gaps, family visits, paperwork deadlines, transitions after appointments. What feels like chaos may, with closer attention, reveal a repeated sequence. And once a sequence can be seen, it can be questioned.

Mapping the care load is not an accusation. It is not a way of proving that the person receiving care is difficult, that relatives are useless, or that the caregiver has suffered more than anyone understands. Blame may feel satisfying for a moment, especially when the work has been unseen for too long, but blame is too blunt a tool for redesign. Accuracy is more powerful. Accuracy shows what is happening, when it happens, who is involved, what it costs, and which pressures keep returning in slightly different clothing.

The work begins with the invisible actions that have been passing as "nothing", then moves towards the difference between urgency and importance, because not every demand deserves the same place in the day. From there, the pressure points become clearer: the times, tasks, conversations, and missing pieces that repeatedly turn care into a scramble. Only then can change be chosen with discipline, not desperation, by identifying what would reduce the greatest strain without trying to rebuild the entire care arrangement at once.

There is a particular kind of relief that comes from naming the load plainly, even before anything has changed. The caregiver stops arguing with themselves about whether they are simply weak, impatient, or poorly organised. The week begins to show its true shape. The scattered fragments become evidence. The question is no longer, "Why am I so tired when I have not done enough to justify it?" It becomes sharper, more useful, and harder to evade: "What am I carrying that has never been counted?"

Capturing Invisible Tasks

The most exhausting part of caregiving is not always the work that other people can see. It is often the work that disappears the moment it is done. A meal is noticed if it is missing, but not if it is quietly planned, bought, prepared, served, adjusted to preference, cleared away, and remembered for next time. A prescription problem becomes visible when the tablets run out, but the routine checks that prevent that from happening can pass without recognition for months. A calm afternoon may look like luck, when in reality it was built from reminders, reassurance, timing, restraint, and careful attention to small signs that trouble was beginning to gather.

This is why caregivers so often feel tired in ways they cannot easily explain. They may look back over the day and struggle to name one large achievement, yet feel as though they have been mentally carrying a tray that could tip at any moment. The phone was checked. The appointment was confirmed. The tone of voice was assessed. The fridge was noticed. The laundry was judged. The mood was managed. The family message was softened before being sent. The possible problem was anticipated before anyone else knew it existed.

Invisible tasks are not imaginary tasks. They are simply tasks that leave little evidence.

Caregiving is full of these hidden actions because much of care is preventive. The caregiver does not only respond to what has happened; they monitor what might happen next. They notice whether someone sounds more confused than usual, whether a bill has been left unopened, whether a walking stick has been moved out of reach, whether the person receiving care is eating less, washing less, sleeping differently, withdrawing socially, becoming more anxious, or repeating a question with a new urgency. These observations may not lead to immediate action every time, but they still demand attention. Attention is labour.

The problem is that attention is hard to count. A lift to an appointment can be placed on a calendar. A phone call can be timed. A shopping trip produces a receipt. But vigilance has no neat border. It begins before the visit and continues after it. It follows the caregiver into work, into conversations, into bed. It interrupts ordinary life with small internal questions: Did I order that? Did they understand? Should I call again? Was that forgetfulness normal? What if no one else notices? This is the mental load of care, and it is one of the reasons a caregiver can feel busy even while sitting still.

Emotional labour is just as easily hidden. Caregivers often spend enormous energy regulating the atmosphere around care. They choose words carefully to avoid shame. They absorb irritation because arguing would make the next task harder. They reassure someone who is frightened while privately feeling frightened themselves. They listen to complaints without reacting to every unfair sentence. They translate medical instructions into language the person can tolerate. They manage relatives who want updates, professionals who need details, and the person receiving care who may resist the very help being offered.

This kind of labour is rarely recorded because it does not look like a task. It looks like patience. It looks like personality. It looks like being "good with them". But patience used repeatedly under pressure has a cost. Staying calm is work when the situation invites panic. Being gentle is work when you are tired. Not snapping is work when the same issue has been explained many times before. A caregiver who appears composed may be spending considerable energy to keep the care relationship from becoming more painful than it already is.

Planning is another invisible layer. Care does not happen only when the caregiver is physically present. It is often prepared elsewhere, in fragments of time stolen from ordinary life. A caregiver thinks through transport, timing, meals, medication, clothing, forms, access, mobility, mood, money, weather, parking, and what might go wrong if one part of the plan fails. They may run through a visit before it happens and replay it afterwards to check what needs following up. This planning may never be seen by the person receiving care, but without it, visible care would frequently collapse into confusion.

The invisibility becomes more dangerous when everyone, including the caregiver, starts to treat these tasks as too small to matter. A reminder seems small. A check-in seems small. A message seems small. A call to clarify a detail seems small. But small tasks become heavy when they are constant, unshared, time-sensitive, emotionally loaded, and connected to risk. A grain of sand is light. A sack of sand is not.

Caregivers often underestimate their workload because they count only the obvious duties and ignore the surrounding labour that makes those duties possible. They may say, "I only visit three times a week," without counting the daily monitoring calls, the pharmacy coordination, the emotional recovery after each visit, the messages with relatives, the background worry, and the planning that turns those visits into functioning support. They may say, "I just help with appointments," without counting the booking, transport, reminders, paperwork, waiting, note-taking, explaining, and follow-up. The word "just" is often where invisible labour hides.

Capturing these tasks begins with a change of attitude. The purpose is not to build a case for resentment. It is not to produce a dramatic inventory designed to shame the person receiving care or accuse everyone else of failing. The purpose is accuracy. A caregiver cannot protect their time, ask for help, set boundaries, or redesign routines while working from a false picture of what they actually do. Accuracy is the beginning of choice.

A useful way to start is to record a normal week as honestly as possible. Not an ideal week. Not a crisis week, unless crisis has become the norm. A normal week. The caregiver writes down every care-related action, including actions that seem too minor to count. The point is to notice the full pattern: calls made, messages answered, items checked, appointments managed, worries tracked, conversations softened, supplies monitored, decisions made, emotions absorbed, tasks remembered, and problems prevented.

This record does not need to be beautiful or complicated. In fact, it should not be. Caregivers already carry enough administrative burden. A plain notebook, a phone note, a printed sheet, or a simple document can work. What matters is that the task is captured close enough to the moment that it is not forgotten. Invisible labour vanishes quickly because it is so woven into the day. Recording it gives the caregiver evidence before memory edits the load down into something smaller and less truthful.

The entries should include more than obvious activity. "Called about appointment" is useful, but "called about appointment, waited on hold, clarified transport, reassured Mum afterwards, updated brother" gives a truer picture. "Checked medication" is useful, but "checked medication, noticed low supply, added refill to list, worried about weekend gap" shows the chain of labour. The goal is not literary detail. It is to reveal that caregiving tasks often travel in clusters. One action generates another. One need pulls a string of smaller responsibilities behind it.

It is also important to capture mental tasks. These can feel strange to write down because no one has asked caregivers to count thinking as work. Yet thinking is often the place where caregiving lives. Remembering that a form is due. Holding a concern until the right person can be contacted. Monitoring whether a symptom has changed. Deciding whether a call is necessary. Anticipating resistance before a conversation. Planning how to phrase a request so it will not cause distress. These are not empty thoughts. They are executive tasks performed inside the mind.

Emotional tasks deserve the same respect. A caregiver might record, "Stayed calm during repeated questioning," or "Listened to complaints after visit," or "Reassured them about the appointment," or "Managed my own frustration before calling back." These entries may feel uncomfortably personal, but they matter. Emotional labour is one of the reasons care can be draining even when the practical task is brief. A ten-minute call can take an hour to recover from if it involves anxiety, criticism, confusion, or guilt.

After a week of recording, many caregivers experience a revealing discomfort. The list looks longer than expected. It may feel excessive, as though writing it down has made the caregiver seem dramatic. That reaction is worth noticing. Many caregivers have been trained to minimise themselves so thoroughly that accuracy feels like exaggeration. But the list is not an argument. It is a mirror. If the mirror shows more than expected, the problem is not the mirror.

The next step is to group the tasks into broad categories. This helps the caregiver see the shape of the load rather than drowning in details. Some tasks relate to practical care: meals, cleaning, transport, shopping, personal items, repairs, household management. Some relate to health: medication, appointments, symptoms, professional communication, monitoring, equipment, safety. Some relate to administration: forms, bills, insurance, benefits, records, passwords, letters. Some relate to emotional and relational care: reassurance, companionship, conflict management, family updates, persuasion, grief support, managing resistance.

This grouping often reveals an important truth: the caregiver may not be doing "a bit of everything"; they may be carrying entire categories that no one else has recognised. One person may be the transport system. Another may be the emotional shock absorber. Another may be the administrative memory. Often, the main caregiver is all three. When the categories are visible, the caregiver can begin to ask more precise questions about what should remain with them and what should be shared, simplified, delegated, delayed, or stopped.

The record should also show timing. When do tasks happen? Are mornings especially demanding? Do most calls arrive during work? Does paperwork happen late at night because there is no other space? Do family messages cluster before visits? Does the caregiver lose evenings to follow-up after appointments? Timing matters because a task is not only its content; it is also its placement in the day. A brief task at the wrong time can be more disruptive than a longer task that is planned and contained.

Frequency matters too. A task performed once may be manageable. A task performed daily, unpredictably, or repeatedly across the week may be a major load. Caregivers are often misled by the apparent size of a single action. "It only takes a minute" is one of the most misleading phrases in care. A minute that interrupts concentration, triggers worry, requires emotional control, or repeats many times is not just a minute. It is a demand on attention, and attention is finite.

Another useful question is who notices the task. In many care arrangements, the main burden is not simply doing the work but being the person who sees that the work exists. The person who notices empty cupboards, unsettled moods, missed letters, dirty clothes, overdue bills, low medication, family tension, or transport gaps is already working before any visible task begins. Noticing creates responsibility unless it is consciously shared. The caregiver who notices everything becomes the person who owns everything.

This is why capturing invisible tasks should include the trigger point. Did the task happen because someone asked? Because you noticed? Because a professional instructed you? Because a relative passed it back to you? Because the person receiving care became distressed? Because you feared the consequence if no one acted? Triggers reveal how work arrives. Some tasks are planned. Others are dumped. Others are pulled from the caregiver by anxiety. Knowing the difference helps identify where the system is leaking.

It is crucial to record not only what was done, but what was prevented. Prevention is the least visible success. When a caregiver orders medication early, no one experiences the crisis of running out. When they prepare someone for a visit, the visit may go smoothly. When they calm a conversation, the family may avoid conflict. When they organise paperwork, a deadline may pass without drama. These outcomes can make the caregiver's labour appear unnecessary because the problem never fully appears. Prevention hides its own evidence.

That is why a caregiver should occasionally ask, "What would probably happen if I did not do this?" This question is not meant to inflate importance. It clarifies risk. If no one would notice for weeks, the task may be less urgent than it feels. If a missed task would create health, safety, financial, or emotional consequences quickly, it belongs in a different category. This is the beginning of prioritisation, but before prioritisation can happen, the task must be seen.

Capturing invisible tasks also brings emotional truth to the surface. Some tasks are not time-consuming, but they are emotionally expensive. A five-minute call with a critical relative may cost more than an hour of quiet household help. A conversation that requires persuasion may drain more than a practical errand. A visit that involves watching someone decline may leave the caregiver heavy for the rest of the day. If the record includes only minutes, it will miss this deeper cost. Time is one measure. Emotional weight is another.

Caregivers often need language for this because many people understand hours better than emotional strain. "It only took half an hour" may be technically true and still incomplete. A better internal question is, "How much of me did that task require?" Some tasks require patience. Some require courage. Some require suppression. Some require grief. Some require vigilance. Some require confrontation. These demands do not show on a clock, but they shape capacity.

The point of mapping invisible tasks is not to prove that every task is equally important. Some tasks may indeed be habits that can be dropped. Some may be driven by anxiety rather than genuine need. Some may be performed to avoid criticism rather than protect wellbeing. Some may belong to other adults. Some may have made sense once and no longer serve the situation. Capturing the task does not automatically justify it. It simply brings it into view so it can be examined.

This distinction protects the caregiver from using the list as a weapon. A care map should not become a scroll of grievances recited in every family conversation. That may be understandable when a caregiver has felt unseen, but it rarely creates useful change. The stronger move is to use the record to make specific decisions: this task is essential; this task can wait; this task should move to someone else; this task needs a routine; this task is emotionally costly and requires recovery afterwards; this task may not need to happen at all.

The record also helps caregivers ask for help more effectively. "I am overwhelmed" is true, but often too broad for others to act on. "I am managing prescriptions, appointment reminders, transport planning, and all family updates" is harder to dismiss and easier to divide. People may still resist, but the conversation becomes more concrete. It shifts from a vague plea for relief to a clear description of work.

For caregivers who are used to being the capable one, this clarity may feel exposing. The list may reveal that the current arrangement depends on their constant competence. It may reveal that others have underestimated the load because the caregiver has been smoothing over the consequences. It may reveal that some help previously offered is too vague to be useful. These discoveries can bring anger, sadness, or fear. That is natural. Seeing the truth can be painful before it becomes freeing.

There is also a private grief in realising how much of one's life has been occupied by uncounted care. The record may show lost evenings, fragmented workdays, interrupted rest, postponed friendships, and an identity increasingly organised around other people's needs. This recognition should be handled with tenderness. The aim is not to shame the caregiver for allowing it to happen. Most caregiving loads expand gradually, through love, urgency, duty, and lack of alternatives. The aim is to stop the expansion from remaining invisible.

Once the invisible tasks are captured, the caregiver can begin to see patterns that were previously hidden by exhaustion. Perhaps most strain comes not from visits, but from messages between visits. Perhaps transport is less burdensome than emotional management. Perhaps paperwork creates dread because it is always left until late. Perhaps a relative's vague involvement creates more work than no involvement at all. Perhaps the person receiving care becomes most anxious when no predictable contact has been agreed. These insights are practical gold.

They also make boundaries more precise. A caregiver who knows the true load does not have to say only, "I need space." They can say, "I cannot continue handling all non-urgent calls during work hours." They do not have to say only, "Everyone needs to help." They can say, "The pharmacy collection and appointment reminders need to move to someone else." They do not have to say only, "I am exhausted." They can say, "The emotional recovery after visits means I need that evening protected." Accurate boundaries come from accurate seeing.

The act of capturing invisible tasks can even change the caregiver's relationship with themselves. Many caregivers carry a quiet suspicion that they are overreacting. They wonder why they are so tired, why they feel resentful, why they cannot simply be kinder, more patient, more organised. A written record often answers with more compassion than any reassurance could. It says: this is not nothing. This is work. This is why you are tired.

That recognition matters because self-doubt consumes energy. A caregiver who spends all day working and all night questioning whether the work counts is being drained twice. Naming the labour reduces that second drain. It gives the caregiver permission to move from shame to assessment, from vague distress to informed decision-making.

However, the list should not become another burden to maintain forever. Capturing invisible tasks is most useful as a focused exercise, repeated when circumstances change or when the caregiver feels lost inside the load again. The aim is not to create a perfect record of every act of care. Perfection would defeat the purpose. The aim is to reveal enough of the pattern to make better choices.

The caregiver should expect the first attempt to be incomplete. Some tasks will be forgotten. Some emotional labour will be hard to name. Some mental load will appear only after reflection. That is fine. The map does not need to capture every grain of sand to prove there is a sack being carried. It simply needs to be honest enough to show the shape and weight of the work.

A care load that remains invisible will keep expanding into whatever space the caregiver leaves undefended. It will fill evenings, interrupt work, colonise sleep, and rename itself as love whenever the caregiver starts to question it. Once captured, it loses some of that power. It becomes discussable. It becomes dividable. It becomes adjustable. It becomes real in a way that others may finally understand and the caregiver can no longer so easily dismiss.

The beginning is simple, but not easy: write down what you do, what you notice, what you remember, what you prevent, what you absorb, and what it costs. Do this without drama and without apology. The truth does not need to shout. It only needs to be seen clearly enough that the next decision can no longer be made from a false picture of the load.

Separating Urgent from Important

One of the most draining features of caregiving is that everything can begin to feel urgent. The phone rings and the body tightens. A message arrives and the mind jumps ahead to the worst possible consequence. A complaint, a change in mood, an unopened letter, a missing item, a request from a relative, a small household problem, a prescription query, a sudden worry about tomorrow's appointment: each one can arrive with the same emotional force. The caregiver may not have time to ask whether the matter is truly time-critical. They simply react, because reaction has become the safest way to keep things from falling apart.

This is how urgency becomes a climate rather than an event.

In a sustainable care arrangement, urgent and important are not the same thing. They may overlap, of course. A genuine medical concern, a safety risk, a missed essential medicine, or a serious breakdown in supervision may be both urgent and important. But many demands feel urgent because someone is anxious, annoyed, lonely, impatient, confused, or accustomed to immediate response. Other tasks are deeply important but do not shout. They sit quietly in the background until neglect turns them into tomorrow's crisis.

The caregiver who cannot separate urgent from important becomes vulnerable to the loudest need in the room. This is exhausting because volume is not the same as priority. The most distressed person may not be pointing towards the highest-risk issue. The most visible task may not be the one that protects wellbeing. The task that makes the caregiver feel guilty may not be the task that most deserves their limited energy. Without a way to distinguish these pressures, caregiving becomes a form of emotional triage performed all day, every day, without a clear method.

The result is a particular kind of fatigue: not only tiredness from doing too much, but tiredness from deciding too often under pressure. Every call becomes a question. Every request becomes a moral test. Every delay feels dangerous. The caregiver is forced to keep asking, "Must I do this now?" while also carrying the fear that the wrong answer might harm someone, disappoint someone, or prove that they do not care enough. Decision fatigue then becomes part of the care load itself.

Separating urgent from important is not about becoming detached. It is about becoming accurate.

Accuracy matters because care is full of competing demands. A kitchen may be untidy, a relative may be offended, a form may be waiting, a person receiving care may want company, a prescription may need checking, and the caregiver may not have slept properly. If all of these demands are treated as equal, the caregiver will be pulled towards whatever creates the strongest immediate discomfort. That may be the untidy kitchen, because it is visible. It may be the offended relative, because their messages are sharp. It may be the request for company, because guilt rises quickly. Meanwhile, the prescription check, which quietly prevents a more serious problem, may be postponed.

This is the danger. Important tasks are often quiet until they have been neglected for too long.

A useful care system protects quiet importance. Medication routines, food supply, hydration, mobility safety, appointment preparation, transport, bills, key documents, rest for the caregiver, and reliable communication may not always feel dramatic in the moment. Yet these are the areas that often prevent avoidable crises. They are less emotionally noisy than a complaint and less visible than a mess, but they carry greater consequences. The caregiver must learn to hear them before they shout.

Urgency should be assessed by risk and time, not by panic alone. Risk asks, "What could happen if this is not addressed?" Time asks, "How soon does it genuinely need attention?" These two questions bring the caregiver out of emotional reflex and into practical judgement. A problem that could cause harm soon deserves swift action. A problem that is uncomfortable but not dangerous may deserve attention later. A problem that someone else can handle should not automatically become the caregiver's interruption. A problem that is recurring should not be solved only in the moment; it should be redesigned.

This distinction can be uncomfortable because it requires the caregiver to tolerate other people's displeasure. Someone may want an immediate answer. Someone may insist that a non-critical issue cannot wait. Someone may present their frustration as an emergency because they have learned that urgency gets a faster response. The caregiver may feel cruel for pausing. Yet pausing is not neglect. Pausing is often the first act of wise care.

A pause creates space for classification. Is this a safety issue? Is health at risk? Is there a deadline with real consequences? Is the person distressed but safe? Is this a preference, a comfort, a habit, or a genuine need? Does it require me specifically? Can it be handled during the next planned check-in? Can another person take it? Has this happened before? If it has happened before, why does it keep arriving as a crisis?

These questions are not bureaucratic. They are protective. They prevent the caregiver's life from being ruled by every emotional surge. They also protect the person receiving care from a chaotic system in which everything depends on the caregiver's immediate availability. When urgency is classified well, true emergencies receive better attention because the caregiver's energy has not been spent on preventable or mislabelled crises.

One of the most common traps is confusing emotional urgency with practical urgency. Emotional urgency is real. A person may feel frightened, lonely, angry, embarrassed, or abandoned. Those feelings deserve compassion. But they do not automatically require instant action from the caregiver. A lonely person may want a long call now, but the important care action may be a predictable contact routine. An anxious person may demand repeated reassurance, but the important action may be clearer information, a written reminder, or a scheduled check-in. A relative may send an accusatory message, but the important action may be refusing to debate in the middle of work.

When emotional urgency is always answered immediately, it can become stronger rather than weaker. The person receiving care may learn that distress is the route to attention. The caregiver may learn that peace is purchased through instant availability. Over time, both people become trapped. The care recipient feels insecure unless the caregiver responds at once. The caregiver feels guilty unless they interrupt their own life. A more stable rhythm requires compassion with boundaries: feelings are acknowledged, but they do not always set the timetable.

Another trap is confusing visible urgency with true importance. A pile of dishes, an unmade bed, a cluttered room, or a minor household mess can feel urgent because it is right there, accusing the caregiver with its physical presence. But visibility is not the same as consequence. Tidying may be worthwhile, especially where hygiene or safety is involved, but it should not automatically outrank a medication refill, a financial deadline, a mobility concern, or the caregiver's protected rest after a difficult appointment. The eye can be a poor judge of priority when it is drawn to what looks messy rather than what matters most.

Caregivers also need to beware of inherited urgency. Some families carry a long-standing habit in which certain people's discomfort has always been treated as more important than everyone else's stability. A demanding relative may expect immediate updates. A parent may have always interpreted delay as disrespect. A sibling may only become involved when there is drama, then criticise decisions made by the person doing the daily work. These patterns can make the caregiver feel as if every response is being judged against old family rules. The urgency may not belong to the care situation at all. It may belong to family history.

Separating urgent from important requires the caregiver to develop an internal standard that is stronger than other people's reactions. This does not mean ignoring feedback. It means not allowing feedback to become the whole decision-making system. The caregiver must be able to say, privately and sometimes aloud, "I understand this feels pressing, and I will deal with it at the appropriate time." That sentence carries a quiet authority. It acknowledges feeling without handing over control.

A practical way to classify tasks is to consider three elements: risk, timing, and ownership.

Risk concerns the consequence of delay. A high-risk task affects health, safety, essential care, money, legal or administrative standing, or serious emotional stability. A low-risk task may be irritating, inconvenient, or embarrassing, but delay will not cause meaningful harm. Timing concerns whether action is needed immediately, soon, later, or as part of a routine. Ownership concerns who is actually best placed to handle it. These three elements help the caregiver avoid the automatic assumption that every task must be done now and by them.

For example, collecting a necessary prescription before supply runs out may be important and time-sensitive. Tidying a drawer because the person receiving care is annoyed may be low-risk and delayable. Confirming transport before an appointment may prevent a crisis. Answering a non-urgent message from a relative during work may create disruption without improving care. Checking whether there is enough food for the next day may be important. Reorganising the entire kitchen because it would look better may not be. The difference is not always glamorous, but it is decisive.

This type of classification can feel unnatural at first. Caregivers are often trained by circumstance to act before thinking. They may fear that any delay is neglect. They may also be carrying memories of times when something small did become serious, which makes every small thing feel threatening. This fear deserves respect, but it should not be allowed to turn all care into permanent emergency response. A mature care system accepts risk without becoming ruled by imagination.

The question "What happens if this waits?" is especially useful. If the honest answer is "someone will be annoyed", that is different from "someone may be unsafe". If the answer is "I will feel guilty", that is different from "an essential task will fail". If the answer is "the house will look untidy", that is different from "a fall risk will remain in the hallway". If the answer is "a relative will complain", that is different from "a deadline will be missed with serious consequences." The caregiver must learn to distinguish discomfort from danger.

That distinction is one of the foundations of sustainable care.

It also helps the caregiver protect their best energy for tasks that prevent future harm. Many caregivers spend the day clearing small emotional fires and then have no capacity left for the quiet administrative or planning work that would reduce tomorrow's pressure. They answer every message but do not update the medication list. They smooth every family feeling but do not confirm the transport plan. They respond to complaints about small household matters but postpone a conversation about shared responsibilities. The day feels full, but the care system is not becoming safer or more stable.

Important tasks often require concentration, not panic. They may need a clear mind, a calm conversation, a written plan, or a scheduled block of time. If the caregiver's attention is constantly hijacked by urgency, these important tasks remain undone until they become urgent too. This is how preventable crises are manufactured. The task was not invisible because it did not matter. It was invisible because it was not screaming.

The caregiver must therefore create protected space for important work. This may be a weekly review, a regular admin hour, a planned supply check, or a fixed time for care-related calls. The form does not matter as much as the principle: some tasks are too important to be left to leftover attention. They need a place in the rhythm of care before they turn into pressure. A care system that never makes room for prevention will keep paying for crisis.

There is also an emotional boundary hidden inside this practice. When the caregiver chooses important over merely urgent, they may have to disappoint someone. They may not answer immediately. They may not tidy what someone wants tidied. They may not enter a circular argument. They may not respond to a relative's dramatic message until later. This can feel harsh, especially for caregivers who have used responsiveness as proof of love. But a caregiver cannot build stability while being endlessly interruptible.

Responsiveness is not the same as reliability. In fact, constant responsiveness can make a caregiver less reliable over time because it fragments their attention and exhausts their capacity. Reliability means that essential things are handled, risks are monitored, commitments are clear, and the caregiver remains functional enough to continue. A person who responds to everything immediately may look reliable in the moment while becoming increasingly unable to sustain the role.

The care recipient may also benefit from a calmer priority system. When the caregiver responds to every issue as though it is equally serious, the atmosphere of care becomes tense. The person receiving care may absorb that tension and become more anxious. They may learn that small problems deserve large reactions. A steadier system communicates something different: some things need immediate action, some can wait, some belong in the next routine check, and some are not the caregiver's responsibility. This clarity can reduce fear, even when it is initially resisted.

Of course, classification is not perfect. Caregivers will sometimes misjudge. A task that seemed minor may become more important. A concern that seemed urgent may turn out to be harmless. This imperfection is not a reason to abandon the practice. It is a reason to review and adjust. Good care does not require flawless prediction. It requires a thoughtful method, willingness to learn, and enough humility to revise the plan when new information appears.

It is also important to recognise that some caregivers live in situations where there are too many genuinely important tasks and too few resources. In such cases, separating urgent from important may reveal a painful truth: the issue is not poor prioritisation, but an unsustainable arrangement. If health, safety, transport, supervision, emotional support, administration, and household functioning all depend on one person, no classification system will make the load humane. Prioritisation can reduce chaos, but it cannot turn an impossible role into a fair one. It may instead provide the evidence needed to ask for more help or reconsider the arrangement.

The caregiver should be wary of using prioritisation as another way to criticise themselves. The purpose is not to prove that they have been doing care badly. Most caregivers are making decisions under pressure, with incomplete information, emotional strain, and limited support. It is unsurprising that urgency takes over. The aim is not self-reproach. The aim is to regain enough distance from the noise to choose with more wisdom.

This distance can begin with a simple habit: before responding, name the task. Not the feeling around it, but the task itself. "This is a safety concern." "This is a comfort request." "This is a family complaint." "This is a deadline." "This is reassurance-seeking." "This is a household preference." "This is prevention." "This is not mine to do." Naming the task strips away some of the emotional fog. It allows the caregiver to respond to what is actually present rather than to the whole history of guilt, fear, and expectation around it.

Once the task is named, the caregiver can decide its proper place. Now. Today. This week. During the planned call. For someone else. Not at all. These categories are not rigid rules, but they give the caregiver a working structure. Without such structure, everything enters the same crowded doorway and the caregiver becomes the doorway.

The phrase "not at all" is worth including because some tasks do not need to be done. Caregivers often inherit unnecessary work because it once served a purpose, because someone prefers it, because it prevents criticism, or because the caregiver has always done it. Separating urgent from important makes space to ask whether a task is still needed. Some routines are essential. Some are comforting. Some are habits. Some are attempts to control anxiety. Some are ways of preserving appearances at the caregiver's expense. Not all deserve continuation.

For instance, doing extra cleaning before a relative visits may reduce judgement but increase exhaustion. Providing lengthy updates to every family member may create the appearance of inclusion but consume time needed for actual care. Reassuring someone repeatedly about the same non-urgent issue may bring temporary calm but reinforce dependency on constant response. These are not simple matters, and compassion is needed. Yet a caregiver has the right to ask whether the task serves care or merely serves the avoidance of discomfort.

This is where importance must be defined with moral clarity. Important does not mean "what keeps everyone pleased". It means what protects health, safety, dignity, stability, essential functioning, and the caregiver's ability to continue. Some pleasing tasks may be lovely when there is capacity. They should not be allowed to displace the tasks that keep the whole arrangement from becoming fragile.

A strong priority system also changes how help is requested. Rather than saying, "I need help with everything," the caregiver can identify the tasks that truly matter and ask for support there. "I need someone to take over prescription refills" is clearer than a general plea. "I need transport confirmed two days before appointments" is more effective than asking people to be more considerate. "I need non-urgent family updates to wait until Sunday evening" is more sustainable than responding to scattered messages throughout the week. Priorities make requests more concrete.

They also make boundaries more defensible. Not defensible in the sense that the caregiver must argue their worth, but defensible internally. When guilt rises, the caregiver can return to the classification. This is not urgent. This is important but not mine. This is emotionally loud but low-risk. This is genuinely time-sensitive. This can wait until the planned check-in. This must be escalated. A clear internal system reduces the power of guilt to rewrite the day.

The hardest test comes when an unimportant task is emotionally intense. A person may be deeply upset about something that does not require immediate action. A relative may be forceful about a matter that is not high priority. The caregiver may feel pressure in the body as though danger is present, even when the actual issue can wait. These moments require steadiness. The caregiver can be kind without being pulled off course. "I hear that this is upsetting. I will deal with it tomorrow." "I am not able to discuss this during work." "That is not urgent, so I am putting it on the list for the next planning time." Simple sentences can protect the care system from being hijacked.

Over time, this practice reshapes the emotional rhythm of care. The caregiver becomes less reactive. The person receiving care begins, perhaps slowly, to encounter a more predictable response pattern. Other relatives learn that pressure does not automatically produce immediate compliance. Important tasks receive more attention before they fail. The caregiver's day becomes less porous. Not easy. Not perfectly calm. But less governed by the suddenness of other people's feelings.

The deeper benefit is that caregiving starts to move from fear to judgement. Fear asks, "What if I do not respond?" Judgement asks, "What response is appropriate?" Fear imagines blame. Judgement considers consequences. Fear treats every demand as a test of love. Judgement recognises that love without prioritisation can become chaos. The caregiver does not become less caring by developing judgement. They become more capable of protecting what care most depends upon.

Separating urgent from important is therefore not a productivity trick. It is a caregiving discipline. It helps the caregiver honour real risk without bowing to every pressure. It protects prevention from being crowded out by noise. It creates room for decisions that are calmer, fairer, and more repeatable. It teaches the caregiver that not every raised voice, anxious message, visible mess, or guilty feeling deserves command of the day.

A sustainable care load is not built by doing everything quickly.

It is built by knowing what must be protected, what can wait, what can move to someone else, and what should no longer be treated as a duty at all.

Identifying Pinch Points and Triggers

Every caregiving arrangement has pressure points. Some are obvious because they arrive with noise: the missed appointment, the angry phone call, the last-minute transport problem, the pile of paperwork discovered too late. Others are quieter, hiding inside ordinary routines until the caregiver begins to notice that the same moments keep becoming difficult. Morning gets tense. Mealtimes unravel. Visits from relatives leave everyone unsettled. Bills create dread. Evenings become emotionally loaded. A simple request somehow turns into a long negotiation.

These patterns matter because repeated strain is rarely random. It may feel random when the caregiver is exhausted, because everything arrives as one more problem in a crowded day. But many caregiving crises have a rhythm. They gather around predictable times, predictable tasks, predictable people, predictable transitions, or predictable gaps in information. Once those patterns are visible, the caregiver can stop treating every flare-up as a fresh disaster and begin asking a more useful question: *where does this arrangement keep breaking down?*

A pinch point is a place in the care system where pressure repeatedly concentrates. It may be a time of day, such as mornings, when medication, washing, dressing, breakfast, transport, and mood all collide. It may be a recurring task, such as booking appointments or managing prescriptions. It may be a relationship pattern, such as a relative who appears only to criticise or a care recipient who resists help until the situation becomes urgent. It may be a practical gap, such as no reliable driver, no written instructions, no backup plan, or no shared calendar.

A trigger is what sets the pressure in motion. It may be an ambiguous instruction. It may be a change in routine. It may be hunger, tiredness, pain, shame, confusion, loneliness, or fear. It may be the arrival of a letter with official language that no one wants to open. It may be a family visit that brings old roles back to life. It may be the caregiver's phone lighting up during work, creating immediate tension before the message has even been read.

Pinch points and triggers are connected, but they are not the same. The pinch point is the recurring place of strain. The trigger is the spark that ignites it. A mealtime may be the pinch point; the trigger may be too many choices, a late start, an empty fridge, a swallowing concern, a change in appetite, or an argument about what is "good" for the person receiving care. A paperwork deadline may be the pinch point; the trigger may be unopened post, missing passwords, unclear responsibility, or the caregiver's dread of dealing with forms late at night. The more precisely the caregiver can distinguish the two, the more intelligently the routine can be redesigned.

This is not an exercise in blame. Blame asks, "Who is causing trouble?" Pattern recognition asks, "What keeps making this moment harder than it needs to be?" That distinction is essential. A person receiving care may become irritable every morning, but the cause may not be bad character. It may be pain, embarrassment, poor sleep, rushed communication, fear of losing independence, or too many instructions delivered too quickly. A caregiver may feel angry every time paperwork appears, but the issue may not be laziness or avoidance. It may be that administrative tasks always arrive without enough information, enough time, or enough emotional space.

Caregiving becomes more manageable when problems are examined as sequences rather than isolated incidents. A difficult morning, for example, may not begin when the person refuses to get dressed. It may begin the previous evening when no clothes are prepared, no transport time is confirmed, no medication routine is agreed, and the caregiver goes to bed already anxious. By the time refusal appears, the system is already under strain. The visible conflict is only the final scene.

This sequence thinking is powerful because it prevents the caregiver from becoming trapped in surface reactions. If the caregiver focuses only on the moment of resistance, they may try to push harder, persuade longer, or absorb more frustration. If they examine the sequence, they may notice that the routine is too compressed, the instructions are unclear, the person feels rushed, or the caregiver is entering the morning without enough support. The solution is not always more effort. Often, it is earlier design.

Mornings are a common pinch point because they carry too many demands at once. The day has not yet found its shape, and already the caregiver may be dealing with medication, hygiene, breakfast, mobility, appointments, transport, mood, and their own responsibilities. If the person receiving care is anxious, slow to start, confused, in pain, or resistant to help, the morning can become a daily test of patience. The caregiver may begin each day feeling as though they are already behind.

The trigger may be less obvious than the tension itself. Perhaps the person receiving care feels embarrassed about needing help with personal tasks. Perhaps they become overwhelmed when given several instructions together. Perhaps breakfast choices create conflict. Perhaps the caregiver arrives too close to departure time because no margin has been built in. Perhaps a relative sends messages early in the day and pulls the caregiver's attention away. Naming the trigger does not remove the difficulty, but it changes the caregiver's relationship to it. What was once "every morning is awful" becomes "mornings become difficult when too many decisions and time pressure arrive together."

Mealtimes can create similar strain. Food is never only food in caregiving. It can carry health concerns, independence, memory, habit, culture, control, appetite, money, grief, and dignity. A caregiver may see a meal as nourishment and safety. The person receiving care may experience it as intrusion, criticism, loss of choice, or another reminder that life has changed. A simple question such as "What do you want for lunch?" can become loaded if the person is tired, indecisive, ashamed of needing help, or unable to manage too many options.

The pinch point may appear as repeated arguments about eating, shopping, cooking, waste, or preferences. The trigger may be choice overload, lack of routine, a fridge that is not stocked with easy defaults, poor timing, physical discomfort, loneliness, or the caregiver's anxiety about nutrition. If every meal is treated as a fresh negotiation, both people may become exhausted. The caregiver may begin to dread what should be a basic act of care. The person receiving care may feel managed rather than respected.

Paperwork is another frequent source of pressure because it combines practical consequence with emotional weight. Forms, letters, bills, appointment notices, assessments, insurance documents, benefit applications, service correspondence, and financial records can gather quietly until they suddenly become urgent. The caregiver may not know what is missing until a deadline is close. The person receiving care may avoid opening letters because they feel overwhelmed or ashamed. Other relatives may assume "someone" is handling it, which usually means the most responsible person is expected to notice, interpret, and act.

The trigger here is often ambiguity. Who opens the post? Who understands the forms? Who keeps passwords? Who knows which letters matter? Who files documents? Who follows up? Who is allowed to speak on behalf of the person receiving care? When these questions remain unanswered, paperwork becomes a recurring ambush. It waits in drawers, bags, envelopes, and half-remembered conversations until the caregiver is forced into late-night administration with a tired mind and a rising pulse.

Family visits can also be pinch points, especially when visitors do not understand the daily care load. A relative may arrive with good intentions and leave behind emotional disruption. They may question routines, criticise decisions, make promises they do not keep, encourage the person receiving care to expect changes that are not practical, or perform a burst of help that creates more work afterwards. The main caregiver may then have to soothe the care recipient, correct misunderstandings, explain the reality, and absorb resentment from all sides.

The trigger may be old family dynamics rather than the visit itself. The sibling who has always been critical may still criticise. The parent who has always preferred one child's opinion may still dismiss the caregiver who does the work. The relative who cannot tolerate guilt may turn brief involvement into grand advice. Caregiving does not erase family history; it often intensifies it. Under stress, people return to familiar roles, even when those roles damage the care system.

Transport is another deceptively simple pressure point. A journey to an appointment sounds like a practical task, but it can include preparation, timing, mobility, parking, waiting, emotional reassurance, note-taking, follow-up, and recovery. If transport is unreliable, every appointment becomes vulnerable. If the caregiver is the only driver, their schedule becomes the hidden infrastructure beneath the entire care arrangement. If no backup exists, any change in the caregiver's work, health, or family life becomes a care crisis.

The trigger may be late booking, unclear appointment details, no shared calendar, underestimating travel time, resistance from the person receiving care, or assumptions that the caregiver will be available. Transport problems often reveal a wider issue: the care system has not separated coordination from physical availability. The caregiver may be willing to arrange appointments, but that does not mean they can personally provide every journey. Unless this distinction is made, transport becomes one of the fastest ways for "helping" to turn into permanent obligation.

Communication itself can become a pinch point. Too many channels create confusion. A text from one relative, a voicemail from another, a note from a professional, a reminder from the person receiving care, and a half-remembered conversation can leave the caregiver holding fragments of information without a clear source of truth. Misunderstandings multiply. Someone believes a task is done. Someone else believes it was never agreed. The caregiver becomes the interpreter, messenger, record-keeper, and emotional buffer.

The trigger is often the absence of a reliable communication rhythm. When people communicate only when anxious, annoyed, or rushed, information arrives already charged. A practical update becomes a family argument. A question becomes an accusation. A delay becomes evidence of neglect. Without a shared method for updates, every message carries the possibility of conflict. The caregiver then has to manage not only the information, but the feeling attached to it.

Caregivers should pay close attention to the body when identifying pinch points. The body often recognises patterns before the mind has named them. A tightening stomach before a certain phone call. A headache after family messages. Restlessness before visits. Irritation at a particular time of day. Dread when a letter arrives. A rush of anger when someone says, "Can you just...?" These reactions are not always proof that the situation is wrong, but they are data. They point towards places where the care system may be demanding too much, too often, or too unclearly.

The caregiver can begin by asking where tension repeats. Not where things are occasionally hard; caregiving will always contain some difficulty. The question is where the same kind of hard keeps returning. Which moments are regularly followed by exhaustion? Which tasks are repeatedly delayed until they become urgent? Which conversations leave the caregiver feeling trapped? Which requests create immediate resentment? Which routines depend on hope rather than structure? Which people leave more confusion behind them than they remove?

These questions turn emotional strain into practical information. Instead of saying, "Everything is too much," the caregiver may discover that the heaviest pressure comes from evening calls, appointment transport, medication uncertainty, family criticism, or mealtime resistance. This is not a small distinction. "Everything" cannot be redesigned. A specific pinch point can.

A simple pattern record can help. For a week or two, the caregiver notes when pressure spikes, what happened just before it, who was involved, what information was missing, what decision had to be made, and what the emotional cost was afterwards. The record does not need to be elaborate. It only needs to reveal repetition. The caregiver is looking for the recurring hinge: the moment where the day turns from manageable to strained.

The most useful observations are often plain. "Calls after 9 p.m. leave me unable to sleep." "Mum becomes distressed when appointment details are discussed too early." "Dad refuses lunch when given too many choices." "My brother's visits create confusion because he promises things without checking." "Paperwork becomes urgent because letters are not opened weekly." "Transport fails when appointments are booked without checking availability." Each sentence turns vague frustration into a practical target.

The aim is not to make care perfectly smooth. Human needs are not a production line. People have moods, fears, preferences, pain, pride, and unpredictable days. But many caregiving arrangements are harder than they need to be because predictable pressure is allowed to remain unnamed. Once a pinch point is identified, the caregiver can stop being surprised by the same problem. They can meet it earlier, with less drama and more structure.

It is important to look for triggers inside the caregiver too. Not every trigger comes from the care recipient, relatives, or logistics. A caregiver may be especially reactive when tired, hungry, rushed, criticised, ignored, or made to feel incompetent. They may become tense when a request resembles old family expectations. They may overreact to small changes because previous crises have taught them to expect the worst. They may feel anger not because the current request is unreasonable, but because it lands on top of many earlier unspoken sacrifices.

This self-awareness is not self-blame. It is self-protection. A caregiver who knows their own triggers can plan with more honesty. If difficult conversations after work lead to harshness, those conversations may need another time. If late-night messages create anxiety, the phone boundary needs attention. If visits after poor sleep cause resentment, the schedule must acknowledge sleep as part of care. If family criticism makes the caregiver over-explain and then over-commit, responses need to become shorter and firmer.

Caregiving pressure also spikes when instructions are ambiguous. "Keep an eye on her." "Make sure he eats properly." "Sort the paperwork." "Check she is okay." "Help more." These phrases may sound caring, but they are operationally weak. They leave too much open to interpretation. The caregiver must decide what "okay" means, how much help is enough, when concern becomes action, and whether they will be judged if something is missed. Ambiguity creates mental labour because the caregiver has to turn vague expectations into actual decisions.

Clear standards reduce triggers. If "check she is okay" becomes "call at 10 a.m. and ask about breakfast, medication, pain, and plans for the day", the task becomes more manageable. If "sort the paperwork" becomes "open post every Friday, photograph urgent letters, and file the rest", the ambiguity shrinks. If "help with appointments" becomes "book appointments, but transport is shared between three people", ownership becomes clearer. Precision may feel less warm, but it is often kinder than leaving the caregiver to interpret every expectation alone.

Another recurring trigger is lack of backup. A care system without backup turns every minor disruption into a threat. If the main caregiver becomes ill, the plan wobbles. If a car breaks down, the appointment is at risk. If a helper cancels, the caregiver absorbs the task. If the person receiving care has a difficult day, there is no margin. This constant fragility keeps the caregiver in a state of alert. They are not only doing the task; they are guarding against the collapse of the task.

Backups do not have to be elaborate. They may be as simple as an alternative driver, a spare key arrangement, a second person who knows the medication routine, a written list of contacts, or an agreed response for missed calls. The point is that the caregiver should not be the only answer to every disruption. When no backup exists, the caregiver's body becomes the backup. That is not sustainable design; it is hidden dependence.

Pinch points should be examined through the lens of safety, frequency, and emotional cost. Safety asks whether the recurring problem creates risk. Frequency asks how often it happens. Emotional cost asks how much it drains the caregiver or damages the relationship. A problem that is low-risk, rare, and mildly irritating may not deserve immediate redesign. A problem that is high-risk, frequent, or emotionally corrosive deserves serious attention. This helps the caregiver avoid trying to fix everything at once.

For example, a weekly argument about medication is not merely annoying if it increases the chance of missed doses and leaves the caregiver anxious for hours. A monthly paperwork panic may deserve attention if it threatens finances or services. A daily mealtime struggle may be more urgent to redesign than an untidy bedroom if it affects nutrition and the emotional tone of the whole day. A relative's occasional irritating comment may be less important than their repeated habit of making promises that disrupt routines.

The caregiver also needs to distinguish between a trigger and a person. This is especially important for preserving relationships. If "Mum is impossible in the mornings" becomes "mornings are difficult when there is time pressure and too many choices", the caregiver has more room to act without contempt. If "my sister makes everything worse" becomes "visits create confusion when she makes promises outside the care plan", the issue becomes more addressable. Language matters because it either hardens resentment or opens a path towards change.

This does not mean excusing harmful behaviour. Some people are manipulative, irresponsible, aggressive, or persistently dismissive. Caregivers should not be asked to soften reality beyond recognition. But even then, identifying the trigger can help. If a relative reliably creates conflict during group discussions, the caregiver may choose written updates instead. If the person receiving care becomes verbally harsh when tired, difficult topics may need a different time. If a professional recommendation creates unrealistic pressure, the caregiver may need to clarify what is actually possible. The goal is not to label people neatly, but to reduce avoidable harm.

Once a pinch point is identified, the caregiver should resist the temptation to leap immediately into a grand solution. The more useful move is to understand the mechanics. What exactly happens? When does it begin? What happens just before it escalates? What information is missing? What assumption is being made? Who is expected to act? What would make the situation easier by a small but meaningful degree? Good redesign begins with observation, not panic.

Small changes often have disproportionate power because they interrupt the sequence early. A written morning routine can reduce repeated instruction. A default meal plan can reduce choice fatigue. A weekly post-opening time can prevent paperwork ambushes. A shared calendar can reduce appointment confusion. A fixed call time can reduce repeated emotional interruptions. A short message after family visits can correct misunderstandings before they spread. These are not glamorous interventions, but caregiving stability is usually built from unglamorous interventions repeated faithfully.

The caregiver should also consider whether a pinch point is signalling a deeper threshold. Sometimes a routine breaks down because it is poorly designed. At other times, it breaks down because the person's needs have changed. More resistance, more confusion, more falls, more missed meals, more medication problems, more distress, or more night-time disruption may indicate that the current level of support is no longer adequate. In such cases, redesigning the routine may help, but it may not be enough. The pinch point is then not merely an inconvenience; it is a signal that the care plan needs reassessment.

This is why identifying triggers should be done with honesty rather than optimism. Caregivers sometimes minimise recurring problems because admitting the pattern feels like opening the door to bigger decisions. They tell themselves it was a bad day, then another bad day, then another. They normalise strain because the alternative is frightening. But a pattern does not disappear because it is inconvenient to name. Naming it early may preserve more options than waiting until the pressure forces a crisis.

There is also relief in recognising that not every difficult moment requires an emotional explanation. Sometimes the problem is not deep family trauma, personality conflict, or lack of love. Sometimes the problem is simply that no one knows who is doing transport. The medication list is out of date. The morning routine is too rushed. The phone boundary is unclear. The post is not being opened regularly. The caregiver has no recovery time after visits. Ordinary design failures can create extraordinary emotional strain.

This realisation can reduce shame. The caregiver is not necessarily failing because the same issue keeps returning. They may be trying to operate without a workable system. The person receiving care may not be "being difficult" so much as responding to a routine that does not match their capacity. Relatives may not be malicious, though they may still be unhelpful; they may be responding to vague expectations. Pattern recognition allows everyone to move away from character judgements and towards practical correction.

Still, practical correction requires courage. Some triggers cannot be reduced without changing expectations. If late-night calls are a pinch point, someone may have to hear that non-urgent calls will wait until morning. If family visits create confusion, visitors may need clearer limits. If transport assumptions are causing strain, the caregiver may have to stop automatically filling the gap. If paperwork keeps becoming urgent, the person receiving care may have to accept a more regular review. These changes can cause discomfort. That discomfort is often the price of leaving crisis care behind.

A caregiver does not need to identify every pinch point at once. In fact, trying to map the entire care system in one sitting can become another form of overwhelm. The best place to begin is usually the moment that keeps stealing peace. The moment that regularly turns a manageable day into a strained one. The task that creates dread before it begins. The person, time, or routine after which the caregiver feels repeatedly depleted. That is often where the system is speaking most clearly.

The deeper purpose is to move caregiving from surprise to anticipation. Surprise says, "This keeps happening to me." Anticipation says, "This tends to happen here, under these conditions, and it needs a better design." That shift does not remove the human difficulty of care, but it gives the caregiver more authority within it. They are no longer only absorbing pressure. They are reading it.

When pinch points and triggers are named, the care load becomes less mysterious. The caregiver begins to see that the chaos has edges. It has times, causes, sequences, and repeated openings. Those openings are where change can enter. Not everywhere at once. Not perfectly. But precisely enough that the next difficult moment is not treated as fate.

The question to carry forward is simple and demanding: where does care keep becoming harder than the need itself requires?

Choosing What Must Change First

Once the real care load becomes visible, a caregiver may feel both relieved and overwhelmed. Relieved, because the exhaustion finally makes sense. Overwhelmed, because the list is longer than expected and every part of it seems to ask for attention. There are medicines to manage, appointments to coordinate, meals to think about, relatives to update, bills to check, moods to steady, safety risks to watch, and a life of your own still trying to exist around the edges.

The temptation is to fix everything at once.

That temptation is understandable. When a caregiver has been under strain for too long, clarity can produce urgency. The mind starts racing. The whole arrangement looks flawed. Every weak point seems connected to every other weak point. If transport were better, appointments would be easier. If relatives helped more, resentment would ease. If paperwork were organised, late-night anxiety would reduce. If the person receiving care accepted routines, mornings would improve. If calls were contained, sleep might return. The caregiver sees the entire web and wants to pull it straight in one decisive movement.

But care systems rarely improve through total overhaul. They improve through intelligent sequence.

Trying to change everything at once often creates another form of chaos. The caregiver, already depleted, becomes the manager of a reform project. New routines are introduced before old patterns are understood. Relatives are asked for too many changes at the same time and respond with confusion or resistance. The person receiving care feels overwhelmed by sudden adjustments. The caregiver then spends more energy explaining, persuading, correcting, and monitoring than they were spending before. What began as a rescue plan becomes a second workload.

This is why the question is not, "What needs to change?" The list may be long. The sharper question is, "What must change first?"

That question requires discipline. It asks the caregiver to resist the emotional pull of the most irritating problem and look instead for the change that will create the greatest relief, protection, or stability. The first change does not need to solve the whole situation. It needs to reduce pressure in a meaningful place. A good first change creates breathing room. It lowers risk, interrupts a repeated crisis, protects recovery time, or removes a task from the caregiver that has become too costly to carry alone.

The order matters because energy is limited. A caregiver who is exhausted cannot afford symbolic improvements that look satisfying but change little. Rearranging a cupboard may feel productive, but if the true pressure comes from missed medication refills, the cupboard is not the starting point. Writing a long message to relatives may feel cathartic, but if no specific task is transferred, nothing has changed except the caregiver's emotional exposure. Buying another planner may feel like control, but if no one else is sharing responsibility, the planner may simply become a neater record of overload.

Choosing what must change first means placing impact above appearance.

A useful first test is safety. Any issue that creates a realistic risk of harm deserves serious attention. This does not mean every worry should be treated as an emergency. Caregivers can imagine endless possibilities, and fear is not the same as evidence. But some areas clearly carry greater consequence than others: medication routines, falls risk, food and hydration, essential appointments, dangerous confusion, unsafe driving, financial vulnerability, missed care needs, or situations where the caregiver's exhaustion is beginning to affect judgement. When safety is genuinely involved, it usually outranks tidiness, preference, family opinion, and appearances.

Safety also includes the caregiver. This is often missed. A care arrangement that leaves the caregiver dangerously sleep-deprived, emotionally volatile, unable to work properly, neglecting their own health, or driving while exhausted contains risk. The caregiver may be tempted to rank their own wellbeing below every practical task, but that ranking is false. If the caregiver is part of care, their deterioration is not a side issue. It is a safety signal. A first change may therefore be a night-time phone boundary, a transport backup, a protected rest period after difficult appointments, or a reduction in tasks that require constant vigilance.

The next test is frequency. Some problems are painful but rare. Others are less dramatic yet happen so often that they quietly drain the whole week. A monthly argument may be unpleasant, but daily morning conflict may be doing more damage. A complicated form may be stressful, but repeated calls during work may be fragmenting the caregiver's life every day. A single missed appointment may matter, but a recurring pattern of last-minute appointment preparation may be the larger problem. Frequency turns small tasks into heavy loads.

Caregivers often overlook frequent irritations because they have become normal. The daily reminder. The repeated question. The constant message. The regular transport assumption. The predictable mealtime resistance. The evening call that derails sleep. These may not look serious in isolation, but repetition gives them weight. A change that reduces a frequent pressure can produce more relief than a change aimed at a rare crisis, even if the rare crisis feels more dramatic in memory.

The third test is emotional cost. Some tasks take little time but consume a great deal of emotional energy. A five-minute call with a critical relative may leave the caregiver tense for hours. A brief conversation about food may trigger shame, resistance, and frustration. A short visit may be exhausting if it requires constant emotional regulation. A practical errand may be manageable, while a family update afterwards becomes the part that drains the caregiver most. Time does not tell the whole truth. Emotional cost must be counted.

This matters because resentment often grows around emotionally expensive tasks that appear small to outsiders. The caregiver may struggle to explain why they dread a simple phone call or why a brief exchange leaves them exhausted. But the body keeps the record. If a task repeatedly produces anger, dread, guilt, or heaviness, it deserves attention. Not because every difficult feeling means the task should disappear, but because repeated emotional cost affects the quality of care and the caregiver's capacity to continue.

The most powerful first change often sits where safety, frequency, and emotional cost overlap. A repeated medication problem that creates anxiety and risk. A daily evening call that disrupts sleep and causes dread. A weekly transport scramble that threatens appointments and damages work. A family communication pattern that repeatedly creates conflict and leaves the caregiver responsible for repair. These are high-impact targets. Changing one of them can alter the emotional climate of the whole arrangement.

The caregiver should be wary of choosing the easiest problem simply because it is available. Easy changes have their place, especially when morale is low, but they should not be confused with meaningful change. Clearing a drawer, buying storage boxes, or making a new list may provide a small sense of order. That can be useful. But if the caregiver is still taking every non-urgent call at night, still providing all transport, still managing all appointments, still absorbing relatives' criticism, or still missing sleep, the main load remains intact. Cosmetic order cannot substitute for structural relief.

At the same time, the caregiver should not choose the hardest problem first simply because it is the most emotionally charged. A long-standing family conflict may be real, but it may not be the best starting point if the caregiver has no energy, no evidence, and no clear request. A major conversation about care arrangements may be necessary, but it may go better after one smaller system has been clarified. Starting with a practical pressure point can build confidence and create evidence. Stability often grows through proof, not declarations.

For example, instead of beginning with "Everyone needs to do more," the caregiver might begin with one defined task: prescription refills, appointment transport, weekly shopping, paperwork scanning, or a scheduled visit. This narrower change is easier to explain, easier to measure, and harder for others to avoid through vague sympathy. It also gives the caregiver a clearer sense of whether someone is genuinely willing to help or merely willing to agree in principle.

A good first change should be specific enough to implement. "I need my life back" is emotionally true, but too large to guide action. "I will not answer non-urgent calls after 8 p.m." is specific. "My siblings need to support me" may be justified, but it is not yet an operational change. "One person needs to take over pharmacy collection every Friday" is operational. "Mornings are impossible" names distress. "Clothes, medication, breakfast, and transport details need to be prepared the evening before appointment days" names a redesign.

The more specific the change, the less emotional labour it requires to maintain. Vague intentions invite negotiation. Specific changes create edges.

The caregiver should also ask whether the proposed change depends mostly on their own behaviour, another person's behaviour, or a shared agreement. This distinction matters. Some changes are within the caregiver's immediate control: not answering non-urgent messages during work, writing down the medication routine, setting a fixed check-in time, refusing to provide transport beyond an agreed limit. Other changes require cooperation: a relative taking over a task, the person receiving care accepting a routine, family members using a shared calendar. Shared changes can be valuable, but they may take longer and require follow-up.

When a caregiver is depleted, it can be wise to begin with a change that gives them some control quickly. This is not because cooperation is unimportant, but because waiting for everyone else to become reasonable can keep the caregiver trapped. A personal boundary or routine can create immediate space. Once there is a little more steadiness, broader negotiation becomes easier. A drowning person does not begin by redesigning the harbour. They first need something solid to hold.

However, personal control should not become another excuse for doing everything alone. Some caregivers choose only changes that depend on them because involving others feels too difficult. They create more systems, more reminders, more notes, more alarms, more careful planning, all designed to compensate for the absence of shared responsibility. This can help temporarily, but it may also deepen the pattern in which the caregiver remains the central engine.

The first change should reduce load, not simply organise the caregiver's over-functioning more neatly.

A useful question is: "Will this change remove work, reduce risk, or merely rearrange the burden?" If a new system requires the caregiver to do more monitoring, more reminding, or more explaining, it may not be true relief. If asking a helper to take a task results in the caregiver checking repeatedly, correcting mistakes, and feeling anxious, the handoff needs a clearer standard or a different person. If a routine adds steps but does not reduce confusion, it may be too complicated. Good change should make the care load lighter, safer, or more predictable. Preferably all three.

The first change should also be small enough to survive a bad week. Caregivers often design ideal routines when they are desperate for order, then feel defeated when real life interrupts them. A sustainable change does not depend on everyone being calm, rested, and cooperative. It must work when someone is tired, when a call runs long, when the person receiving care is irritable, when a helper forgets, when the caregiver has their own obligations. The minimum workable version is often better than the perfect version.

For instance, a complete family care platform may be too much to introduce, but a shared weekly message with appointments, tasks, and urgent notes may work. A detailed meal plan may collapse, but three default meals that are easy to repeat may reduce daily stress. A full paperwork archive may be unrealistic, but one folder for current letters and essential contacts may prevent panic. A complex rota may fail, but one fixed transport commitment from one helper may create real relief.

The caregiver should measure progress by fewer crises and more recovery time, not by whether the care arrangement looks impressive. This is an important standard. Some changes look modest but transform the week. A fixed call time may reduce interruptions. A pharmacy routine may prevent last-minute panic. A transport backup may make appointments less frightening. A written list of key information may allow someone else to step in. These changes may not impress an outsider, but they create practical stability where it matters.

Recovery time is a particularly honest measure. If a change does not create any space for the caregiver to rest, think, work, sleep, or return to themselves, it may not be sufficient. The purpose of redesign is not simply to make the caregiver more efficient at carrying too much. It is to make the load more humane. A better system should return some capacity to the caregiver. If every saved minute is immediately swallowed by another task, the care plan has not yet changed enough.

It is also necessary to decide what not to change yet. This can feel uncomfortable, especially when many things are clearly imperfect. But not every problem can be the starting point. Some can be parked. Some can be tolerated for now. Some can be revisited after the first pressure point improves. This is not avoidance; it is sequencing. A caregiver who tries to address all weaknesses at once may lose the ability to address any of them well.

Parking a problem does not mean pretending it is fine. It means saying, "This matters, but it is not the next move." That sentence can reduce the mental clutter of constant unfinished concern. The caregiver may keep a short "later" list so that issues are not forgotten, but they are not allowed to dominate the present. The current focus remains on the chosen change. Stability requires attention, and attention is weakened when scattered across every possible improvement.

Choosing the first change may bring guilt. The caregiver may think, "How can I focus on phone boundaries when the house is messy?" or "How can I prioritise my sleep when they are lonely?" or "How can I ask someone else to manage prescriptions when I know I would do it better?" These thoughts are common. They are also part of the old system defending itself. Guilt often rises when a caregiver begins to act strategically instead of reactively.

The response to guilt is not surrender. It is return to criteria. Safety. Frequency. Emotional cost. What reduces risk? What repeats most often? What drains capacity? What would create room for steadier care? These questions help the caregiver move from guilt to judgement. They do not remove feeling, but they prevent feeling from becoming the only decision-maker.

The person receiving care may also resist the first change. They may prefer the familiar arrangement, even if it is harming the caregiver. They may distrust new helpers, dislike routines, or interpret a boundary as abandonment. Their response matters, but it cannot be the sole measure of whether change is necessary. A system that relies on the caregiver's depletion will often object when depletion is interrupted. That objection may deserve compassion, but it should not automatically govern the plan.

Relatives may resist as well. Some may minimise the problem. Some may agree but fail to act. Some may criticise the chosen priority because it is not the issue they personally notice. Some may prefer broad emotional discussions over specific responsibilities. This is why the caregiver's chosen change must be clear. The more precise the request or boundary, the less room there is for the conversation to dissolve into sympathy, defensiveness, or debate about whether the caregiver is really overwhelmed.

For example, "I am no longer able to manage all appointment transport" may invite argument about why. "Starting next month, I can coordinate appointment dates, but I can only drive once a month. The remaining journeys need assigned drivers or another transport option" is harder to blur. It defines the change, the limit, and the gap that must be addressed. The caregiver does not need to prove total collapse. They need to state the new terms.

The first change should be given enough time to work, but not so much time that failure is ignored. Some adjustments need practice. People forget. Routines wobble. The person receiving care may need repetition. Helpers may need clearer instructions. The caregiver may need to hold the boundary several times before it becomes believable. Early discomfort does not automatically mean the change is wrong.

But repeated failure is information. If the same person keeps missing the task, the task may need to move. If the routine is too complex, it needs simplifying. If the boundary is constantly breached because there is no consequence, it needs reinforcement. If the change reduces one problem but creates a larger one, it needs review. Sustainable care is not about rigidly defending the first idea. It is about staying loyal to the goal: less crisis, lower risk, more recovery, clearer responsibility.

The caregiver should expect emotional turbulence during the shift. Any meaningful change disturbs the system that made the old pattern feel normal. The caregiver may feel selfish on the first evening they do not answer a non-urgent call. A relative may sound annoyed when asked to take a defined task. The person receiving care may test whether the boundary is real. The caregiver may feel tempted to retreat to the familiar role because familiar exhaustion can feel safer than unfamiliar firmness.

This is where the chosen priority becomes an anchor. The caregiver can remind themselves, "This is the change I am practising now." Not every complaint requires a new decision. Not every uncomfortable feeling requires a reversal. Not every imperfect attempt means the old arrangement was better. Change becomes sustainable when the caregiver stops renegotiating with themselves every time discomfort appears.

It may help to name the reason for the change in a single clear sentence. "This will prevent prescription crises." "This will protect my sleep." "This will stop appointment days becoming emergencies." "This will reduce daily interruptions." "This will make it possible for someone else to help." "This will lower the emotional cost of family communication." A sentence like this keeps the focus on function rather than guilt. It gives the caregiver something to return to when the old pattern pulls hard.

The chosen change should also be visible enough to evaluate. After a reasonable period, the caregiver can ask: Are there fewer last-minute scrambles? Is the task clearer? Has risk reduced? Am I recovering more quickly? Is someone else actually carrying part of the load? Is the person receiving care more settled, or at least no less safe? Is the emotional cost lower? Has this change revealed a deeper issue that now needs attention?

These questions prevent the caregiver from mistaking effort for improvement. Many caregivers work extremely hard on changes that do not actually reduce strain. They create documents no one uses, plans no one follows, boundaries they do not hold, or routines that are too fragile to survive real life. Evaluation is not criticism. It is care for the care plan. A plan deserves review because the people inside it deserve something that works.

There is a quiet confidence that grows when one high-impact change begins to hold. The caregiver sees that the care system is not fixed by fate. Some parts can move. Some assumptions can be challenged. Some tasks can be transferred. Some routines can be simplified. Some emotional patterns can be interrupted. This confidence matters because caregiving often teaches helplessness: the feeling that every demand is inevitable and every limit impossible. One successful change disproves that story.

Still, change must remain humane. The purpose is not to make the care arrangement efficient at the expense of dignity. The person receiving care is not a problem to be processed. They may be frightened by changes, especially if those changes touch independence, contact, or familiar routines. A good first change is firm about the need but respectful in its implementation. It explains enough, repeats calmly, and allows adjustment where possible without surrendering the core limit.

Humane change also includes the caregiver's dignity. The caregiver should not have to perform total desperation to justify one practical adjustment. They should not have to beg for a night of sleep, a shared task, a predictable call time, or relief from a repeated crisis. The need for change is legitimate before collapse. This is one of the central shifts in sustainable care: prevention is allowed to speak before disaster speaks louder.

Choosing what must change first is, in the end, an act of strategic compassion. It recognises that love has limited energy and must be directed wisely. It refuses the fantasy that doing more everywhere is the same as caring well. It honours the person receiving care by protecting the structures that keep care steady. It honours the caregiver by insisting that their capacity is not an endlessly renewable resource.

The first change will not fix everything. It is not meant to. Its purpose is to create a foothold: one place where the load becomes lighter, one pattern that stops repeating, one risk that is reduced, one pocket of recovery that is protected, one responsibility that no longer lives only in the caregiver's head.

From there, the next change can be chosen with less panic.

The question is not which problem hurts the most in this moment. The question is which change will give the care system the greatest chance of becoming safer, calmer, and more liveable. That is where the work should begin.

Chapter 3
Boundaries That Do Not Break Relationships

How can a limit preserve a relationship when it feels, at first, like a threat to it? This is the question many caregivers meet with a tightening chest. They know something has to change. The late calls, the assumed availability, the errands that swallow work hours, the emotional demands that leave them raw, the repeated expectation that they will adjust because they always have: all of it has become too much. Yet the thought of saying so feels dangerous. A boundary seems less like a practical limit and more like a betrayal waiting to be named.

The fear is understandable. Caregiving relationships are not ordinary transactions. They carry love, history, dependence, gratitude, grief, duty, and often old family roles that were formed long before care was needed. A simple sentence such as "I cannot do that tonight" may land in a room already crowded with memory. The person receiving care may hear rejection. A sibling may hear criticism. The caregiver may hear their own guilt before anyone else says a word. No wonder many limits remain unspoken until they burst out as anger, exhaustion, or withdrawal.

The paradox is that avoiding boundaries in order to protect a relationship often damages the relationship more deeply. Silence may keep the peace for a day, but it quietly feeds resentment. Over-explaining may prevent one argument, but it teaches others that every limit is open to appeal. Saying yes to avoid disappointment may feel kind in the moment, but repeated false consent turns care into a private ledger of unpaid emotional debts. A relationship built on one person's collapse is not secure. It is merely unchallenged.

The central tension is between being available enough to remain caring and being boundaried enough to remain whole. Caregivers are often asked, implicitly or directly, to confuse the two. If they care, they should answer. If they love, they should come. If they understand the seriousness of the situation, they should adapt. But availability without limit is not love's highest form. It is a fragile arrangement that depends on the caregiver never becoming ill, overwhelmed, angry, needed elsewhere, or entitled to a life that is not constantly interrupted.

The stakes are relational as much as practical. Without boundaries, the caregiver may begin to experience the person receiving care not as someone they love, but as the source of endless demand. That shift is painful. It may be hidden beneath politeness, but it changes tone, patience, and tenderness. A request that might once have been easy begins to feel like an invasion. A phone call becomes a threat. A visit becomes something to endure. The relationship narrows until it is made mostly of tasks, pressure, and guilt. This is not because the caregiver lacks devotion. It is because devotion has been asked to operate without protection.

There is another cost: unclear limits invite repeated conflict. When no one knows where the edges are, every situation must be negotiated from scratch. Can the caregiver take calls during work? Can they drive to every appointment? Can they stay late after every difficult visit? Can they absorb anger, tears, or panic whenever they appear? If the answer changes only when the caregiver is already depleted, others experience the limit as sudden and personal. Clear boundaries, stated before collapse, are less dramatic than desperate refusals. They give relationships a structure strong enough to carry disappointment without turning every disappointment into a crisis.

A boundary begins with a clear understanding of what it is and what it is not. It is a limit on the caregiver's own time, actions, energy, and availability, not an attempt to control another person's feelings or choices. From there, the caregiver must name the non-negotiables that protect basic functioning: sleep, work, parenting, health, recovery, and the private spaces where a person returns to themselves. Those limits then need to be held under pressure, because the first challenge to a boundary is rarely logical disagreement; it is emotion, habit, fear, and the old belief that the caregiver will eventually give way.

This work requires firmness, but not hardness. A boundary does not have to be delivered like a locked door slammed in someone's face.

It can be plain, warm, and steady. The image is less a wall than a front gate: there is still relationship, still access, still care, but not every person may enter at every hour, in every mood, for every reason. The gate matters because without it, the home is no longer a home. It becomes a passageway for everyone else's urgency.

The difficult question is not whether boundaries will cause discomfort. They will. Someone may feel disappointed. Someone may test the limit. Someone may accuse, plead, cry, or insist that no one else can help. The sharper question is whether the relationship can survive the truth that the caregiver is not endlessly available. If it cannot, then the problem is larger than the boundary itself. The next step begins with a simple distinction that changes everything: what is a boundary, and what has only been mistaken for one?

What Boundaries Are and Are Not

A boundary is often misunderstood because it arrives at the exact point where someone else wants more than you can give. In that moment, it can look like refusal, distance, punishment, rejection, selfishness, or disloyalty. The caregiver says, "I cannot come tonight," and the other person hears, "You do not matter." The caregiver says, "I do not answer non-urgent calls during work," and a relative hears, "You are making this difficult." The caregiver says, "I can help with appointments, but I cannot manage every journey," and the family hears, "You are stepping back."

This confusion is one reason caregivers delay boundaries until they are already angry. They do not want to seem harsh, so they keep bending. They do not want to upset the person receiving care, so they keep answering. They do not want conflict with relatives, so they keep absorbing. Then, when the strain becomes unbearable, the boundary comes out with the heat of everything that should have been said earlier. What might have been a clear limit becomes a desperate announcement. What might have protected the relationship now sounds like an accusation.

The first task is to remove the moral fog around the word itself. A boundary is a limit on your own actions, time, availability, body, attention, money, space, or participation. It says what you will do, what you will not do, when you are available, how you can be contacted, what conditions you need, and where your responsibility ends. It does not dictate another person's feelings. It does not require them to approve. It does not control their choices. It simply defines the terms under which you can remain involved without being consumed.

This distinction matters. Many caregivers avoid boundaries because they think a boundary means telling someone else what to do. They imagine saying, "You must stop calling me," or "You cannot be upset," or "You have to accept this." Those statements attempt to manage the other person. They invite resistance because they place the caregiver in charge of another adult's behaviour or emotions. A cleaner boundary says, "I answer non-urgent calls between 6 p.m. and 7 p.m." or "If a conversation becomes insulting, I will end the call and try again tomorrow." The focus returns to the caregiver's own conduct.

Boundaries are not ultimatums, although they are often confused with them. An ultimatum usually tries to force someone into compliance by threatening a consequence the speaker may or may not be willing to carry out. It often arrives dramatically, under pressure, with the emotional message: "Do what I want, or else." A boundary is quieter and more self-responsible. It says: "This is what I can do. This is what I cannot do. This is what I will do if the limit is crossed." The aim is not to win control. The aim is to protect what is necessary.

For example, "If you keep complaining, I will never help you again" is not a useful caregiving boundary. It is a threat shaped by exhaustion. "I want to help, but I will not stay in a conversation where I am being shouted at. I am going to end this call now, and we can speak tomorrow" is a boundary. It is specific, immediate, and within the caregiver's control. It does not demand that the other person become calm. It simply refuses to make the caregiver available for harm.

A boundary is also not a punishment. This is essential in caregiving, because the person receiving care may already feel frightened, dependent, ashamed, or powerless. If a caregiver sets a limit without clarity, the other person may interpret it as retaliation: "You are doing this because I was difficult," or "You are trying to teach me a lesson." That interpretation may not be accurate, but it is emotionally understandable. A strong boundary therefore needs a calm centre. It should not be used to wound, withdraw affection, or make the other person suffer for having needs. It should protect the caregiver's capacity so that care can continue in a healthier form.

Nor is a boundary an argument. Caregivers often weaken their boundaries by turning them into long explanations. They state the limit, then defend it, apologise for it, justify it, soften it, rephrase it, invite debate, and finally negotiate against themselves. This usually happens because they want the other person to understand and agree. Understanding is welcome when it comes, but it cannot be the price of a boundary. Some limits must stand even when the other person does not like them.

This is hard because caregivers often want emotional harmony before they act. They want everyone to feel comfortable with the change. They want the person receiving care to recognise the strain. They want siblings to say, "Of course, that makes sense." They want permission, not merely from others but from the entire emotional atmosphere. Yet many caregiving systems are built around the caregiver's willingness to adapt. When that willingness becomes less automatic, discomfort is inevitable. Waiting for no one to be upset can mean waiting forever.

A boundary may be kind, but it will not always feel kind to the person meeting it. This is not a sign that the boundary is wrong. A child may dislike a parent's need to work. A parent may dislike an adult child's evening phone limit. A spouse may dislike a respite arrangement. A sibling may dislike being asked to take responsibility. Dislike is not proof of harm. Disappointment is not proof of cruelty. A caregiver must learn to hold the difference between causing pain and allowing another person to experience the discomfort of reality.

Boundaries are not walls, either. This matters because some people imagine that boundary-setting means becoming cold, distant, or emotionally unavailable. In unhealthy forms, people can use the language of boundaries to avoid all responsibility, refuse repair, or excuse indifference. That is not what sustainable caregiving requires. A good boundary is more like a gate than a wall. It allows connection, but not without shape. It allows care, but not endless access. It allows closeness, but not intrusion into every hour and every reserve of the caregiver's life.

The gate image is useful because it preserves relationship while protecting entry points. A gate can open at agreed times. It can remain closed when entry would damage the household. It can have conditions. It can be predictable. The person outside the gate may not always like that it exists, but without a gate the home is no longer a home. It becomes a passageway. Many caregivers have become passageways for other people's urgency, fear, frustration, and unfinished responsibilities. A boundary restores the idea that the caregiver also has an inside life worth protecting.

A boundary is not a feeling, although feelings often announce the need for one. Resentment, dread, irritation, anxiety, numbness, and exhaustion can all signal that something is wrong. But the feeling itself is not the boundary. "I feel overwhelmed" is true, but it does not tell anyone what must change. "I cannot take non-urgent calls after 8 p.m." is a boundary. "I am resentful that I do all the transport" is useful information. "I can drive to one appointment each month, and the rest need another arrangement" is a boundary. Feelings reveal the pressure. Boundaries define the limit.

This difference protects the caregiver from making emotional pleas. A plea says, "Please understand how hard this is for me." A boundary says, "This is what I can reliably do." Pleas depend on sympathy. Boundaries depend on clarity. Sympathy may be absent, inconsistent, or short-lived. Clarity can remain even when sympathy fails. A caregiver may still choose to explain, especially when the relationship is tender, but the explanation should not become the foundation. The foundation is the limit itself.

Boundaries are also not selfishness. This accusation has unusual power in caregiving because the person receiving care may genuinely need help. The caregiver is not turning away from a trivial request. They may be dealing with illness, ageing, disability, grief, confusion, or serious vulnerability. Because the need is real, the caregiver may conclude that any limit is selfish. But this is false. Selfishness ignores the other person's humanity. A boundary includes the caregiver's humanity alongside it.

There is a profound ethical difference between "I do not care what happens to you" and "I cannot be the only answer to what is happening." There is a difference between "Your needs are inconvenient to me" and "Your needs require a plan larger than my constant availability." There is a difference between abandonment and sustainable involvement. Caregivers must hold these differences firmly, because guilt will often blur them at the exact moment a boundary is most needed.

A boundary is not a denial of love. It may be one of love's more honest forms. Love without limits can become controlling, resentful, fearful, or performative. It can begin to say yes while inwardly withdrawing. It can keep showing up physically while emotionally leaving the room. It can preserve appearances while quietly destroying warmth. A boundary makes love more truthful by refusing to pretend that the caregiver has infinite capacity. It says, "I care enough to tell the truth before bitterness tells it for me."

This is especially important where family roles are old and deeply grooved. Some caregivers have always been the responsible one, the calm one, the available one, the mediator, the fixer, the person who can be relied upon to adjust. In such families, a new boundary may feel like a personality change to everyone else. They may ask, "What has got into you?" or "Why are you suddenly being difficult?" The honest answer is that the limit is not sudden. Only the statement of it is new.

A boundary that has not been spoken is often still present in the body. The caregiver may already be paying for crossed limits through headaches, poor sleep, irritability, avoidance, fatigue, resentment, or a shrinking sense of self. The system may appear peaceful because the caregiver is absorbing the consequences privately. When the boundary is finally named, the discomfort moves from inside the caregiver into the relationship where it can be seen. This is why boundaries often feel disruptive. They do not create all the discomfort; they reveal where discomfort has been hidden.

A boundary is also not a guarantee that others will behave well. This is a painful but necessary truth. Caregivers sometimes believe that if they find the perfect wording, the other person will accept the limit calmly. Good wording helps. Timing helps. Warmth helps. Specificity helps. But no sentence can guarantee another person's maturity. Someone may cry, sulk, accuse, manipulate, withdraw, argue, or behave as though the boundary is negotiable. Their reaction is information, but it is not the measure of whether the boundary is legitimate.

The measure is whether the boundary protects something necessary and whether it is within the caregiver's rightful control. Sleep is necessary. Work hours may be necessary. Parenting duties may be necessary. Medical appointments may be necessary. Recovery time may be necessary. Emotional safety may be necessary. Financial limits may be necessary. Time with a partner, children, friends, or oneself may be necessary. The caregiver does not need to prove that they are broken before these needs count.

There is a dangerous pattern in caregiving where limits are considered acceptable only after collapse. The caregiver must become visibly ill, furious, tearful, or desperate before others take the request seriously. This pattern trains caregivers to distrust calm limits. They feel they must produce evidence of suffering to justify a change. But prevention is more humane than collapse. A boundary stated while the caregiver is still steady is not premature. It is wise.

A boundary is not necessarily permanent in every detail. Care situations change. A limit that works during one season may need revision later. A caregiver may be able to offer more support during a short crisis, then return to the usual boundary when the crisis passes. They may need stricter limits when their own health, work, or family responsibilities change. Flexibility can be part of sustainable care. But flexibility must be conscious, not extracted through pressure. An exception should be named as an exception, or it will often become the new expectation.

This is where caregivers must be especially careful with "just this once". Sometimes "just this once" is appropriate. Life is unpredictable, and care requires humanity. But if the same exception repeats, it is no longer an exception. It has become an informal agreement, usually one the caregiver never consciously accepted. A boundary protects against this drift by giving the caregiver language to say, "I can do this today because it is urgent, but I cannot make this my regular role."

A boundary is not merely a sentence. It is a repeated practice. The first statement matters, but consistency makes it real. If the caregiver says they do not answer non-urgent calls after 8 p.m., then answers every time guilt rises, the boundary becomes a preference. If they say they cannot provide weekly transport, then rearrange their life each week when no one else steps in, the care system learns that the stated limit can be overridden. This does not mean the caregiver must become rigid or punitive. It means the boundary must have enough consistency to become believable.

Consistency is difficult because pushback often targets the caregiver's softest places. "No one else will do it." "You know how anxious they get." "It will only take a minute." "I thought you cared." "You are the only one they trust." "After everything they did for you." These statements may contain fragments of truth, but they are also pressure. A caregiver can hear the concern without letting it erase the limit. The test of a boundary is rarely whether it can be stated once. The test is whether it can survive the first wave of emotional weather.

Boundaries are not a substitute for compassion. They need compassion to be humane. The caregiver can acknowledge distress: "I know this is upsetting." They can offer what is available: "I can talk tomorrow morning." They can validate the relationship: "I love you, and I am still not able to come tonight." They can be clear without being sharp. But compassion should not be confused with surrender. If every expression of distress results in the boundary being withdrawn, distress becomes the key that unlocks the caregiver's life.

A boundary is also not the same as withdrawal. Withdrawal often happens when boundaries have been absent for too long. The caregiver becomes so depleted that they pull away emotionally, avoid contact, delay responses, or fantasise about disappearing from the role. Withdrawal may feel like the only available protection, but it can damage trust and intensify guilt. Boundaries, by contrast, aim to protect connection by making continued involvement possible. They say, "Here is how I can remain present," rather than silently vanishing under the weight of unspoken resentment.

This is why boundaries should be as concrete as possible. Abstract limits invite argument because they can be interpreted in many ways. "I need you to respect me" may be true, but what does that mean in behaviour? "I will end a call if I am shouted at" is clearer. "I need more time for myself" is important, but too vague. "Sunday morning is not available for care tasks unless there is a true emergency" gives shape. "I cannot be responsible for everything" may express the truth, but "I will handle appointment booking, not transport" changes the arrangement.

Concrete boundaries reduce emotional labour because the caregiver does not have to renegotiate the same issue repeatedly. They also reduce the chance that others will claim confusion. People may still dislike the boundary, but dislike is different from not understanding it. A clear boundary gives everyone a visible edge. It turns the caregiver's invisible limit into shared information.

There is another common misunderstanding: that a boundary must be justified by the other person's bad behaviour. Many caregivers wait until someone has been unreasonable enough to "deserve" a boundary. This is a mistake. Boundaries are not only responses to misconduct. They are ordinary structures for sustainable life. You may need a boundary around work hours even if the person receiving care is polite. You may need a boundary around sleep even if the late calls are loving. You may need a boundary around transport even if the appointments are important. A boundary can be necessary even when no one has done anything wrong.

This point can reduce blame. If boundaries are only created when someone is at fault, every limit becomes an accusation. The person receiving care may feel punished, and the caregiver may feel forced to prove wrongdoing. But if boundaries are understood as design requirements, the tone changes. The question becomes not "Who is being unreasonable?" but "What structure allows care to continue without harm?" That question is more mature, and often more effective.

Boundaries are also not failures of generosity. Genuine generosity requires freedom. When a caregiver gives from choice, the act can strengthen connection. When they give from fear, guilt, coercion, or exhaustion, the act may look generous while inwardly breeding resentment. A boundary creates the space in which yes can become honest again. Without no, yes loses moral value. It becomes compliance.

This is one of the most liberating truths in caregiving: limits do not only protect the caregiver from doing too much; they protect the meaning of what the caregiver does choose to give. A visit offered freely feels different from a visit extracted through guilt. A phone call made within a sustainable rhythm feels different from a call answered with dread. A task accepted deliberately feels different from a task absorbed because no one else would act. Boundaries return dignity to giving.

A boundary is not always comfortable for the caregiver either. Even a necessary limit may feel awkward, sad, or frightening. The caregiver may grieve the fact that such a limit is needed. They may wish they could be more available. They may feel sorrow when the person receiving care struggles with the change. These feelings do not invalidate the boundary. They simply reveal that caregiving is emotionally complex. The caregiver can feel compassion, sadness, and guilt while still holding the line.

The goal is not to become someone who never feels pulled. The goal is to stop letting every pull become a command.

Some boundaries will concern time. "I am available for care calls between these hours." Some will concern tasks. "I can coordinate appointments, but I cannot provide daily transport." Some will concern emotional safety. "I will not continue conversations where

I am insulted." Some will concern roles. "I cannot be the messenger between family members." Some will concern money. "I cannot cover costs without prior agreement." Some will concern recovery. "I need the evening after hospital appointments free from additional care tasks." All are ways of making the care role more truthful.

A boundary should be stated before it is enforced where possible. Sudden enforcement may sometimes be necessary, especially if a situation is harmful, but advance clarity is usually better. It allows the person receiving care and others involved to adjust. It reduces the sense of shock. It also helps the caregiver feel more grounded because they are not inventing the limit in the middle of conflict. The best boundaries often sound almost boring. They are policies, not performances.

For example: "I do calls after 6 p.m. only for true emergencies." "I am not available during work unless there is a safety issue." "I can visit on Saturday, but I cannot stay overnight." "I will discuss care plans with the family once a week, not through scattered messages every day." "I can help with forms if they are ready by Thursday, but I cannot manage last-minute paperwork." These statements are not dramatic. Their strength lies in their plainness.

The caregiver may be tempted to soften the boundary so much that it becomes unclear. "I might not always be able to answer, if that is okay, unless you really need me, but I will try" is not a boundary. It is a fog. It communicates guilt more than guidance. A clearer version would be: "I do not answer non-urgent calls during work. I will call back after 5 p.m." Clarity may feel less affectionate, but in practice it is often kinder because it reduces confusion, testing, and disappointment.

Boundaries should be paired with reality, not fantasy. It is not enough to say, "I cannot do this anymore," if no alternative is being considered for an essential task. Some limits reveal the need for a new plan. If the caregiver cannot provide transport, then transport must be reassigned, booked, paid for, reduced, or reconsidered. If the caregiver cannot manage night-time distress, a different support arrangement may be needed. The boundary does not solve every practical problem, but it tells the truth that the old solution is no longer available.

This truth-telling is the heart of boundaries in caregiving. A boundary says, "This is the real edge of my capacity." That edge may be inconvenient. It may be disappointing. It may force others to participate. It may expose gaps that have been hidden by the caregiver's effort. But a hidden edge is still an edge. Ignoring it does not make the caregiver limitless. It only increases the chance that the edge will be discovered through breakdown.

A boundary is not the opposite of care. It is one of the conditions that allows care to remain human. Without boundaries, the caregiver may become resentful, the person receiving care may become over-dependent, and relatives may remain comfortably vague. With boundaries, the system has to encounter reality. This encounter may be uncomfortable, but it is also where sustainable care begins.

The caregiver does not need to become hard to have boundaries. They need to become clear. They do not need to stop loving. They need to stop treating love as proof that they should be endlessly available. They do not need to control how others react. They need to decide how they will act when their limits are crossed. They do not need to win every argument. They need to stop turning every limit into an argument.

A boundary, at its simplest, is the sentence that prevents care from becoming self-erasure.

It says, "I am here, and I have edges."

For many caregivers, believing both halves of that sentence is the beginning of a different kind of relationship: one with more truth, less hidden resentment, and enough structure for care to continue without requiring the caregiver to disappear.

Writing Your Non-Negotiables

A non-negotiable is not a dramatic announcement. It is not a threat, a protest, or a final warning issued after months of silent resentment. In caregiving, a non-negotiable is a clear limit that protects the caregiver's basic ability to function. It marks the conditions without which care becomes unsafe, unstable, or personally damaging. It is the difference between a preference and a requirement, between "I would like this to be easier" and "This cannot continue in this form without consequences."

Many caregivers struggle with this distinction because care often trains them to treat their own needs as adjustable. Sleep can be shortened. Meals can be delayed. Work can be interrupted. Exercise can be abandoned. Friendships can be postponed. Medical appointments can be moved. Downtime can be sacrificed. The caregiver becomes the flexible part of the system, the person whose life bends so that everything else can remain in place. At first, this may seem loving. Over time, it becomes dangerous.

A non-negotiable begins with the recognition that some parts of your life are not luxuries. They are foundations. Sleep is not a reward for completing every task. Work hours are not optional because someone else is anxious. Parenting duties do not disappear because an older relative needs support. Your own health does not become less important because another person's needs are more visible. Recovery time is not selfish decoration; it is maintenance. Without these foundations, the caregiver may continue performing tasks, but the quality of presence, judgement, patience, and emotional steadiness will begin to decline.

This is why non-negotiables must be written, not merely felt. A feeling can warn you that something is wrong, but it cannot by itself create a care boundary. "I cannot keep doing this" may be true, but it is too broad to guide action. "I do not answer non-urgent calls after 8 p.m." is usable. "I need people to respect my time" may be justified, but it is too vague to hold under pressure. "I am unavailable during work hours unless there is a genuine safety issue" gives the care system a clear instruction. Written limits turn distress into policy.

The word "policy" may sound too formal for family life, but caregiving often becomes complicated precisely because everything is handled informally for too long. Informality has warmth, but it can also hide expectations. Someone assumes you can drive. Someone assumes you will answer. Someone assumes you will cover the gap. Someone assumes that because you did something once, you can do it again. A personal policy is not coldness. It is a way of making your capacity visible before resentment has to speak for it.

A useful non-negotiable has three qualities: it is concrete, it is within your control, and it protects something essential. "Everyone must stop stressing me out" is not a non-negotiable because it tries to control other people's behaviour and is too broad to enforce. "If a conversation becomes insulting, I will end the call and speak again later" is a non-negotiable because it defines your action. "My siblings must care more" is not a workable limit. "I will no longer be the messenger between relatives; care updates will go in one shared message" is clearer. The boundary must live where your authority actually exists.

Caregivers often write non-negotiables too softly at first because they are afraid of sounding harsh. They produce sentences full of apology, hesitation, and escape routes. "I might not be able to take calls quite so late unless it is really important, but I will try if you need me" sounds kind, but it leaves the whole arrangement open to interpretation. What counts as late? What counts as important? Who decides? A clearer version would be: "I take calls after 8 p.m. only for true emergencies. Everything else waits until the next day." That sentence may feel firmer, but it is also fairer because people know what to expect.

The most common areas for non-negotiables are the areas caregivers most often sacrifice: sleep, work, parenting, health, money, emotional safety, personal time, and recovery. These are not selfish categories. They are load-bearing categories. If your sleep collapses, your care becomes more brittle. If your work is repeatedly interrupted, your financial stability and professional identity may suffer. If your children or partner receive only the leftovers of your attention, the cost of caregiving spreads through the household. If your own medical needs are delayed, the care system is quietly consuming the person it depends upon.

Sleep boundaries are often among the hardest to claim because late-night contact can feel emotionally urgent. A person receiving care may be lonely, frightened, confused, or unsettled. A relative may send anxious messages because they have finally found time to think about the situation. The caregiver may feel cruel ignoring the phone. Yet sleep is one of the first foundations to protect because it affects nearly every other capacity. A non-negotiable around sleep might be: "I do not discuss non-urgent care issues after 9 p.m." Or: "My phone is off overnight except for agreed emergency contacts." Or: "Evening calls must be arranged before 7 p.m. unless there is a safety issue."

The strength of these statements lies in their plainness. They do not argue that the caregiver is tired enough to deserve rest. They simply establish the condition. This matters because once a caregiver tries to prove exhaustion, the conversation can become a trial. Someone may say they are tired too. Someone may insist this situation is different. Someone may minimise the effect. A policy avoids this trap. It says, "This is the arrangement," rather than, "Please decide whether my need is legitimate."

Work boundaries require the same clarity. Caregiving can easily invade paid work because messages and calls appear small from the outside. A quick question. A short update. A reminder. A sudden request. But interruptions during work carry hidden costs: lost concentration, stress, embarrassment, reduced performance, and the sense that the caregiver is never fully present anywhere. A work boundary might be: "I am not available for non-urgent care calls during work hours." Or: "Messages sent during work will be answered after 5 p.m." Or: "Appointments need to be planned with at least one week's notice if I am expected to attend."

Such limits do not mean work always outranks care. Genuine emergencies require response. But most care-related communication is not a genuine emergency. It has simply become accustomed to immediate access. A non-negotiable helps separate urgency from habit. It teaches the care system that the caregiver's employment is not an endlessly interruptible resource.

Parenting and household responsibilities also need protection. Caregivers who are adult children, partners, or relatives often feel pulled between generations or households. They may leave their own children waiting while they respond to another family member's distress. They may become physically present at home but mentally occupied by care. They may promise themselves they will make it up later, only to find that later keeps being claimed by the next demand. A non-negotiable in this area might be: "I am not available for care calls during my children's bedtime unless there is an emergency." Or: "Sunday lunch is family time and is not used for routine care tasks." Or: "I do not cancel my child's commitments for non-urgent appointments."

These boundaries can provoke guilt because the person receiving care may also be family. But caregiving should not require the caregiver to continually rob one relationship to pay another. The caregiver's household is not a reserve fund for everyone else's needs. Protecting those relationships is not abandonment of the care recipient. It is recognition that the caregiver has existing commitments that deserve dignity too.

Medical non-negotiables are especially important because caregivers often delay their own care. They miss check-ups, postpone treatment, ignore symptoms, or cancel therapy because someone else's appointment seems more urgent. This is a quiet form of self-neglect, often disguised as devotion. A caregiver's health cannot remain indefinitely secondary without consequence. A useful non-negotiable might be: "I do not cancel my own medical appointments for routine care tasks." Or: "If a care need conflicts with my treatment, another arrangement must be found." Or: "My health appointments go on the shared calendar as fixed commitments."

The caregiver may need to repeat this principle often, especially if others are used to treating them as the default backup. Your health is not spare capacity. It is part of the care system's stability. A caregiver who becomes unwell because they never protect their own care has not been selfless in a sustainable way; they have become another point of crisis.

Financial boundaries deserve the same directness. Many caregivers quietly spend money on petrol, groceries, equipment, prescriptions, household items, parking, takeaways during hospital visits, missed work, or small emergencies. Because each expense may be modest, the total impact can remain unseen until resentment grows or money becomes tight. A financial non-negotiable might be: "I do not cover care expenses without agreement." Or: "All shared costs must be discussed before they are incurred." Or: "I can contribute time, but I cannot provide ongoing financial support." Money boundaries can feel awkward, but silence around money often creates deeper conflict later.

Emotional safety is another category caregivers frequently overlook. They may tolerate shouting, accusations, guilt trips, insults, manipulation, or repeated circular conversations because the person is ill, frightened, old, distressed, or dependent. Compassion is necessary. Endurance of harm is not. A non-negotiable around emotional safety might be: "I will not stay in conversations where I am being shouted at." Or: "I will discuss care plans, but I will not respond to insults." Or: "If the conversation becomes circular, I will pause it and return later." These are not punishments. They are conditions for respectful contact.

It is important to write these limits before the next difficult conversation if possible. Under pressure, the caregiver's mind may become crowded with guilt, fear, old family roles, and the desire to make the discomfort stop. A written non-negotiable provides a sentence to return to. It keeps the caregiver from improvising their boundaries in the middle of emotional weather. The sentence does not have to be elegant. It has to be clear enough to survive stress.

The process begins privately. Before telling anyone else, the caregiver should ask: What must be protected for me to continue providing care without becoming depleted, resentful, or unsafe? The answer should be practical, not abstract. "I need respect" may be true, but it needs translation. Does respect mean no shouting? No calls during work? No last-minute transport assumptions? No discussing care through hostile group messages? No criticism from relatives who are not helping? The more specific the translation, the more useful the boundary.

A second question follows: What have I been treating as optional that is actually essential? This question often reveals the areas where caregivers have been most self-abandoning. Perhaps they have treated sleep as flexible when it is not. Perhaps they have treated paid work as interruptible when it should be protected. Perhaps they have treated their own grief, health, or marriage as something to handle later. Perhaps they have treated every request as urgent because saying no feels unbearable. Non-negotiables begin where false flexibility ends.

A third question is: What am I willing to repeat without defending myself each time? This is crucial. A non-negotiable should not require a long speech whenever it is tested. It must be simple enough to repeat. "I am not available for routine calls after 8 p.m." "I can visit on Saturdays, not weekdays." "I do not discuss care matters while being shouted at." "I can organise appointments, but I cannot provide regular transport." These sentences are not designed to win approval. They are designed to hold shape.

Caregivers should aim for a short list. Too many non-negotiables can become overwhelming and may be difficult to maintain. The first list should focus on the limits that protect basic functioning. If everything becomes non-negotiable, the term loses force. The question is not, "What would make caregiving ideal?" The question is, "What must be protected so that caregiving does not damage me or the people who depend on me?" This keeps the list grounded.

A short list might include one boundary around sleep, one around work, one around emotional safety, and one around a major recurring task such as transport or paperwork. Another caregiver's list might focus on health appointments, childcare, money, and recovery time. There is no universal template because each care situation has its own pressure points. The test is whether the boundary protects something essential and responds to a real pattern, not a passing irritation.

Once the non-negotiables are written, they should be phrased as policies rather than pleas. A plea asks for permission: "Please try not to call so late because I am really struggling." A policy states the arrangement: "I do not take non-urgent calls after 8 p.m." A plea depends on the other person's empathy. A policy depends on the caregiver's clarity. Empathy is welcome, but it cannot be required for the boundary to exist.

This does not mean the caregiver must sound cold. Warmth and firmness can sit in the same sentence. "I care about what happens, and I am not available for routine calls during work." "I know evenings can feel lonely, and I do not take non-emergency calls after 9 p.m." "I want appointments to go smoothly, and I cannot be the regular driver." The warmth acknowledges the relationship. The firmness protects the limit. Neither has to cancel the other.

It is also wise to define key terms where confusion is likely. "Emergency" is one of the most important. If a caregiver says they are available only for emergencies, but everyone has a different definition of emergency, the boundary will be tested constantly. A practical definition may include immediate safety concerns, serious health changes, urgent medication issues, or situations where professional help is needed. It should not include loneliness, frustration, routine questions, family complaints, minor preferences, or issues that can wait until the next agreed contact.

The caregiver does not need to create a legal document. They simply need enough clarity to prevent emotional pressure from relabelling every discomfort as a crisis. A sentence such as "By emergency, I mean immediate health or safety concerns that cannot wait until morning" can save many future arguments. It gives the caregiver a standard to return to when guilt begins to blur the line.

Non-negotiables also need consequences, though the word can sound harsher than the practice. A consequence is not revenge. It is the action that follows when the boundary is crossed. Without it, the boundary becomes a request. "If I am shouted at, I will end the call." "If a non-urgent message comes during work, I will answer after work." "If transport is not arranged in advance, I cannot guarantee I will drive." "If paperwork is given to me after the deadline, I may not be able to complete it." The consequence should be realistic, proportionate, and within the caregiver's control.

A boundary without a consequence often invites repeated testing. The person receiving care or relatives may not do this maliciously. They may simply be accustomed to the old pattern. If the caregiver says one thing and does another, the system learns from the behaviour, not the words. Consistency teaches the new arrangement. This is why the caregiver should not write a non-negotiable they are not prepared to practise. It is better to start with one boundary that can be held than a dozen that collapse under pressure.

There will be moments when the caregiver breaks their own boundary. This is not a reason to abandon it. Care is complex, and change is rarely perfect. The important thing is to name the exception rather than let it redefine the rule. "I answered tonight because the situation was urgent. Routine calls will still wait until the agreed time." Or: "I drove today because there was no safe alternative, but I cannot be the regular driver." Naming the exception protects the non-negotiable from quiet erosion.

The caregiver should expect internal resistance. Writing non-negotiables may bring up guilt, fear, grief, and embarrassment. It may feel strange to put one's own sleep or work on the same page as someone else's care needs. It may feel disloyal to write, "I am not available for this." These feelings are not proof that the limits are wrong. They are often evidence that the caregiver is stepping out of an old role in which their value depended on being endlessly adaptable.

There may also be external resistance. People who benefited from the caregiver's lack of limits may not welcome the new clarity. The person receiving care may feel anxious. Relatives may feel inconvenienced. Someone may claim the caregiver has changed. Someone may insist the boundary is unnecessary. Someone may test it immediately. None of this is surprising. A non-negotiable changes the care arrangement from assumption to agreement, and systems built on assumption often resist becoming explicit.

The caregiver does not need to over-explain. Over-explaining usually weakens a non-negotiable because it invites debate. A brief reason may be helpful: "I need to sleep properly so I can function tomorrow." "I cannot risk interruptions during work." "I need this time with my children." But the reason should not become a negotiation. If the other person disagrees with the reason, the limit still stands. The caregiver's basic functioning is not a courtroom matter.

It can help to write two versions of each non-negotiable: the private truth and the public sentence. The private truth may be raw: "Late calls make me anxious and ruin my sleep." The public sentence is steadier: "I do not take non-urgent calls after 8 p.m." The private truth helps the caregiver understand why the boundary matters. The public sentence communicates the boundary without exposing more vulnerability than is necessary. This distinction protects the caregiver from turning every limit into an emotional confession.

Non-negotiables should also be reviewed when circumstances change. A new diagnosis, increased care needs, a change in work, a school holiday, the caregiver's illness, a move, or a shift in available support may all require adjustment. A boundary is not a stone tablet. It is a living protection. But adjustment should be deliberate, not forced by guilt or crisis. The caregiver can ask, "Does this limit still protect what it needs to protect? Does it need to be firmer, clearer, or more flexible in a defined way?"

The list should remain connected to the wider care plan. A non-negotiable may reveal a gap that needs to be filled. If the caregiver cannot provide daily transport, another transport solution is needed. If they cannot be available overnight, an emergency plan is needed. If they cannot manage all paperwork, responsibilities must be assigned or support found. A boundary does not pretend the need disappears. It says the need cannot continue to be met in the old way.

This is where some caregivers become frightened. They worry that naming a limit will expose the absence of alternatives. Sometimes it will. But the absence of alternatives is not a reason to pretend the caregiver has unlimited capacity. It is a reason to confront the system honestly. If the entire arrangement depends on the caregiver violating their own non-negotiables, the arrangement is already unstable. The boundary is not the cause of the instability. It is the first truthful sign of it.

A well-written non-negotiable should feel both firm and slightly relieving. It may still be uncomfortable, but it should make internal sense. The caregiver should be able to say, "This protects something necessary." It should reduce ambiguity. It should create a clearer expectation. It should be possible to repeat without a speech. It should be specific enough that the caregiver knows when it has been crossed.

For example: "I do calls after 6 p.m. only for true emergencies." This protects evening recovery. It defines the time. It separates routine contact from emergency contact. It can be repeated. It gives the caregiver a standard. Another example: "I can attend one appointment a month, but I cannot be responsible for every appointment." This protects time and work. It offers a defined contribution without accepting the whole category. Another: "I will not continue a conversation where I am being insulted." This protects emotional safety and provides a clear action.

These sentences are not elaborate. That is their strength. A non-negotiable that requires a paragraph of explanation every time it is used is unlikely to hold. The caregiver needs language that can be spoken while tired, anxious, or challenged. The simpler the sentence, the more durable it becomes.

Writing non-negotiables is ultimately an act of care for the whole care system. It prevents the caregiver from silently overextending and then exploding. It gives the person receiving care more predictable access rather than unreliable over-availability followed by withdrawal. It makes relatives face real capacity rather than imaginary capacity. It turns hidden resentment into visible structure. It allows help to be offered from steadier ground.

The deeper change is internal. The caregiver begins to move from asking, "What will people think of me if I set this limit?" to asking, "What will happen to care if I do not?" That question changes the moral frame. It recognises that limitless giving is not the same as faithful care. It recognises that the caregiver's life has load-bearing walls. It recognises that a relationship protected by honest limits may be more durable than one preserved by denial.

A non-negotiable is not the sentence that proves you care less.

It is the sentence that makes continued care possible without requiring you to vanish from your own life.

Keeping Boundaries Under Pressure

A boundary is not proven by the moment it is spoken. It is proven by what happens after it is challenged.

This is where many caregivers are caught off guard. They may spend days finding the right words, preparing the conversation, softening the tone, choosing a careful moment, and explaining the limit with as much kindness as they can manage. They may say, calmly and reasonably, "I cannot take non-urgent calls after 8 p.m." or "I can help with appointments, but I cannot provide regular transport." Then the response comes: tears, anger, silence, accusation, panic, pleading, or the familiar sentence that lands like a hook in the chest: "No one else will do it."

The caregiver had prepared for the boundary. They had not prepared for the pressure.

Pressure is the natural test of a boundary because boundaries usually interrupt an established pattern. Someone has been used to immediate access. Someone has been used to the caregiver saying yes. Someone has been used to emotional distress producing a practical response. Someone has been used to the caregiver absorbing inconvenience rather than making it visible. When the caregiver changes the pattern, the system often tries to pull them back into their old role.

This does not always happen through cruelty. Sometimes the person receiving care is genuinely frightened. Sometimes a relative truly feels guilty and does not know how to respond except by pushing responsibility back towards the person who has always carried it. Sometimes the pressure is not calculated; it is habitual. People repeat what has worked before. If tears have brought the caregiver back, tears may appear. If anger has made the caregiver over-explain, anger may rise. If helplessness has led the caregiver to rescue, helplessness may become louder.

The caregiver must understand this without becoming cynical. Pressure is information, not always manipulation. But even when pressure is sincere, it does not automatically make the boundary wrong.

This distinction is essential. Caregivers often confuse the intensity of someone else's reaction with the moral status of the limit. If the person cries, the boundary must be cruel. If a sibling becomes angry, the boundary must be unreasonable. If the care recipient says they feel abandoned, the boundary must be too harsh. If the caregiver feels guilty, the boundary must be selfish. These conclusions are emotionally understandable, but they are not reliable. A necessary boundary can cause distress. A kind boundary can be disliked. A sustainable limit can be met with panic precisely because the old arrangement depended on its absence.

The first skill in keeping boundaries under pressure is to expect pushback. Not as a sign of failure, but as part of the process. A boundary that changes nothing may meet no resistance because it costs no one anything. A boundary that redistributes time, access, work, emotional labour, or responsibility is likely to be felt. Someone may have to wait. Someone may have to do a task. Someone may have to tolerate uncertainty. Someone may have to find another source of support. Someone may have to face the fact that the caregiver's capacity has limits.

Expectation matters because surprise weakens resolve. When a caregiver believes that a well-stated boundary should be calmly accepted, the first emotional reaction can feel like evidence that the boundary has gone wrong. But when the caregiver expects resistance, they can meet it with steadiness. They can think, "This is the difficult part I knew might come," rather than, "I have made a terrible mistake." The boundary is not failing simply because someone is testing it. It is entering the stage where consistency begins.

The second skill is to stop over-explaining. Over-explaining is one of the most common ways caregivers accidentally weaken their own limits. It often begins as kindness. The caregiver wants to be understood. They want the other person to know they are not being cruel. They want to reduce hurt. They want to prove that the boundary is reasonable. So they explain their tiredness, their work pressure, their lack of sleep, their family responsibilities, their emotional strain, their worry, their good intentions, and their regret.

The problem is that too much explanation can turn a boundary into a debate.

Every extra detail gives the other person something to challenge. If the caregiver says they are tired, someone may say everyone is tired. If they mention work, someone may say the appointment is more important. If they talk about their children, someone may say the care recipient once sacrificed for them. If they admit guilt, someone may press directly into that guilt. The caregiver then finds themselves defending the boundary instead of holding it. The conversation becomes less about what is possible and more about whether the caregiver has earned the right to say no.

A strong boundary needs a short reason, not a full defence. "I need to sleep, so I do not take non-urgent calls after 8 p.m." "I cannot interrupt work for routine issues, so I will reply after 5 p.m." "I can organise the appointment, but I cannot drive every week." These sentences are not cold. They are clear. They give enough context to be humane without offering the boundary up for negotiation.

Under pressure, the caregiver should use repetition rather than expansion. This is sometimes called the broken-record approach, but the phrase can sound mechanical. In practice, it means returning calmly to the same core sentence instead of inventing new arguments. "I hear that this is upsetting. I am still not available tonight." "I know you are worried. I will call in the morning." "I understand you want me to drive. I cannot be the regular driver." "I can see this feels difficult. The arrangement is still the same."

Repetition is powerful because it refuses the invitation to enter a courtroom. The caregiver does not become harsher. They do not attack. They do not escalate. They simply stop treating every objection as a new decision. This is vital because many caregivers have been trained to reconsider their limits whenever someone else becomes distressed. Repetition teaches the nervous system that discomfort does not automatically require reversal.

The third skill is to separate empathy from compliance. Caregivers often believe that if they truly understand someone's distress, they must respond by giving way. This is not empathy. It is surrender disguised as compassion. Real empathy can say, "I know this is hard," without adding, "therefore I will abandon the limit." It can say, "I understand you feel frightened," without becoming endlessly available. It can say, "I can hear that you are angry," without accepting insults or changing the arrangement to make the anger stop.

This separation is particularly important when tears appear. Tears can be sincere and moving. The person receiving care may feel real fear, grief, loneliness, or loss of control. The caregiver may feel almost physically pulled to soothe the pain by withdrawing the boundary. But comfort does not always mean compliance. Sometimes comfort means staying gentle while the limit remains intact. "I am sorry this feels painful. I am not leaving you. I am also not able to come tonight." That sentence protects both truths.

Anger requires a different steadiness. An angry response can frighten a caregiver into retreat, especially if family history has taught them that anger means danger, rejection, or lasting punishment. The caregiver may rush to explain, apologise, or offer a compromise they do not mean. But anger is not an instruction. It is an emotion, sometimes a tactic, sometimes a protest, sometimes fear wearing armour. The caregiver does not need to defeat it. They need to refuse to be governed by it.

A calm response might be: "I will not discuss this while I am being shouted at." Or: "I can continue when we can speak respectfully." Or: "I am going to end the call now and try again tomorrow." These responses are not designed to shame the other person. They protect the conditions under which a conversation can remain useful. A boundary about tone is often necessary because care conversations can easily become dumping grounds for everyone's anxiety.

Guilt trips are more subtle and often more difficult to resist. "After everything I have done for you." "You know I have no one else." "I did not think you would be like this." "A good daughter would not say no." "You are making me beg." These statements strike at identity. They do not merely ask for a task; they question the caregiver's character. That is why they are so effective. The caregiver may feel an immediate urge to prove goodness by giving in.

The best response to guilt pressure is not a counter-argument about whether the caregiver is good. That path leads nowhere. The stronger response is to return to the limit. "I know you are disappointed. I am still not able to do that." "I care about you, and the answer is still no." "I am not discussing whether I care. I am telling you what I can do." These sentences refuse the false trial. The caregiver's love is not on the witness stand every time they set a limit.

The phrase "no one else will" deserves special attention because it may be partly true. Sometimes other relatives are absent. Sometimes services are limited. Sometimes friends are willing in theory but unreliable in practice. Sometimes the caregiver really is the most capable person. This reality can make the boundary feel impossible. If no one else will step in, how can the caregiver step back?

The answer is not simple, but it begins with honesty: another person's refusal to help does not create unlimited capacity in the caregiver. A gap in the system is still a gap, even when the caregiver has been filling it. If a task is essential, the gap must be named and addressed. If the caregiver cannot do it, pretending they can is not a plan. "No one else will" may explain why the situation is hard, but it does not prove that the caregiver must carry the task indefinitely.

A useful response is: "That may be true, and I still cannot do this in the current way." This sentence can feel frightening because it allows the problem to remain visible. Caregivers often rush to close gaps because visible gaps create anxiety, criticism, and guilt. But when the caregiver automatically fills every gap, no one else has to face the inadequacy of the arrangement. Keeping a boundary under pressure sometimes means allowing the system to see the problem it has been outsourcing to you.

This is not the same as abandoning urgent safety needs. If there is immediate risk, action may be required. But once the immediate risk has passed, the caregiver should avoid letting every emergency response become a permanent obligation. They can say, "I handled this today because it was urgent. We need another plan because I cannot be the ongoing solution." Naming the exception protects the boundary from being quietly overwritten.

A boundary is also tested through delay. The caregiver may state a limit, and others may behave as though they did not hear it. A relative may continue sending messages during work. The person receiving care may keep calling late at night. A sibling may agree to take over a task and then leave it undone until the caregiver steps in. This kind of pressure is not always dramatic. It can be passive. The old system waits to see whether the caregiver will resume their usual role.

Consistency becomes crucial here. If a non-urgent message arrives during work, the caregiver answers after work. If a late call is not an emergency, it waits. If a relative fails to complete an agreed task, the caregiver does not automatically absorb it without comment. The response must match the boundary often enough for the system to learn. A boundary that is stated but not practised becomes a suggestion.

This is where caregivers often face their own internal pushback. The hardest pressure may not come from outside at all. It may come from the caregiver's own body: the racing heart after not answering, the guilt after holding the line, the urge to check, the fear of being judged, the loneliness of being firmer than people expect. Old roles live inside the nervous system. A caregiver who has spent years being available may feel unsafe when they become less available, even if the boundary is reasonable.

Internal pressure should be treated with care, not contempt. The caregiver does not need to shame themselves for feeling guilty. They can name the feeling without obeying it. "This is guilt. It does not mean the boundary is wrong." "This is fear. It does not decide the plan." "This is the old role pulling at me." Such private language helps the caregiver stay anchored while the emotional body catches up with the practical decision.

It can help to prepare a small set of boundary sentences in advance. Not a script to recite robotically, but a set of steady phrases that reduce the need to think under pressure. Under emotional strain, the mind often forgets its own clarity. Prepared sentences provide a bridge between intention and action.

"I am not able to do that."

"I can help with this part, not that part."

"That does not work for me."

"I know this is upsetting, and the answer is still no."

"I will talk about this when we can both speak calmly."

"I am ending this call now. We can try again tomorrow."

These sentences are plain because pressure does not require poetry. It requires steadiness.

The caregiver should also decide in advance what counts as an emergency. This prevents every emotional spike from being treated as a reason to suspend the boundary. Emergency might mean immediate health or safety risk, sudden serious deterioration, urgent medication concern, or a situation where professional help may be needed. It should not automatically include loneliness, frustration, inconvenience, routine questions, family anxiety, or discomfort with waiting. Without this distinction, a boundary around availability will be repeatedly breached by rebranded urgency.

When boundaries involve communication, timing can help. A caregiver may say, "I am not available for scattered messages during the day, but I will check and respond at 6 p.m." This gives the person receiving care or relatives a reliable point of contact while protecting the caregiver from constant interruption. Predictability often reduces panic. The goal is not to vanish; it is to replace chaotic access with structured access.

Some boundaries need a consequence that is immediate and calm. If the person shouts, the call ends. If the conversation becomes circular, it pauses. If a relative sends hostile messages, the caregiver replies only to practical information. If a task is not provided by the agreed deadline, the caregiver cannot guarantee completion. The consequence should not be inflated or dramatic. It should be the natural action needed to protect the limit.

The caregiver must avoid consequences they are not willing to carry out. Empty consequences teach the opposite of boundaries. "I will never help again" may be said in anger, but if it is not true or not desirable, it damages trust without improving the system. Better to use smaller, real consequences: "I am leaving now." "I will respond tomorrow." "I will not continue this conversation." "I cannot complete paperwork given to me at the last minute." Small, enforceable consequences are stronger than dramatic threats.

It is also important to recognise when a boundary conversation has become circular. A circular conversation repeats the same objections, explanations, guilt, reassurance, and counter-arguments without movement. Caregivers can lose hours in these loops because they believe the right words will finally create understanding. Sometimes understanding is not the issue. Acceptance is. The other person may understand the boundary and still dislike it. The caregiver does not need to keep explaining until dislike disappears.

A useful closing line is: "I have explained what I can do. I am not going to keep discussing it tonight." Or: "We are repeating ourselves now, so I am going to pause this conversation." This kind of ending may feel abrupt to someone who is used to endless negotiation, but it protects the caregiver from being worn down by repetition. Under pressure, boundaries are often defeated not by one strong argument, but by sheer conversational exhaustion.

Some situations require documentation. After a boundary is discussed, the caregiver may send a brief message confirming the arrangement: "Just to confirm, I can visit on Saturdays, but I cannot do weekday transport. Non-urgent calls after 8 p.m. will wait until the next morning." This is not cold. It reduces later confusion. It also prevents memory from being reshaped by emotion. When people are distressed, they may sincerely misremember what was said. Written confirmation gives the care system a stable reference point.

Documentation is especially useful with relatives. Family care can become a fog of informal promises and shifting interpretations. A sibling may say they will "help more" but never define how. A relative may agree in principle, then later claim the boundary was not clear. A short written summary turns a conversation into an arrangement. It does not guarantee compliance, but it makes avoidance easier to see.

The caregiver should expect that some people will accuse them of being rigid. This accusation can be powerful because caregivers often pride themselves on flexibility. But flexibility without limits becomes self-erasure. The issue is not whether the caregiver can ever make exceptions. The issue is whether exceptions remain conscious, rare, and named. A caregiver can be flexible in a true emergency without reopening every boundary for routine pressure.

A phrase such as "I can make an exception today, but this does not change the usual arrangement" is valuable. It allows humanity without surrendering the structure. The caregiver should use it whenever they choose to bend a boundary for a good reason. Otherwise, others may treat the exception as evidence that the boundary was never real.

There will also be times when the caregiver realises a boundary needs adjustment. Holding boundaries under pressure does not mean clinging stubbornly to every sentence ever written. Care situations change. The caregiver may learn that a boundary is too vague, too strict, too hard to practise, or not aimed at the true pressure point. Revision is allowed. The difference is that revision should come from reflection, not from panic, guilt, or intimidation. A boundary can be changed without being abandoned.

The caregiver can ask: Is this limit protecting what it was meant to protect? Is it specific enough? Is it within my control? Is it being tested because it is unclear, or because others dislike it? Am I bending because the situation genuinely requires flexibility, or because I am afraid of someone's reaction? These questions keep the caregiver in adult judgement rather than emotional reflex.

Sometimes pressure becomes manipulation. The difference can be difficult to name, but patterns matter. If someone repeatedly uses guilt, threats, exaggerated helplessness, silent treatment, rage, or emotional collapse to force the caregiver back into compliance, the issue is no longer a single difficult reaction. It is a relationship pattern that may require stronger boundaries, support from a neutral third party, or reduced direct engagement. The caregiver should not minimise persistent coercion simply because care is involved.

A person's vulnerability does not give them unlimited rights over the caregiver's life.

This sentence may feel uncomfortable, but it is necessary. Care recipients may be frightened, ill, dependent, or grieving. They may also behave in ways that harm the caregiver. Both truths can exist. Compassion for their vulnerability should not erase the caregiver's right to emotional safety, sleep, work, health, and dignity. Keeping boundaries under pressure means refusing to let one person's need become a total claim on another person's life.

The caregiver may need support to hold this position. A trusted friend, counsellor, support group, professional adviser, or practical ally can help the caregiver reality-check the boundary and recover after difficult pushback. Isolation makes boundaries harder because the caregiver is left alone with guilt and other people's reactions.

Supportive witnesses can remind the caregiver of the bigger picture when the emotional moment feels overwhelming.

It is also useful to track what happens after a boundary is held. Did the feared disaster occur? Did the person eventually manage? Did another helper step in? Did the issue wait until morning? Did the caregiver sleep better, work more calmly, or feel less resentful? Sometimes the caregiver's fear predicts catastrophe, but reality shows that the system can tolerate more than expected. This evidence builds confidence. It teaches the caregiver that not every limit produces harm.

At other times, holding a boundary reveals a serious gap. Perhaps no one else does step in. Perhaps the person receiving care is not safe with the current level of support. Perhaps the caregiver's limit exposes that the care arrangement has been relying on an impossible amount of unpaid, unshared labour. This can be frightening, but it is also important information. The boundary has revealed the need for a different plan. It has not created the need.

The caregiver should be careful not to interpret every difficult outcome as proof that they should return to over-functioning. If a boundary reveals instability, the answer may be escalation, redistribution, professional input, a new routine, or a clearer emergency plan. Returning to the old pattern may restore temporary calm, but it also hides the problem again. Hidden problems do not disappear. They wait.

Keeping boundaries under pressure is not about winning. It is about becoming consistent enough that the care system can no longer pretend the caregiver has no edges. This consistency may change how others relate to the caregiver. Some may become more respectful. Some may become more resentful. Some may test harder before adapting. Some may never approve. Approval is not the measure. Sustainability is.

The caregiver's tone matters, but tone is not everything. A kind tone can help preserve dignity and reduce unnecessary escalation. But even the warmest tone will not make every boundary welcome. The caregiver should not spend their life searching for a tone so perfect that no one feels disappointed. That tone does not exist. The aim is to be clear, respectful, and steady, not magically free from other people's discomfort.

There is a kind of grief in this work. The caregiver may have to grieve the fantasy that love, reason, and kindness will always be met with fairness. They may have to grieve the hope that others will notice the strain before being told. They may have to grieve the identity of being endlessly available. They may even grieve the relationship they wished care would create, one in which everyone became more tender, more responsible, and more grateful. Boundaries often ask caregivers to live in the relationship as it is, not as they hoped it would be.

Yet there is freedom on the other side of that grief. A caregiver who can hold a boundary under pressure becomes less controlled by emotional weather. They can hear tears without drowning. They can hear anger without surrendering. They can feel guilt without treating it as an order. They can remain kind without becoming available for everything. They can give from a clearer place because their yes is no longer extracted by fear.

This does not make caregiving easy. It makes it more honest.

A boundary kept under pressure becomes a message to the whole care system: this caregiver is committed, but not limitless. They can be loving, but not endlessly accessible. They can respond to real need, but not to every demand disguised as need. They can tolerate disappointment without rushing to erase it. They can remain in the relationship without handing over the whole of their life.

The first time a boundary is held, it may feel unnatural. The second time, it may still feel uncomfortable. Over time, the boundary begins to do what it was meant to do. It creates predictability. It reduces argument. It protects recovery. It exposes gaps that need real solutions. It makes care less dependent on the caregiver's silent collapse.

Pressure does not mean stop.

Often, pressure means the boundary has reached the very place it was needed.

Chapter 4
Guilt: Useful Signal, Not a Ruler

How can an emotion that proves you care also push you towards choices that harm you? Guilt is one of the most persuasive forces in caregiving because it rarely sounds foolish from the inside. It does not arrive as a stranger. It speaks in the language of love, duty, gratitude, memory, and fear. It reminds you of what someone once did for you. It asks what other people will think. It compares you with siblings, neighbours, friends, and imagined better versions of yourself. It points to the person receiving care and whispers that their need is greater than yours, so your limit must be wrong.

The difficulty is that guilt often contains a grain of truth. You do care. You may have responsibilities. Your choices do affect another person. There may be moments when an apology is needed, a repair should be made, or a task genuinely belongs to you. Guilt can sometimes be a useful signal, a small internal alarm that asks for attention. But a signal is not a ruler. It can alert you to something worth examining; it should not be allowed to govern every decision, define every duty, or redraw the limits of your life whenever someone is disappointed.

This is where caregivers become vulnerable. They mistake the presence of guilt for the presence of wrongdoing. They feel bad, so they assume they have behaved badly. They feel pulled, so they assume the request must be theirs to meet. They feel ashamed, so they say yes before asking whether the yes is safe, sustainable, or even useful. The feeling becomes the verdict. The caregiver stops making decisions and starts obeying emotional pressure, one guilty agreement at a time.

The central tension is between listening to guilt and being ruled by it. Caregiving requires moral sensitivity; a caregiver who feels nothing when another person is struggling would have a different problem. Yet sensitivity without discernment becomes a hazard. It can lead a person to carry responsibilities that are not theirs, compensate for choices other adults refuse to make, cover gaps that require a wider plan, and absorb loneliness, grief, decline, or family dysfunction as though love could personally solve them all. Guilt then stops being evidence of conscience and becomes a mechanism of overwork.

The stakes are high because guilt-driven care does not stay emotionally private. It shapes calendars, sleep, conversations, money, health, and the tone of relationships. A caregiver who says yes from guilt may look generous while becoming resentful. They may visit when exhausted, answer when unavailable, apologise when they have not done wrong, and take on tasks simply to silence the inner accusation that they are failing. The person receiving care may receive more hours, but not necessarily better care. What enters the room is not only help, but strain.

Over time, guilt can make unsafe workloads feel morally necessary. It can convince the caregiver that a limit is cruelty, that rest is abandonment, that another person's loneliness is a personal assignment, that a sibling's absence must be covered without protest, that cultural expectation is the same as practical capacity, and that being judged would be worse than being depleted. This is how guilt becomes dangerous: not because it feels unpleasant, but because it can make unsustainable care feel righteous.

A healthier relationship with guilt begins by understanding why it appears, because a feeling becomes less commanding when its sources are named. From there, responsibility has to be sorted with a cooler eye: what belongs to your role, what exceeds your capacity, what consequences are real, and where you have been compensating for someone else's refusal, absence, or an imperfect system. Only then can guilt be answered without surrender, so that a caregiver can make deliberate choices, repair when needed, and refuse the old habit of saying yes simply to make discomfort disappear.

This work is not about becoming guilt-free. That promise would be dishonest and, for many caregivers, unnecessary. The aim is steadier than that. A caregiver can feel guilty and still make a wise decision. They can feel sad and still hold a boundary. They can disappoint someone and still remain loving. They can recognise another person's suffering without accepting total responsibility for it. They can say no, then return with kindness, rather than saying yes and quietly withdrawing in resentment.

Guilt will still knock. It may arrive after a declined request, after a tense conversation, after a sibling's comment, after seeing the person receiving care look smaller, older, more frightened, or more alone than you can bear. The question is not whether the knock will come. The question is whether guilt will be treated as a visitor with information, or handed the keys to the whole house.

Why Guilt Shows Up in Caregiving

Guilt is one of the most common emotional companions in caregiving because care is never only practical. It is not merely a set of tasks arranged around appointments, medicines, meals, washing, transport, and paperwork. It is also a relationship under pressure. It contains memory, obligation, affection, fear, grief, comparison, and the painful awareness that another person's life may have become smaller, harder, or more uncertain. In that emotional field, guilt can grow quickly. Sometimes it appears after a reasonable boundary. Sometimes it appears after a moment of irritation. Sometimes it appears before anything has happened, simply because the caregiver is thinking about what they cannot do.

This is why guilt can feel so convincing. It rarely arrives with nonsense. It often arrives holding something recognisable. You do care. The person may truly need help. There may be tasks that matter. There may be promises, spoken or unspoken, that still carry weight. There may be a long family history in which love has always been measured by sacrifice. There may be grief beneath the surface, because the person you are caring for is not as they once were, and neither is the relationship. Guilt gathers these truths together and turns them into a blunt command: do more.

But guilt is not always proof that you have done wrong. Often, guilt means that your conscience is awake. It means that you are emotionally connected to the consequences of your choices. It means that another person's discomfort affects you. That capacity is not a flaw. A caregiver with no capacity for guilt might become careless, dismissive, or harsh. The problem is not that guilt appears. The problem begins when guilt is given authority it has not earned.

A signal is useful because it asks for attention. A ruler is dangerous because it governs without question. Guilt should be treated as a signal. It can say, "Look here." It can ask, "Have you been fair?" It can nudge you to apologise if you spoke sharply, follow up if you forgot something important, or reconsider if you acted from impatience rather than judgement. In that form, guilt has value. It keeps you morally responsive. But when guilt becomes a ruler, it no longer asks. It dictates. It tells you to ignore capacity, override limits, accept every request, and treat another person's distress as your personal failure.

Caregivers often fall under guilt's rule because the situations they face are genuinely uneven. The person receiving care may be ill, frail, frightened, grieving, confused, in pain, or losing independence. The caregiver may still have mobility, work, choices, and a life beyond the care role. That imbalance can create a deep discomfort. The caregiver may think, "How can I complain when they are the one suffering?" or "How can I say no when their life is harder than mine?" These questions come from compassion, but they can become traps. Someone else's suffering does not make your capacity infinite.

The first major source of caregiving guilt is love itself. When you love someone, you may feel pain at their pain. You may wish you could remove their loneliness, restore their health, repair their fear, or soften every indignity. When you cannot, guilt may step into the gap between what you wish you could give and what you can realistically provide. This kind of guilt is often grief in disguise. It is not saying, "You have failed." It is saying, "This situation hurts, and you cannot make it whole."

That distinction matters. Grief asks to be felt. Guilt demands repayment. If grief is mistaken for guilt, the caregiver may begin trying to compensate through overwork. They visit when exhausted, answer every call, take on more tasks, spend money they cannot spare, and apologise for limits they need. None of this cures the underlying grief. It simply gives the caregiver a temporary sense of action in the face of loss. The care recipient may still be lonely, unwell, or afraid, and the caregiver is now more depleted than before.

Cultural expectations can intensify this guilt. Many people are raised with strong beliefs about what a good daughter, son, spouse, sibling, or relative should do. These beliefs may contain deep wisdom about loyalty, respect, family responsibility, and the dignity of elders or vulnerable people. They may also contain unrealistic assumptions about availability, gender, sacrifice, obedience, and silence. A caregiver may not simply be responding to the present situation. They may be carrying generations of expectation about what love is supposed to look like.

In some families, the "good" person is the one who does not complain. In others, the responsible person is expected to absorb the needs of everyone else. Some caregivers have been taught that saying no to a parent is disrespectful, that rest is indulgent, that family matters should remain private, or that asking for help shows weakness. These beliefs can be powerful even when the caregiver intellectually disagrees with them. They live in the body as hesitation, shame, and fear of judgement.

Guilt also grows through comparison. A caregiver may compare themselves with a sibling who seems less burdened and feel resentful, then guilty for feeling resentful. They may compare themselves with another caregiver who appears more patient, more organised, more cheerful, or more selfless. They may imagine that other families manage better, other adult children visit more, other spouses cope with more tenderness, other people would never feel the irritation or dread they sometimes feel. Comparison is especially cruel because it usually compares the caregiver's inner reality with someone else's outer performance.

Sibling comparison is particularly charged. One sibling may live nearby while another lives farther away. One may have more money, another more time, another better emotional resilience, another a more complicated relationship with the person receiving care. Yet families often reduce these complexities to simple judgements: who does more, who visits more, who calls more, who seems more devoted. The caregiver who carries the daily load may feel guilty for wanting others to do more, then guilty again for believing they have the right to ask.

There is a strange loneliness in being the most available person. Because you are present, you see more. Because you see more, you feel more responsible. Because you feel more responsible, you do more. Because you do more, others may step back. Then, if you set a limit, you may be treated as though you are withdrawing from a role that somehow became yours by default. Guilt thrives in this arrangement because it convinces the most involved person that any gap is their failure, even when the gap exists because responsibility was never properly shared.

Fear of judgement is another powerful source. Caregivers often imagine being watched by relatives, neighbours, professionals, friends, or the person receiving care. They fear being seen as cold, neglectful, selfish, impatient, ungrateful, or dramatic. Sometimes this fear is based on real comments. A relative may say, "I would never leave Mum alone that long." A professional may make a suggestion without understanding the caregiver's actual capacity. A friend may offer a casual judgement because they have not seen the hidden labour. The caregiver absorbs these remarks and begins to anticipate criticism before it arrives.

Judgement hurts because caregiving is morally exposed work. Most caregivers are making difficult choices with limited resources, incomplete information, and emotional strain. There is rarely a perfect answer. If they visit, something else is neglected. If they work, they feel absent. If they rest, they feel indulgent. If they say yes, they may resent it. If they say no, they may worry they have caused pain. In such conditions, judgement from others can feel unbearable because the caregiver is often already judging themselves.

Guilt may also appear when the caregiver feels anger. This is one of the most misunderstood emotional experiences in care. A caregiver may love the person and still feel irritated by repeated questions, resistance, criticism, neediness, or disrupted plans. They may feel anger at relatives who do not help, at professionals who do not understand, at systems that leave families carrying too much, or at the unfairness of the situation itself. Then guilt follows quickly: "How can I be angry when they cannot help needing care?" or "What kind of person resents someone who is suffering?"

The answer is: a human one. Anger does not automatically mean cruelty. It may be a signal that a boundary has been crossed, a task has become unsustainable, a need is being ignored, or a loss has not been grieved. Caregivers get into trouble when they treat anger as proof of moral failure instead of information. If anger is buried under guilt, it often returns as sharpness, avoidance, sarcasm, emotional numbness, or sudden outbursts. Acknowledging anger privately can prevent it from damaging the relationship publicly.

Another source of guilt is the caregiver's own relief. This can be especially difficult to admit. A caregiver may feel relief when a visit ends, when someone else takes over, when the phone does not ring, when the person receiving care sleeps, when an appointment is cancelled, or when they imagine a future with fewer responsibilities. Relief can trigger shame because it seems to suggest that the caregiver wants to escape the person rather than the pressure. But relief is not the same as lack of love. Often, relief simply means the nervous system has been allowed to stand down.

Caregiving can also awaken old family wounds. A person may be caring for a parent who was critical, emotionally absent, controlling, unpredictable, or difficult long before care was needed. They may feel guilty because the cultural image of caregiving assumes tender reciprocity: the parent gave, now the child gives back. But real families are not always so clean. Some caregivers are trying to provide practical support to someone with whom the emotional history is complicated. They may feel duty, affection, anger, grief, and resistance all at once. Guilt can become the emotion that tries to silence every other truth.

In these situations, guilt may say, "You should not still be hurt." But care needs do not erase the past. A person can become vulnerable without becoming easy to be close to. A caregiver can behave responsibly without pretending the relationship has always been safe or loving. Realistic caregiving must allow emotional complexity.

Otherwise, the caregiver is forced to perform a purity of feeling that no honest human being can maintain.

Guilt also appears when the caregiver has a life outside care. This sounds simple, but it is profound. Work, children, friends, rest, ambition, pleasure, privacy, holidays, hobbies, marriage, health, study, and ordinary freedom can all become guilt triggers. The caregiver may feel guilty for laughing, sleeping, going out, enjoying food, making plans, or having a future that the person receiving care may not share. The contrast can feel cruel. But giving up every source of aliveness does not heal another person's suffering. It only spreads the loss.

This is where guilt becomes confused with loyalty. The caregiver may believe that to be loyal, they must reduce their own life in proportion to the care recipient's loss. If the other person cannot travel, the caregiver should not enjoy travel. If the other person is lonely, the caregiver should not spend time with friends. If the other person is ageing, the caregiver should not think about their own future. This is not loyalty. It is emotional mirroring turned into self-denial. Loyalty means showing up responsibly. It does not mean shrinking until your life matches another person's pain.

Guilt often intensifies around loneliness. Many caregivers feel personally responsible for the loneliness of the person receiving care. This is understandable. Loneliness is painful to witness, especially when someone has lost a partner, mobility, confidence, social circles, or independence. A caregiver may become the main source of company, reassurance, and emotional contact. But one person cannot cure another person's loneliness through constant availability. Companionship can be offered. Connection can be encouraged. Routines can be created. But loneliness may still remain, because it belongs partly to loss, ageing, illness, personality, circumstance, and a wider social world that one caregiver cannot replace.

If the caregiver treats loneliness as their personal assignment, guilt will become endless. There will always be one more call, one more visit, one more hour, one more reassurance, one more reason to postpone their own life. The tragedy is that this may not even solve the loneliness. It may simply make the caregiver resentful and the care recipient more dependent on one source of comfort. Compassion requires acknowledging loneliness. False responsibility requires becoming the entire answer to it.

Another guilt trigger is the gap between what the caregiver thinks they should feel and what they actually feel. They may expect tenderness and find irritation. They may expect patience and find fatigue. They may expect gratitude for the chance to care and find grief over their lost freedom. They may expect confidence and find dread. Because these feelings do not match the idealised image of caregiving, guilt rushes in to punish the difference.

But caregiving is not an idealised role lived by an idealised person. It is demanding human work performed under changing conditions. Feelings will vary. A caregiver can feel tenderness in the morning and resentment by evening. They can be proud of helping and angry that help is needed. They can love the person and dislike the role. They can want to do the right thing and wish someone else would take over for a while. Emotional contradiction is not hypocrisy. It is often the honest texture of care.

Guilt becomes less dangerous when the caregiver stops treating it as a verdict and starts asking what kind of guilt it is. Is it corrective guilt, pointing to something that genuinely needs repair? Is it inherited guilt, repeating family or cultural messages? Is it comparison guilt, based on an imagined standard? Is it grief-guilt, arising from helplessness in the face of loss? Is it boundary guilt, appearing because the caregiver is no longer over-functioning? Is it manipulated guilt, triggered by someone else's pressure? Is it false-responsibility guilt, asking the caregiver to carry what no one person can carry?

This classification is not a mental trick. It is moral clarity. Different guilt requires different responses. If guilt is corrective, the caregiver may need to apologise, adjust, or follow through. If guilt is inherited, it may need to be questioned. If it is grief-guilt, it may need tenderness rather than action. If it is boundary guilt, it may need to be tolerated while the new limit becomes normal. If it is manipulated guilt, it may need a firmer response. If it is false responsibility, it may need to be returned to reality.

One of the most useful distinctions is between responsibility and concern. A caregiver can be concerned about many things without being responsible for all of them. They may be concerned that a relative is lonely, that a sibling avoids involvement, that the person receiving care is unhappy with a decision, that a professional system is slow, that family history is painful, that ageing is unfair. Concern means the issue matters. Responsibility means the issue is yours to act on in a specific and realistic way. Guilt often collapses the two. It says, "Because this matters to you, it belongs to you."

That is false. Many things matter that are not yours to carry alone.

Capacity is another essential part of the distinction. Even when something does fall partly within your responsibility, your capacity still matters. A caregiver may be responsible for helping arrange medical appointments, but not capable of attending every one. They may be responsible for checking in regularly, but not capable of being available all day. They may be responsible for speaking kindly, but not for absorbing verbal harm. They may be responsible for contributing to care, but not for replacing every absent person and every missing service.

Role matters too. Are you the only decision-maker? One of several relatives? A spouse with shared obligations? An adult child with work and children? A friend offering support? A neighbour helping practically? Different roles carry different responsibilities. Guilt often ignores role and speaks as though every caregiver is responsible for everything that would be good. But responsibility must be tied to role, authority, relationship, capacity, and consequence. Otherwise, it becomes limitless.

Consequence matters because not every unmet preference is harm. The person receiving care may be disappointed if you cannot visit on a particular day. That disappointment may be real, but it is not the same as danger. A relative may be annoyed if you do not answer immediately. That annoyance is not proof of urgent need. A house may not be as tidy as someone prefers. That may be uncomfortable, but it may not be important. Guilt often treats discomfort as disaster. Mature care learns to tell the difference.

Caregivers also need to recognise when guilt is compensating for other people's choices. If a sibling repeatedly refuses to help, guilt may push the main caregiver to cover the gap. If another relative promises and fails, guilt may tell the caregiver to step in quietly because the person receiving care should not suffer. If professionals suggest tasks without considering workload, guilt may persuade the caregiver to try harder rather than say the plan is unrealistic. Over time, the caregiver becomes the shock absorber for everyone else's avoidance.

This is not sustainable. Compassion may lead the caregiver to prevent immediate harm, but it should not require them to permanently absorb the consequences of other adults' choices. If someone else will not help, the problem should remain visible. If a system has gaps, those gaps should be named. If a plan requires more labour than the caregiver can provide, the plan must be challenged. Guilt tries to solve the discomfort by making the caregiver bigger than human. Honesty solves it by admitting that the current arrangement is not enough.

Guilt can be especially strong after saying no. The moment after refusal is often emotionally noisy. The caregiver may replay the conversation, imagine the other person sitting sadly, worry about being judged, and search for a way to soften the decision. This rumination can become a second care shift, performed entirely inside the mind. The caregiver may not be doing a task, but they are still paying emotionally. If they do not understand this pattern, they may eventually say yes simply to end the rumination.

A more grounded response is to expect the aftershock. The caregiver can say privately, "Guilt is here because I set a limit, not because the limit is wrong." This kind of self-talk is not sentimental. It is a stabilising practice. It prevents guilt from rewriting the decision before the body has had time to settle. The nervous system may protest a new boundary even when the boundary is wise. Discomfort is not always evidence. Sometimes it is withdrawal from over-functioning.

There is also guilt after anger, especially if the caregiver snapped, used a harsh tone, or withdrew sharply. In those moments, guilt may have a useful message: repair the impact. But repair does not mean surrendering the boundary that anger may have been trying to protect. A mature repair might sound like, "I am sorry I spoke sharply. I was overwhelmed. I am still not able to take calls that late, and we need to keep the evening boundary." This separates behaviour from limit. The caregiver can apologise for the tone without apologising for having a human edge.

This distinction is vital because many caregivers respond to guilt by overcorrecting. They snap, feel ashamed, then become extra available to compensate. They say no, feel guilty, then offer more than they can sustain. They set a boundary, feel bad, then soften it until it becomes meaningless. The emotional swing from refusal to over-giving creates instability. The caregiver becomes harder for others to understand and harder for themselves to trust. Steadiness requires repair without self-erasure.

Guilt may never disappear completely, and that is not the goal. The goal is to reduce its authority. A caregiver can learn to listen without obeying immediately. They can pause before saying yes. They can ask whether the guilt is pointing to true responsibility or false responsibility. They can check capacity. They can consider consequences. They can choose a deliberate yes, a clear no, or a smaller offer that fits reality. The feeling may still ache, but it no longer holds the steering wheel.

The deeper truth is that caregiving guilt often shows up because the caregiver is standing at the edge of several painful realities at once. Someone they care about needs more than they can give. Family expectations may be heavier than actual support. Love may be real, but capacity limited. The past may be unresolved, the present demanding, and the future uncertain. Guilt tries to simplify all of that into one instruction: do more. But complex realities deserve better than a single emotional command.

The caregiver does not need to become guiltless to become wise.

They need to become discerning.

They need to ask, "What is this guilt telling me?" and then, just as importantly, "Is it telling the whole truth?"

Sorting True Responsibility from False

Guilt becomes most dangerous when it attaches itself to the wrong responsibility. A caregiver may feel guilty because a parent is lonely, because a spouse is frightened, because a sibling is absent, because a relative criticises, because a service is slow, because a routine failed, because the house is not as tidy as someone thinks it should be, or because the person receiving care is unhappy with a decision. The feeling is real. The question is whether the responsibility is real.

This distinction is not emotional nit-picking. It is one of the central survival skills of caregiving. Without it, the caregiver can end up carrying everything that hurts, everything that is missing, everything that disappoints, and everything that no one else wants to face. The result is not better care. It is moral overload. The caregiver becomes the place where other people's choices, limits, absences, fears, and system failures are deposited.

True responsibility has shape. False responsibility spreads like water.

True responsibility can be named clearly. It has a task, a role, a realistic degree of influence, and a proportionate consequence. False responsibility is vague, limitless, and emotionally inflated. It sounds like, "I should make them happy," "I should stop them feeling lonely," "I should prevent anyone from being upset," "I should make the family cooperate," "I should be able to manage this without needing more help," or "If something goes wrong, it will be my fault." These statements may feel morally serious, but they are often impossible assignments disguised as conscience.

The caregiver needs a practical test: is this mine to carry?

That question is not an excuse to withdraw from care. It is a method for staying honest. Some things are yours to carry. If you agreed to order medication, it is your responsibility to do it or to communicate clearly if you cannot. If you spoke harshly, it may be your responsibility to repair the impact. If you are the named contact for an appointment, it is your responsibility to pass on essential information. If you said you would visit at a certain time, it is your responsibility to either arrive or give notice. True responsibility asks for follow-through.

False responsibility asks for self-erasure.

A useful starting point is capacity. Can you realistically do this without damaging your functioning, safety, health, work, family life, or emotional stability? Capacity is not the same as willingness. A caregiver may be willing to drive to every appointment, answer every late call, manage every form, and provide daily emotional support. Willingness does not make the load sustainable. The body, the calendar, the bank account, the nervous system, and the household all have their own vote.

Many caregivers ignore capacity because they believe need outranks every limit. If the person receiving care needs something, the caregiver assumes the task must be done by whoever cares most. But capacity is part of reality, not a selfish preference. A person cannot responsibly promise what they cannot reliably provide. If a task requires more time, emotional steadiness, physical strength, money, or availability than the caregiver has, the answer cannot simply be "try harder". The answer must include redesign.

Capacity also changes. What was possible during a short crisis may not be possible over months. What was possible before work changed, before the caregiver became unwell, before children needed more support, before sleep collapsed, or before the care recipient's needs increased may no longer be possible now. False responsibility freezes the caregiver in an old version of themselves. True responsibility updates the plan when capacity changes.

The next test is role. What is your actual role in this situation? Are you the main caregiver, one of several relatives, a spouse, an adult child, a friend, a neighbour, a helper for specific tasks, or the person everyone has informally made responsible because you are dependable? Role matters because responsibility must match authority. A caregiver may be expected to solve problems they have no power to control. That is a recipe for guilt without agency.

For example, you may be concerned that a relative is lonely. You may be able to call regularly, arrange visits, suggest community contact, or coordinate with others. But you may not be responsible for becoming their entire social world. You may be concerned that a sibling refuses to help. You may be able to make a clear request or document the gap. But you are not responsible for transforming that sibling into a reliable person. You may be concerned that the person receiving care rejects support. You may be able to explain consequences and offer options. But you may not be able to make another adult accept what they do not want to accept.

Role also protects the caregiver from emotional overreach. A daughter is not a full medical team. A spouse is not an entire care service. A sibling is not a professional mediator for every family wound. A friend is not a permanent emergency plan. A neighbour is not a substitute for structured support. Love may draw someone close to the problem, but closeness does not automatically create total responsibility.

The third test is consequence. What will actually happen if you do not carry this? Caregivers often feel guilt before examining consequences clearly. They imagine disaster, abandonment, judgement, or irreversible harm. Sometimes the risk is real and immediate. Often, the consequence is discomfort, disappointment, inconvenience, criticism, or the need for someone else to act.

These are not the same.

If a medication issue is left unresolved and the person may be unsafe, the consequence is serious. If a non-urgent call waits until morning and the person is disappointed, the consequence is emotional discomfort. If a bill deadline is missed and services or money may be affected, the consequence matters. If a relative is annoyed because they did not receive an instant update, the consequence is not the same kind of risk. If the caregiver does not tidy a room before a visitor arrives, the consequence may be embarrassment or judgement. That may feel unpleasant, but it may not be important enough to override rest, work, or essential care.

False responsibility often treats all negative reactions as equal. Someone's sadness, anger, boredom, disappointment, and anxiety all become proof that the caregiver should act. True responsibility sorts consequences. It asks what is unsafe, what is merely uncomfortable, what is urgent, what can wait, what belongs to someone else, and what is being amplified by guilt.

A fourth test is influence. Can your action genuinely change the outcome, or are you trying to control something no one person can control? Caregivers often feel responsible for outcomes that are only partly within their influence. They may try to keep someone calm, prevent decline, maintain family unity, remove loneliness, preserve independence, or make care feel dignified at every moment. These are worthy hopes, but they are not fully controllable outcomes.

You can create conditions that support calm. You cannot guarantee calm. You can encourage safe routines. You cannot prevent every risk. You can offer companionship. You cannot cure loneliness. You can communicate clearly with relatives. You cannot make them fair. You can treat someone with dignity. You cannot remove every humiliation that illness, ageing, or dependence may bring. When caregivers confuse influence with control, guilt becomes endless because life will keep producing outcomes beyond their power.

This is especially painful when the person receiving care is unhappy. A caregiver may do the practical tasks well and still face sadness, anger, complaint, fear, or dissatisfaction. The temptation is to interpret unhappiness as evidence that the caregiver has not done enough. But some unhappiness belongs to the situation itself. Losing independence is painful. Needing help can feel humiliating. Physical decline can be frightening. A smaller life can be lonely. The caregiver may soften these experiences, but cannot erase them.

True responsibility says, "I will act with care within my role and capacity." False responsibility says, "If they suffer, I have failed." The second sentence sounds loving, but it is a trap. It makes the caregiver responsible not only for actions, but for the emotional weather of another person's life.

Another useful test is consent. Did you consciously agree to this responsibility, or did it drift towards you because no one else took it? Many caregiving duties are never assigned; they accumulate. You handled one appointment, so appointments became yours. You collected one prescription, so prescriptions became yours. You calmed one family dispute, so emotional mediation became yours. You answered late calls once or twice, so late availability became assumed. The role expanded without a real conversation.

A responsibility that drifted towards you may still be important, but it should not be treated as sacred simply because it has become familiar. The caregiver is allowed to review inherited tasks. They are allowed to ask whether they still consent to carrying them. They are allowed to separate what they deliberately choose from what the care system silently placed on their shoulders.

This is where many caregivers discover that guilt is protecting an old arrangement, not a true duty. The feeling says, "You cannot stop now." But the more accurate statement may be, "This task has never been properly shared." Guilt says, "They rely on you." Reality may say, "The system has been allowed to rely on you too much." Guilt says, "You are letting them down." Reality may say, "A hidden workload has finally become visible."

False responsibility often grows around other people's choices. A sibling chooses not to visit, and the main caregiver feels guilty for not visiting more. A relative refuses to learn the medication routine, and the caregiver feels guilty for not being constantly available. The person receiving care rejects outside help, and the caregiver feels guilty for not compensating personally. A family member creates conflict, and the caregiver feels guilty for not smoothing it over. In each case, guilt turns someone else's choice into the caregiver's burden.

This does not mean the caregiver should allow preventable harm just to make a point. Care often requires practical judgement. But there is a difference between responding to an immediate need and permanently absorbing the consequences of other people's refusal. If a sibling will not help, that is a family problem, not proof that the caregiver has unlimited responsibility. If the person receiving care refuses reasonable support, that refusal has consequences that cannot always be neutralised by the caregiver's sacrifice. If a system leaves gaps, those gaps must be named, not hidden inside one person's exhaustion.

Systemic gaps are another source of false responsibility. Caregivers may feel personally guilty because services are delayed, professional advice is impractical, paperwork is confusing, transport is limited, paid support is unaffordable, or information is fragmented. The caregiver may say, "I should be able to sort this." But some problems are not personal failures. They are structural shortages, administrative burdens, financial constraints, or coordination problems that have landed in the caregiver's lap.

Recognising systemic gaps does not solve them instantly, but it changes the emotional meaning. The caregiver can stop converting every obstacle into self-blame. They can say, "This is a gap in support," rather than, "I am failing." That distinction matters because shame drains energy that is needed for practical action. A caregiver who sees the gap clearly is more likely to ask for help, escalate concerns, simplify routines, document needs, or make a realistic plan. A caregiver buried in false guilt may simply work harder until they break.

Sorting responsibility also requires a clear distinction between care and rescue. Care is deliberate, proportionate, and as sustainable as possible. Rescue is immediate, emotionally driven, and often repeated without redesign. A caregiver may rescue because the situation is genuinely urgent. That is sometimes necessary. But if rescue becomes the standard response, false responsibility expands. The caregiver begins to believe that every problem must be solved by their personal intervention.

A useful question is: "Am I responding to a true emergency, or am I preventing others from facing a needed change?" If the house is unsafe today, action may be necessary. If the same unsafe pattern keeps returning because no one will discuss a higher level of support, the repeated rescue may be hiding the real problem. If a late-night panic happens once, compassion may be needed. If late-night panic becomes the usual route to contact, a communication boundary may be needed. If transport fails once, stepping in may be kind. If transport fails repeatedly because no one else plans, the task needs reassignment.

False responsibility also appears as emotional substitution. The caregiver tries to feel guilty instead of feeling grief, anger, helplessness, or disappointment. Guilt can be oddly attractive because it implies control. If you are guilty, then perhaps you could fix the problem by doing more. Grief is harder because it admits that some losses cannot be fixed. Anger is harder because it may require boundaries. Helplessness is harder because it exposes limits. Disappointment is harder because it reveals other people's failures.

For instance, feeling guilty about a relative's loneliness may be easier than admitting sadness that their world has narrowed. Feeling guilty about a sibling's absence may be easier than feeling angry that responsibility is unequal. Feeling guilty after saying no may be easier than accepting that someone you love will be disappointed and you cannot prevent it. Guilt offers action. "Do more." But action is not always the appropriate response. Sometimes the honest response is mourning, naming, adjusting, or tolerating discomfort.

A caregiver can test responsibility by asking five plain questions.

Is this within my role?

Do I have the capacity to carry it?

What are the real consequences if I do not?

Am I the only person who can do this, or simply the person most likely to do it?

Am I responding to a need, or compensating for someone else's choice, avoidance, or a wider gap?

These questions slow guilt down. They make it answerable. They move the caregiver from emotional reflex to moral judgement.

Consider the example of a relative's loneliness. The caregiver may already be managing appointments, medication, shopping, paperwork, and safety checks. Yet after every visit, the person says, "I hardly see anyone. I sit here all day." The caregiver leaves feeling crushed. They consider adding more visits, longer calls, weekend time, perhaps cancelling their own plans. The guilt says, "They are lonely. You must go more."

The responsibility test gives a fuller answer. Is companionship part of care? Yes, to some degree. Is curing loneliness entirely within the caregiver's role? No. Does the caregiver have capacity for daily emotional support without damage? Perhaps not. What are the consequences if they do not add more visits? The person may remain lonely, disappointed, or sad, but not necessarily unsafe. Is the caregiver the only possible source of connection? Maybe they have become the default, but other options may need exploration. Is the caregiver compensating for wider loss, absent relatives, limited mobility, or lack of community? Very likely.

The result is not indifference. The caregiver may still act. They may create a predictable call schedule, ask another person to visit, explore social contact, arrange practical support, or speak honestly about what they can provide. But they no longer accept the impossible assignment of becoming the full cure for loneliness. That is the difference between realistic accountability and false responsibility.

Realistic accountability is not cold. It is ethically cleaner than guilt-driven overpromising. It says, "I will do my part and tell the truth about its limits." False responsibility says, "I will try to fill the whole gap and resent the cost later." The first position may disappoint someone in the short term. The second often damages the relationship over time.

Sorting responsibility also helps with sibling resentment. A caregiver may feel trapped between anger and guilt: angry that siblings do little, guilty for being angry, guilty for asking, guilty for not asking well enough, guilty for considering doing less. The responsibility test clarifies the issue. The caregiver is responsible for making clear requests where appropriate. They are responsible for communicating essential information. They are responsible for not using resentment as an excuse for cruelty. They are not responsible for making siblings fair, available, emotionally mature, or willing.

This clarity can be both freeing and painful. It frees the caregiver from believing they can fix another adult's character. It is painful because it may reveal that some people will not become the helpers the caregiver hoped they would be. But accepting that truth allows better planning. A caregiver can stop waiting for vague fairness and start asking for specific tasks, seeking other support, adjusting expectations, or setting firmer limits around what they will no longer compensate for.

Sorting responsibility also matters when the person receiving care resists help. The caregiver may feel responsible for the consequences of that resistance. If the person refuses to use a walking aid, rejects meal support, will not share information, ignores advice, or declines outside assistance, the caregiver may feel compelled to monitor more closely, argue more often, or personally absorb the risk. Sometimes cognitive changes or vulnerability complicate this, and safety may require further action. But even then, responsibility must be realistic.

Where the person receiving care has decision-making capacity, their choices remain part of the picture. The caregiver can explain risks, offer help, document concerns, involve appropriate professionals where needed, and decide what they can safely participate in. But they cannot always prevent another adult from making choices they dislike. False responsibility says, "If they refuse help, I must make up the difference." True responsibility says, "Their refusal changes what is possible, and the plan must reflect that."

The caregiver must also sort responsibility for emotions after boundaries. If someone cries because the caregiver cannot visit, whose responsibility is the crying? The caregiver may be responsible for speaking kindly. They may be responsible for offering a realistic alternative if one exists. They may be responsible for not dismissing the person's feelings. But they are not automatically responsible for removing the sadness by reversing the boundary. Another person's distress deserves compassion. It does not always create obligation.

This is difficult because many caregivers have spent years managing the emotional temperature of others. They may feel that if someone is upset, they must soothe, explain, fix, or concede. But emotional responsibility has limits. Adults can be disappointed and still survive. People can dislike a decision and still be cared for. A person receiving care can feel sad about a limit and still not be abandoned. The caregiver can stay connected without becoming controlled by another person's feelings.

A useful internal sentence is: "I am responsible for my behaviour, not for preventing every feeling my behaviour causes." This does not excuse harshness. It simply restores proportion. If the caregiver is cruel, they should repair. If the caregiver is clear and kind but the other person is upset by the limit, the upset is part of adjustment, not proof of wrongdoing.

True responsibility often requires action. False responsibility often requires rumination. This is another way to tell the difference. If the guilt points to a clear repair, task, or conversation within your capacity, it may be useful. If it leads only to repetitive mental loops, imagined judgement, endless self-accusation, and vague pressure to do more, it is probably not guiding you well. Useful guilt becomes a next step. False guilt becomes a fog.

For example, useful guilt says, "I forgot to call when I said I would. I need to apologise and set a better reminder." False guilt says, "I am a terrible person because I did not call, and maybe I should now offer extra visits I cannot sustain." Useful guilt says, "I sounded impatient. I should repair the tone." False guilt says, "Because I snapped, I have no right to keep the boundary." Useful guilt corrects behaviour. False guilt bargains away limits.

A caregiver sorting responsibility should also ask whether a proposed action is sustainable. A response that can be given once may not be responsible if it creates an expectation that cannot be maintained. Offering daily calls after one emotional conversation may feel compassionate, but if the caregiver cannot keep it up, it may lead to future disappointment and guilt. Agreeing to every appointment may solve this month but destroy work stability. Paying for repeated costs may prevent a difficult conversation now but create financial strain later. True responsibility considers the future. False responsibility seeks immediate relief from guilt.

Another marker is resentment. If a responsibility repeatedly produces resentment, it may not be false, but it needs examination. Perhaps the task is necessary but unsupported. Perhaps it belongs partly to someone else. Perhaps it is being done at the wrong time or in the wrong way. Perhaps the caregiver has never consciously agreed to it. Perhaps it is emotionally loaded because of old family wounds. Resentment should not automatically decide the matter, but it should not be ignored. It often indicates that responsibility and capacity are out of alignment.

Caregivers may fear that questioning responsibility will make them selfish. In reality, it often makes them more reliable. A person who knows what is theirs can carry it more cleanly. They are less likely to say yes and then seethe. Less likely to overpromise and withdraw. Less likely to confuse help with control. Less likely to accept tasks and then punish others emotionally for needing them. Clear responsibility produces cleaner care.

It also produces cleaner refusals. When a caregiver has sorted responsibility, they can say no without turning the conversation into a moral drama. "I cannot be responsible for daily transport." "I am not able to manage that paperwork at short notice." "I cannot be the only person providing company." "I will not be the messenger between siblings." "I can help with this part, but not the whole arrangement." These sentences may still be difficult, but they are grounded in reality rather than defensiveness.

Sometimes the sorting process reveals that a task truly is yours. This matters. The goal is not to shrink every responsibility until nothing remains. Sustainable care requires integrity. If a caregiver has been avoiding a necessary conversation, they may need to have it. If they have let resentment make them unreliable, they may need to reset. If they promised to do something and cannot, they need to communicate clearly rather than disappear. If they caused hurt, they may need to repair. True responsibility is not always light. It is simply proportionate.

The word "proportionate" is crucial. Caregiving does not remove proportionality from moral life. A small mistake may need a small repair, not weeks of self-punishment. A real responsibility may need a defined contribution, not total availability. A difficult family situation may need honest communication, not lifelong emotional mediation. A care recipient's loneliness may need thoughtful support, not the caregiver's entire social and emotional life. Proportion protects both people from the excesses of guilt.

When responsibility is sorted well, the caregiver becomes less reactive to accusation. If someone says, "You do not care," the caregiver can return internally to the truth: "I care, and I am not responsible for everything." If someone says, "You are the only one who can help," the caregiver can ask whether that is fact or habit. If someone says, "They will be lonely without you," the caregiver can recognise the sadness without accepting total ownership. If someone says, "You should do more," the caregiver can measure that claim against capacity, role, consequence, and sustainability.

This inner steadiness does not make external pressure vanish, but it reduces its power. The caregiver is no longer forced to treat every emotional statement as an accurate moral judgement. They can listen, consider, and decide. That pause is where freedom enters.

Sorting responsibility is ultimately the work of returning burdens to their proper size. Some burdens are yours. Some are shared. Some belong to other adults. Some belong to systems, circumstances, illness, ageing, grief, or chance. Some are not burdens at all, but discomforts that can be felt without being fixed. The caregiver's task is not to carry the entire landscape of suffering. It is to carry their part with honesty, skill, and limits.

Guilt will resist this sorting because guilt prefers simple commands. "Do more." "Say yes." "Fix it." "Prevent the pain." "Be better." Responsibility is more nuanced. It asks, "What is mine? What is possible? What is fair? What is safe? What is repeatable? What belongs elsewhere?" These questions may not produce easy answers, but they produce truer ones.

A caregiver who learns to sort responsibility does not become less loving. They become less available to false assignments. They stop mistaking every ache for an obligation. They stop carrying loneliness as if it were a package addressed only to them. They stop covering every gap without naming it. They stop treating another person's distress as automatic proof of their failure.

The result is not guilt-free caregiving. It is clearer caregiving.

And clarity is what allows a caregiver to say, with compassion and firmness, "This matters, but it is not all mine to carry."

Responding to Guilt Without Surrendering

Guilt is persuasive because it asks for action. It does not merely sit in the mind as discomfort; it pushes. Call now. Go today. Apologise again. Say yes. Stay longer. Cancel your plan. Answer the message. Explain yourself until they understand. Do the task because no one else will. The feeling may begin as a small ache, but if left unquestioned it can become a command system, directing the caregiver's time, body, money, attention, and emotional availability.

The problem is not that guilt appears. In caregiving, guilt will appear. It appears because the stakes are human. Someone may be vulnerable, lonely, frightened, unwell, confused, or disappointed. You may be tired, limited, impatient, or unavailable at the very moment they want more from you. The collision between need and capacity creates emotional heat. Guilt often rises from that heat and announces itself as truth.

But guilt is not always truth. Sometimes it is a signal. Sometimes it is grief. Sometimes it is old family conditioning. Sometimes it is fear of judgement. Sometimes it is the echo of being called selfish too many times. Sometimes it is simply the discomfort of doing something new after years of over-functioning. A caregiver who treats every guilty feeling as an instruction will eventually build a life around avoiding guilt rather than providing wise care.

Responding to guilt without surrendering begins with one critical pause: *what is this guilt asking me to do, and is that action wise?* Not kind-looking. Not immediately soothing. Not likely to keep everyone calm for the next hour. Wise. A guilt-driven yes can look generous while creating future resentment, exhaustion, and instability. A wise response may feel uncomfortable while protecting the caregiver, the relationship, and the care arrangement over time.

Many caregivers skip this pause because guilt feels urgent. The body wants relief. Saying yes can quiet the feeling temporarily. Answering the call, making the visit, giving the money, accepting the task, or apologising for a boundary may reduce the immediate emotional pressure. The caregiver feels less cruel, less anxious, less exposed. Yet this relief is often short-lived. The same demand returns. The same resentment grows. The same exhaustion deepens. Guilt is quieted for a moment, but the pattern that produced it remains untouched.

This is why guilt-driven decisions are so costly. They are usually made to escape an emotion, not to solve the real problem. The caregiver says yes to avoid feeling like a bad daughter, son, spouse, sibling, or friend. They agree to a task because refusing would make them feel guilty. They abandon a boundary because someone cried. They over-explain because someone seemed disappointed. They offer extra help because a relative implied they were not doing enough. In each case, guilt becomes the decision-maker.

A healthier pattern begins by separating the feeling from the choice. "I feel guilty" is not the same as "I have done wrong." "I feel pulled" is not the same as "this is mine to carry." "They are upset" is not the same as "I must change my answer." "I wish things were different" is not the same as "I must sacrifice more." These distinctions may sound simple, but under pressure they are radical. They return authority to judgement rather than emotion.

The caregiver can begin with a short internal sentence: "Guilt is present, and I can still choose deliberately." This does not deny the feeling. It does not shame the caregiver for having it. It simply places guilt in its proper position. Guilt may sit at the table, but it does not chair the meeting.

A second useful sentence is: "Feeling bad does not automatically mean I have behaved badly." This is especially important after setting a boundary. A caregiver may say, "I cannot take non-urgent calls after 8 p.m.," then spend the evening feeling restless, cruel, and anxious. The feeling may be intense. But intensity is not evidence. The guilt may be the nervous system adjusting to a new limit. It may be the old role protesting. It may be fear of another person's reaction. The caregiver needs to ask whether the boundary was harmful or simply uncomfortable.

A third sentence is: "I can care about their distress without making myself the solution to all of it." This is vital when the person receiving care is lonely, anxious, disappointed, or angry. Compassion does not require total availability. A caregiver can acknowledge pain without volunteering for an unsustainable role. They can say, "I know this feels hard," while still saying, "I am not able to come today." They can offer a planned call instead of immediate access. They can remain loving without becoming endlessly reachable.

Responding well to guilt also requires a decision rule. Without one, the caregiver must negotiate with guilt from the beginning every time it appears. That is exhausting. A decision rule gives the caregiver a standard to return to when emotion rises. One rule might be: "I do not say yes while I am panicking." Another might be: "I check capacity before agreeing." Another: "I do not reverse a boundary in the moment because someone is upset." Another: "If the task is not urgent, I give myself time to decide."

These rules are not rigid for the sake of rigidity. They protect the caregiver from emotional ambush. Guilt often demands immediate relief, but many caregiving decisions do not require an immediate answer. A caregiver can say, "I need to check what is possible and come back to you." Or: "I cannot decide that right now." Or: "I will think about it and reply tomorrow." This pause alone can break the cycle of guilt-driven agreement.

The pause is particularly important when a request comes wrapped in emotional pressure. "You are the only one who can do this." "I do not know what I will do if you say no." "After everything they did for you." "Your sister would come if she cared." "I suppose I will just manage alone." These statements may provoke a rush of guilt, but they should not be allowed to bypass judgement. The caregiver can hear the pressure and still ask: Is this urgent? Is it mine? Do I have capacity? What are the consequences if I say no? Who else could be involved? Is this a one-off need or another repetition of a pattern?

The difference between guilt and responsibility becomes clearest at the point of action. Responsibility usually points towards a specific, proportionate next step. Guilt often points towards a vague demand to do more. If you forgot a promised call, responsibility may say, "Apologise and call now if appropriate." Guilt may say, "You are awful; offer extra visits to make up for it." If you snapped during a hard conversation, responsibility may say, "Repair the tone." Guilt may say, "Withdraw the boundary to prove you are kind." If you cannot attend an appointment, responsibility may say, "Give notice and help arrange an alternative if that is your role." Guilt may say, "Cancel your own essential commitments because disappointment is unbearable."

A practical question helps: "What is the smallest responsible action?" This question prevents guilt from expanding a situation beyond proportion. If you spoke sharply, the smallest responsible action may be an apology, not an entire surrender of your limits. If you cannot visit, the smallest responsible action may be a clear message and a planned alternative, not abandoning your own rest day. If a relative is angry, the smallest responsible action may be to acknowledge the concern and restate the arrangement, not enter a long defence of your character.

This matters because guilt often pushes towards excessive repair. The caregiver does not merely apologise; they overcompensate. They do not merely clarify; they justify for an hour. They do not merely decline; they offer three other things they cannot sustain. They do not merely acknowledge disappointment; they take responsibility for removing it. Excessive repair may look loving, but it teaches everyone that the caregiver's guilt can be converted into more labour.

Repair is important. Surrender is different.

Repair says, "I see the impact of my behaviour, and I will address it honestly." Surrender says, "Because someone is upset, I will give up the limit that was protecting me." Repair strengthens trust. Surrender trains the relationship to treat guilt as the route around every boundary. A caregiver must learn the difference, especially after conflict.

A mature repair might sound like: "I am sorry I sounded impatient yesterday. I was tired, and I should have spoken more calmly. I am still not able to take calls after 9 p.m., so we need to keep that boundary." This sentence does three things at once. It acknowledges harm. It avoids self-excuse. It preserves the limit. That combination is the heart of responding to guilt without surrendering.

Another version might be: "I know it was disappointing that I could not drive you. I should have told you earlier that I was unavailable. Going forward, I can help coordinate appointments, but I cannot be the regular driver." Again, the caregiver accepts responsibility for communication without accepting a role they cannot sustain. This is emotionally cleaner than either defensiveness or collapse.

Caregivers often fear that maintaining a boundary after apologising will seem insincere. In truth, the opposite is often the case. An apology that secretly purchases self-erasure is not healthier. It may sound generous, but it creates resentment. A clear apology paired with a clear limit tells the truth. It says, "My behaviour can improve, and my capacity still has edges." Both can be true.

Guilt also needs to be answered differently depending on its source. If the guilt is corrective, the caregiver should act. If the guilt is inherited, the caregiver should question it. If the guilt is grief, the caregiver should feel it rather than pay it with extra labour. If the guilt is triggered by manipulation, the caregiver should strengthen the boundary. If the guilt comes from comparison, the caregiver should return to the reality of their own role and capacity. A single feeling may require very different responses.

Inherited guilt often appears as a "should" with no clear origin. "I should never say no to my mother." "I should be able to cope." "A good spouse would not need breaks." "Family should not need outside help." These statements may have been absorbed from culture, religion, family history, gender expectations, or childhood roles. They may feel sacred simply because they are old. But old does not always mean wise. The caregiver can ask, "Who taught me this, and does it fit the reality I am living now?"

This question is not disrespectful. It is responsible. A belief that may have functioned in one context can become damaging in another. Respect for family does not require unlimited availability. Loyalty does not require silence. Love does not require the caregiver to become the sole answer to complex needs. A caregiver can honour what is good in their values while rejecting the parts that demand self-erasure.

Comparison guilt needs a different response. The caregiver may think, "Other people would do more," or "My sibling seems less troubled by this," or "I should be as patient as that person." Comparison usually ignores context. It does not account for health, money, distance, work, emotional history, temperament, hidden support, or the private cost another person may be paying. The caregiver needs to return to the only useful measure: what is true in this care situation, with this load, this capacity, this relationship, and these consequences?

A grounded self-response might be: "I do not need to match an imagined caregiver. I need to make a sustainable decision in the real situation." That sentence cuts through the fantasy standard. The goal is not to perform caregiving in a way that would satisfy every possible observer. The goal is to provide care that is honest, safe, proportionate, and sustainable.

Grief-guilt is more tender. It may arise when the caregiver sees the person receiving care decline, sit alone, struggle with ordinary tasks, or lose parts of the life they once had. The caregiver may feel guilty because they cannot reverse the loss. They may do more in an attempt to soften the grief, but the grief remains. In these moments, guilt may not be asking for a task. It may be asking to be mourned.

A caregiver can say privately, "This hurts because I love them and because I cannot fix everything." That sentence is different from, "I must do more." Sometimes the most honest response to grief-guilt is not action but tenderness: a quiet acknowledgement, a moment of sadness, a conversation with someone trusted, a pause after a visit, a small ritual of recovery. Not every ache is an instruction. Some aches are evidence of love meeting reality.

Manipulated guilt requires firmer handling. If someone repeatedly uses shame, accusation, helplessness, comparison, silent treatment, or emotional escalation to force the caregiver into compliance, the caregiver must stop treating every guilty feeling as morally reliable. The feeling may be real, but it has been triggered by pressure. A useful sentence is: "This guilt has been activated by someone else's demand; I will not decide from it." The caregiver can then return to the boundary.

For example: "I understand you are unhappy. I am still not available tonight." Or: "I am not going to discuss whether I care. I have told you what I can do." Or: "I will speak with you when the conversation is respectful." These responses do not accuse the other person of manipulation, which may only escalate the exchange. They simply refuse to let pressure determine the outcome.

One of the most powerful practices is delaying the yes. Caregivers who struggle with guilt often say yes too quickly because the discomfort of hesitation feels unbearable. A delayed yes protects against this. It does not mean refusing everything. It means refusing to commit before checking reality. "I need to look at my week." "I cannot answer that now." "I will let you know tomorrow." "I need to see whether that is possible." These sentences create enough distance for guilt to settle and judgement to return.

A delayed yes also reveals the nature of the request. If the task is genuinely urgent, that will become clear. If the requester becomes angry simply because the caregiver will not answer instantly, that is useful information. If the caregiver feels calmer after a pause and can offer a limited form of help, the yes becomes more deliberate. If the pause reveals that the task is unsustainable, the caregiver can decline with more confidence.

Deliberate yeses are essential because the aim is not to become a person who always says no. Caregiving requires generosity. There will be times when the caregiver chooses inconvenience, sacrifice, or extra effort because the need is real and the choice is aligned with their values. But a deliberate yes has a different quality from a guilt-driven yes. It is clearer. It knows the cost. It has limits. It does not secretly expect gratitude as repayment for self-betrayal.

A deliberate yes might sound like: "I can stay late tonight because this is urgent, but I cannot do late evenings regularly." Or: "I can help with this form on Saturday, but I need the documents ready before then." Or: "I can call each evening this week after the appointment, but next week we return to the usual check-in." These yeses preserve choice. They help without giving guilt permission to write a permanent contract.

Sometimes the right response is a partial yes. Guilt tends to think in extremes: either do everything or you are abandoning them. Partial yeses break that false choice. "I cannot drive, but I can help book transport." "I cannot visit today, but I can call at 6 p.m." "I cannot manage all the paperwork, but I can help sort the urgent letter." "I cannot be available every evening, but I can do a planned call twice a week." A partial yes honours care without pretending capacity is unlimited.

Sometimes the right response is a clean no. This is the hardest for many caregivers. A clean no does not mean a cruel no. It means a no without excessive justification, hidden apology, or compensatory over-giving. "I am not able to do that." "That does not work for me." "I cannot take that on." "No, I am not available." These sentences may feel too short to someone accustomed to explaining. But shortness can be merciful. It reduces the number of openings for debate.

The caregiver may choose to add warmth: "I know this is disappointing, and I am not able to do that." "I care about what happens, and I cannot take this on." "I understand why you are asking, and the answer is no." The warmth protects the relationship; the clarity protects the boundary. Neither should be sacrificed.

After a no, guilt often begins its second shift: rumination. The caregiver replays the conversation, imagines the other person's disappointment, predicts judgement, wonders whether they were too harsh, and mentally rehearses alternative responses. Rumination can feel like responsibility, but often it is anxiety seeking certainty. The caregiver wants to know they did the right thing. Care rarely offers that kind of perfect certainty.

To reduce rumination, the caregiver can use a post-decision check. Was I clear? Was I respectful? Did I consider real risk? Did I check capacity? Did I offer what was reasonable, if anything was reasonable? Did I avoid promising what I cannot sustain? If the answer is largely yes, the decision does not need to be retried all night. The guilt may still be present, but the decision has been made with care.

A useful closing sentence for the mind is: "I have made a considered decision. I do not need to keep re-deciding it." This matters because guilt often keeps dragging the caregiver back to the same doorway. The mind knocks and asks, "Are you sure?" again and again. At some point, the caregiver must stop reopening the case unless new information appears. Otherwise, guilt becomes a private court that never adjourns.

Caregivers should also learn to identify guilt that belongs to transition. When a caregiver begins setting boundaries, redistributing tasks, or reducing over-functioning, guilt may increase temporarily. This does not mean the changes are wrong. It may mean the caregiver is stepping out of a familiar role. The family system may protest. The person receiving care may feel unsettled. The caregiver's identity may feel shaky. The guilt belongs to the adjustment period.

A transition sentence can help: "This feels wrong because it is new, not necessarily because it is harmful." The caregiver can pair this with observation. Is the person unsafe, or just displeased? Is a real need unmet, or is the old pattern being challenged? Am I abandoning care, or changing how care is provided? These questions keep the caregiver from confusing discomfort with danger.

Responding to guilt without surrendering also requires attention to the body. Guilt is not only a thought. It can be a heaviness in the chest, a knot in the stomach, a restless urge to act, a headache, a sense of being watched, a rush of heat, or a hollow feeling after saying no. If the caregiver acts immediately from that bodily state, they may choose relief over wisdom. A simple physical pause can help: breathe slowly, place both feet on the floor, unclench the jaw, take a short walk, drink water, wait before replying. This is not decorative self-care. It is decision protection.

The caregiver needs enough calm to distinguish a true moral signal from emotional pressure. No one makes their best care decisions while flooded with guilt and fear. A pause does not remove responsibility. It improves the quality of response.

There will be occasions when guilt reveals that the caregiver should change course. This must be acknowledged. Sometimes the caregiver has been avoiding a necessary task. Sometimes they have become too abrupt. Sometimes a boundary has been stated unclearly. Sometimes a no was given from irritation rather than judgement. Sometimes the person receiving care has a need that deserves more attention. Responding to guilt without surrendering does not mean dismissing guilt. It means examining it honestly.

The test is whether guilt points to a specific repair or simply demands self-punishment. If there is a specific repair, make it. Apologise. Clarify. Follow through. Ask a better question. Adjust the plan. But do not add unnecessary sacrifice as proof of remorse. The repair should fit the issue. A small wound does not require a huge repayment. A genuine mistake does not erase every boundary.

For example, if a caregiver forgot to send an appointment reminder, they can apologise and create a reminder system. They do not need to take over every appointment forever. If they spoke impatiently during a stressful call, they can apologise for the tone. They do not need to become available for unlimited calls. If they delayed a response too long, they can acknowledge it and state a clearer response window. Repair should improve the care system, not feed guilt's appetite.

Guilt is also easier to manage when the caregiver has already defined their values. Without values, guilt becomes the loudest moral voice. With values, the caregiver can ask, "Which response best fits the kind of care I am trying to give?" Values might include steadiness, honesty, respect, sustainability, dignity, fairness, and kindness. These are deeper than momentary comfort. A guilt-driven yes may preserve comfort but violate sustainability. A firm no may cause discomfort but honour honesty and fairness.

The caregiver can use values as a compass: "I want to be kind, but not dishonest. I want to be reliable, but not endlessly available. I want to be loving, but not resentful. I want to be responsible, but not self-erasing." These sentences help the caregiver stay connected to a larger moral frame when guilt narrows the whole world to one request.

It is important to understand that some people will not experience the caregiver's response as enough. They may want more access, more reassurance, more time, more sacrifice, more proof. The caregiver may respond thoughtfully and still be judged. This is one of the painful realities of boundaries. Good decision-making does not guarantee approval. A caregiver who makes approval the measure of right action will always be vulnerable to guilt.

The stronger measure is integrity: did I act within my role, capacity, values, and the real needs of the situation? Integrity may still feel uncomfortable. It may still leave sadness. It may still require repair later. But it is steadier than approval, because approval is controlled by other people's expectations, fears, and habits.

When guilt remains after a good decision, the caregiver can practise letting it be present without feeding it. This may sound simple, but it is difficult. The caregiver may want to solve the feeling by taking action. Instead, they can say, "Guilt is here. I am not going to bargain with it tonight." They can redirect attention to something grounding.

They can speak to a trusted person who understands the larger context. They can write down the decision and the reasons for it. They can rest even while guilt complains.

Resting while guilty is one of the most important skills in sustainable care. Many caregivers allow guilt to cancel recovery. They sit down and immediately think of what they should be doing. They take an evening off and spend it mentally apologising. They protect a morning and then feel ashamed for enjoying it. The body is away from care, but the mind is still working. Responding to guilt without surrendering means refusing to let guilt confiscate the recovery time that the boundary was meant to protect.

A practical phrase is: "This rest is part of the care plan." Not a reward. Not an indulgence. Part of the plan. If guilt argues, the caregiver can return to the principle: depleted care is not better care. Resentful care is not warmer care. A caregiver who never recovers becomes less able to provide steadiness. Rest may feel morally uncomfortable at first, but discomfort does not make it wrong.

The same applies to joy. Caregivers often feel guilty for enjoying themselves while someone else is struggling. They may feel disloyal laughing, going out, reading, exercising, travelling, or spending time with friends. Yet joy is not betrayal. A caregiver's life does not need to shrink in order to prove the seriousness of another person's suffering. Joy can be a form of resilience. It returns the caregiver to personhood, which makes care less likely to become a prison.

Responding to guilt without surrendering also improves relationships. At first, this may seem unlikely. Surely saying yes keeps relationships smoother. Sometimes it does, briefly. But repeated guilt-driven yeses create hidden accounts. The caregiver begins to remember every sacrifice no one noticed. They become more sensitive to requests. They may give with a tight heart. They may appear helpful while inwardly withdrawing. The relationship becomes crowded with unspoken resentment.

A deliberate no, or a limited yes, may cause discomfort now, but it can prevent deeper corrosion later. It gives others a more accurate understanding of the caregiver's capacity. It makes the caregiver's yes more trustworthy. It reduces the emotional whiplash of over-giving followed by resentment. It allows repair to be specific rather than theatrical. Over time, steadiness becomes more relationally honest than guilt-driven compliance.

The person receiving care may also benefit from a caregiver who is not governed by guilt. They receive care from someone less likely to swing between over-involvement and withdrawal. They encounter clearer expectations. They are less likely to be made the unconscious cause of the caregiver's exhaustion. They may not always like the limits, but they are living inside a more truthful arrangement. Truth is not always comfortable, but it is kinder than a care relationship built on silent self-betrayal.

There is no perfect method that will make guilt vanish. Some decisions will still ache. Some noes will feel heavy. Some repairs will be awkward. Some people will be disappointed. Some responsibilities will remain genuinely hard. The aim is not emotional purity. The aim is to stop guilt from making every decision alone.

The caregiver can respond to guilt with a sequence: notice it, name it, test it, choose deliberately, repair if needed, and then stop renegotiating unless new information appears. This sequence turns guilt from a ruler into data. It restores proportion. It allows conscience to remain active without allowing conscience to be hijacked by fear, habit, or pressure.

A caregiver who can do this becomes less reactive and more reliable. They no longer need to escape guilt at any cost. They can feel the ache and still keep the boundary. They can apologise without surrendering. They can say yes without self-erasure. They can say no without cruelty. They can make room for another person's disappointment without treating that disappointment as a verdict.

This is not indifference. It is mature care.

Guilt may still knock after a boundary, after a refusal, after a hard visit, after a relative's comment, after a quiet evening taken back for yourself. But the knock does not have to become an order. The caregiver can open the door, listen for what is useful, and refuse to hand over the keys.

Chapter 5
Hard Conversations and Clear Requests

How can a conversation be necessary and still feel almost impossible to begin? The caregiver knows what needs to be said. The late calls cannot continue. The transport assumptions are no longer workable. The sibling who sends advice but not help needs a specific task. The person receiving care must be told, gently but plainly, that a certain pattern is not sustainable. The words may be rehearsed while washing dishes, driving home, lying awake, or staring at a message that has already taken too much of the day. Yet when the moment arrives, the sentence shrinks.

The fear is rarely just about the topic. It is about what the topic may unleash. A request for help can become a family argument. A boundary can become an accusation of selfishness. A practical concern can become proof, in someone else's eyes, that the caregiver is cold, dramatic, or ungrateful. The caregiver may enter the conversation intending to speak clearly and leave having apologised, over-explained, softened the point, accepted another task, or promised to "manage for now" simply to end the discomfort.

Hard conversations in caregiving are hard because they are never only about logistics. They carry old roles, private guilt, fear of decline, unequal labour, resentment, grief, and the painful truth that someone's needs may be larger than one person can meet. A sentence about appointment transport may also be a sentence about who has always been responsible. A request for shared tasks may expose years of avoidance. A boundary around evening calls may bring up loneliness, anxiety, and the care recipient's fear of being left. The practical issue is the doorway; the emotional room behind it may be crowded.

The central tension is between clarity and persuasion. Caregivers often believe they must persuade others before they are allowed to change anything. They gather evidence, prepare emotional arguments, explain the full history, describe how tired they are, and try to prove that the limit is reasonable beyond dispute. But persuasion can become a trap. The more the caregiver tries to win agreement, the more the conversation becomes a trial in which their needs must be defended. Clarity has a different aim. It does not demand that everyone approve before reality is named.

The stakes are significant because unclear conversations create future emergencies. A vague agreement becomes a failed handoff. An emotional discussion without a specific request becomes another week of disappointment. A boundary stated as a plea becomes an invitation to negotiate. A family meeting that ends with "we will all do more" may feel hopeful for an hour, then dissolve because no one knows who is doing what, when, or how. Caregiving pressure thrives in the space between good intentions and explicit commitments.

There is also a relational cost when hard conversations are avoided for too long. Silence does not keep resentment from forming; it merely keeps resentment unspoken. The caregiver may become shorter, colder, more avoidant, or more easily provoked, while others remain confused about why the mood has changed. The person receiving care may sense strain but not understand its source. Relatives may underestimate the workload because no one has described it concretely. Avoidance protects the surface of the relationship while allowing the structure underneath to weaken.

Clear requests are not acts of aggression. They are acts of respect. They give other people a real opportunity to respond rather than forcing them to guess what help means. They also protect the caregiver from the exhausting habit of hoping others will notice, infer, volunteer, and follow through without being asked directly. In caregiving, unsaid needs often become silent tests that other people fail without realising they were being tested. A clear request may not guarantee help, but it replaces fog with information.

The work begins before the conversation itself, with deciding what must be said, what outcome is needed, and what limit cannot be traded away mid-sentence. From there, language becomes a tool rather than a burden: prepared phrases for the arguments that return again and again, steady responses when emotion rises, and calm endings for conversations that have stopped being useful. The final piece is making agreements visible, because memory under stress is unreliable and family systems are skilled at turning vague promises into future conflict.

The dining table may hold a notebook, a phone, a half-finished cup of tea, and the message you have not yet sent. The temptation will be to wait until you feel braver, calmer, less guilty, or more certain that no one will react badly. That moment may not arrive. The more useful question is sharper and less forgiving: what conversation has your silence been postponing, and what is that silence now costing the care arrangement?

Preparing for Boundary Conversations

A boundary conversation usually begins long before anyone speaks. It begins in the body: the tightness when the phone rings late, the irritation when another request arrives as though your availability is assumed, the heaviness after agreeing to something you already know you cannot sustain. It begins in the sentences you rehearse privately and then swallow. It begins in the familiar bargain: not tonight, not now, not when they are upset, not when the family is tense, not when I am this tired.

Avoidance is understandable. Caregiving conversations carry more than the visible topic. A discussion about transport may also carry years of family expectation. A conversation about late calls may carry loneliness, fear, and the care recipient's worry that limits mean abandonment. A request for shared help may carry old sibling rivalries, resentment, denial, or guilt. The caregiver is not simply asking for a practical adjustment. They are touching a system that may have survived precisely because certain things were never said clearly.

That is why preparation matters. It does not remove discomfort, and it cannot guarantee that others will respond maturely. It does something more realistic: it prevents the caregiver from entering a difficult conversation with only exhaustion, guilt, and hope as their tools. Hope is not enough. Hoping that people will understand, hoping the right words will appear, hoping no one gets upset, hoping the conversation somehow leads to change without pressure or awkwardness - these hopes are human, but they are not a plan.

A prepared caregiver is not a cold caregiver. Preparation is not manipulation, strategy in the ugly sense, or an attempt to defeat the other person. It is a way of staying truthful when emotion rises. It allows the caregiver to know the purpose of the conversation before someone challenges it. It helps them say what matters without building a courtroom case. It gives them a clearer path through tears, anger, interruptions, and guilt-laden appeals. It protects the boundary from being negotiated away simply because the caregiver becomes uncomfortable.

The first step is to decide what the conversation is actually about. This sounds obvious, but many caregiving conversations fail because the caregiver enters with a general feeling rather than a specific point. They begin with "I cannot keep doing this" when what they mean is "I cannot provide transport every Tuesday." They say "I need more help" when what they mean is "Someone else needs to handle prescription collection by Friday." They say "You do not respect my time" when what they mean is "I will not answer non-urgent calls during work." The emotional truth may be large, but the spoken request must be clear enough to act upon.

A boundary conversation should not try to solve the entire history of the relationship. This is a common trap. The caregiver begins with one practical issue, then feels pulled to explain every earlier sacrifice, every disappointment, every unhelpful relative, every ignored message, every night of broken sleep, every occasion when they felt unseen. Much of this may be true. It may deserve recognition somewhere. But if it all enters the same conversation, the boundary can disappear beneath the weight of evidence. The other person may become defensive, overwhelmed, ashamed, or argumentative, and the practical change may never be agreed.

Clarity begins with a single sentence: "What do I need to be different after this conversation?" That sentence brings the caregiver back from emotional sprawl. The answer might be: late calls stop unless there is a true emergency. A sibling takes over a defined task. The person receiving care agrees to a fixed check-in time. Appointment transport is no longer assumed. Family updates move to one shared message. Paperwork must be given with enough time to handle it. The caregiver no longer stays in conversations where they are shouted at. A clear outcome gives the conversation a spine.

The next question is: "What is my limit if they do not agree?" This is where many caregivers discover whether they are setting a boundary or making a plea. A plea says, "Please understand and change so I do not have to hold this alone." A boundary says, "This is what I will do from now on." The difference is not emotional distance; it is authority. If the caregiver says, "Please stop calling so late," the arrangement still depends on the other person's restraint. If the caregiver says, "I do not answer non-urgent calls after 8 p.m.; I will respond the next morning," the caregiver has defined their own action.

This distinction is essential because other people may not agree at once. They may argue that the issue is not serious. They may say the caregiver is overreacting. They may promise to change but continue as before. They may insist that the limit is inconvenient. A boundary that depends entirely on agreement can collapse under the first objection. A boundary rooted in the caregiver's own behaviour has more strength. It can be maintained even when others dislike it.

Preparation also requires choosing the right moment, though "right" should not be confused with perfect. Caregivers often wait for a time when no one is tired, anxious, defensive, busy, or emotionally raw. Such a moment may never arrive. The aim is not perfection. The aim is to avoid the worst conditions: the middle of a crisis, the end of a long argument, late at night, in front of an audience, or when the caregiver is so depleted that any pushback will overturn them. A planned conversation is usually better than a boundary blurted out from the edge of resentment.

The caregiver should consider who needs to be present. Some conversations belong directly with the person receiving care. Others belong with relatives, partners, adult children, friends, or paid helpers involved in the arrangement. Sometimes speaking to everyone at once creates accountability. At other times, a group conversation becomes a stage for defensiveness and old alliances. A caregiver should not automatically choose the most emotionally dramatic format. The format should serve the outcome.

The environment matters too. A hard conversation held while one person is rushing out the door, while the television is on, while messages are arriving, or while the caregiver is preparing a meal is less likely to stay clear. A quieter setting reduces unnecessary friction. This is not about ceremony. It is about attention. Caregiving conversations already carry enough emotional weight; they do not need avoidable distractions.

Before speaking, the caregiver should reduce the message to three parts: what is happening, what the limit is, and what will happen next. For example: "The late calls are affecting my sleep. I will only answer after 8 p.m. if there is a true emergency. Non-urgent issues can wait until our morning call." Or: "I have been doing all the appointment transport, and I cannot continue. I can coordinate dates, but the driving needs to be shared or arranged another way." Or: "When I am shouted at, I cannot continue the conversation. If it happens, I will end the call and we can try again later."

These sentences are strong because they do not overreach. They do not accuse the other person of being selfish. They do not ask permission for the caregiver to have limits. They do not pretend the change is optional. They name the reality, state the boundary, and define the next step. A caregiver may add warmth, but warmth should not dilute the message. "I care about you" can sit beside "I cannot do this after 8 p.m." The first sentence protects connection. The second protects capacity.

Many caregivers believe they need to persuade before they can set a boundary. They prepare evidence as though facing a judge. They collect examples, anticipate objections, explain their tiredness, describe their other responsibilities, and try to make the other person see the situation exactly as they do. Some explanation is reasonable. Endless evidence is not. The more the caregiver tries to prove the boundary is justified, the more the other person may treat the conversation as a debate.

Clarity over persuasion is a difficult but necessary principle. The caregiver does not need unanimous agreement that the limit is fair before the limit can exist. They do not need the person receiving care to fully understand the emotional cost. They do not need siblings to admit that the workload has been unequal. They do not need a relative to apologise for being absent. Those things may be welcome, but the boundary cannot depend on them. The immediate goal is not to win a moral case. It is to state what will change.

This does not mean the caregiver should be dismissive. A respectful conversation allows space for response. The other person may have information the caregiver has missed. They may be frightened. They may need clarification. They may suggest an alternative that works. Listening matters. But listening is not the same as surrendering the core limit. A caregiver can say, "I hear that this worries you, and the evening boundary still has to stand." Or: "I understand that transport is difficult, and I still cannot be the regular driver."

Preparation should include likely objections. Not because the caregiver must defeat them, but because predictable comments should not knock the conversation off course. If the family often says, "You are the only one who can do it," the caregiver can prepare: "I may be the person who has done it most often, but I cannot continue being the only person responsible." If someone says, "You are overreacting," the caregiver can say: "You may see it differently. This is still the limit I need." If the person receiving care says, "So you are abandoning me," the caregiver can say: "I am not abandoning you. I am changing what I can safely provide."

Prepared language reduces cognitive load. This matters because caregivers are often tired before the conversation begins. Under stress, the mind tends to revert to old habits: appeasing, explaining, apologising, becoming sharp, agreeing too quickly, or promising to think about it when the limit was already clear. A prepared sentence is a handrail. It gives the caregiver something to hold when the emotional staircase becomes steep.

The caregiver should also prepare a closing line. Many boundary conversations fail not at the beginning but at the end, when the discussion becomes circular. The same points repeat. The other person pushes harder. The caregiver explains again. The tone worsens. The original boundary becomes buried under fatigue. A closing line protects the conversation from becoming a battle of endurance. "I have explained what I can do. I am going to pause this now." "We are repeating ourselves, so I will end the call and we can return to it tomorrow." "The decision is not changing tonight."

A closing line is not rude when used calmly. It is a boundary around the conversation itself. Caregivers need this because some people process distress by continuing to talk until someone gives way. Others may not intend harm, but they keep circling because they cannot tolerate the answer. The caregiver does not have to stay in a conversation until the other person feels satisfied. They need to stay long enough to be clear, respectful, and accountable. After that, ending the exchange may be the healthiest choice.

Another part of preparation is deciding what can be offered instead, if anything. A boundary does not always need an alternative, but alternatives can help when the need is real and the caregiver has some capacity. "I cannot visit tonight, but I can call tomorrow morning." "I cannot drive weekly, but I can help set up a rota." "I cannot manage daily updates, but I can send one summary each Sunday." "I cannot talk while being shouted at, but I will try again later when the conversation is calmer." These alternatives show continued care without erasing the limit.

However, the caregiver must be careful not to offer alternatives from guilt. A substitute offer should be sustainable. If the caregiver says no to late-night calls and then offers long morning calls every day, the boundary may simply move the burden rather than reduce it. If they cannot provide transport and offer to coordinate every detail for everyone else without help, they may remain the hidden manager. A good alternative should support the boundary, not secretly undo it.

The caregiver also needs to prepare emotionally for the possibility of disappointment. This is perhaps the hardest part. Many caregivers can plan the words but not tolerate the other person's reaction. They want to say the sentence and be met with understanding. Sometimes that happens. Often it does not. The person may cry. A sibling may become defensive. A parent may make a painful comment. A spouse may withdraw. A friend may minimise. A professional may underestimate the load. These reactions can hurt, but they are not automatic proof that the boundary is wrong.

The caregiver can remind themselves before the conversation: "My task is to be clear and respectful. I cannot control their reaction." This sentence is not emotional armour against compassion. It is a truth that prevents over-responsibility. The caregiver is responsible for tone, timing where possible, clarity, and follow-through. They are not responsible for ensuring that every person feels calm, pleased, or convinced by the end of the conversation.

It can help to write the boundary down beforehand. The act of writing exposes vagueness. It reveals whether the caregiver is making a request, setting a limit, offering a preference, or trying to express resentment. A written sentence can be refined until it becomes direct enough to use. Some caregivers may even read from notes during the conversation. There is no shame in this. A conversation that matters deserves more than improvised survival.

A written plan should include the desired outcome, the core sentence, the likely objections, the prepared responses, the closing line, and the next practical step. This need not be elaborate. A few lines can be enough. The point is not to script every word. The point is to prevent the caregiver from losing the thread when pressure rises.

Preparation also includes deciding what not to say. This is often overlooked. The caregiver may need to avoid character attacks: "You never appreciate me." "You are selfish." "No one in this family cares." These statements may express genuine pain, but they are likely to ignite defensiveness. The caregiver may also need to avoid absolute claims that can be debated: "I do everything." "You never help." "No one ever listens." The other person may seize on one exception and derail the conversation.

More effective language focuses on the arrangement. "I am currently handling appointment booking, transport, prescriptions, and family updates, and this is no longer sustainable." "I need one person to take over prescriptions." "I will not continue late-night care discussions." "Transport needs a different plan." This kind of language keeps the conversation close to the change required. It is harder to argue with a clear description of roles, tasks, and limits than with a sweeping accusation.

The caregiver should avoid beginning with apology. This does not mean they should be unkind. It means the boundary should not be introduced as though it is wrongdoing. "I am sorry, but I cannot keep doing this" may feel polite, but it can signal uncertainty and invite reassurance or pressure. A firmer opening is: "I need to change how we handle evening calls." Or: "I need to talk about appointment transport." Or: "This arrangement is no longer workable for me." Apology belongs where harm has been done, not where a limit is being named.

Tone matters, but tone should not become performance. Some caregivers worry so much about sounding kind that their actual message disappears. Others become overly formal because they fear emotion will undermine them. The healthiest tone is steady, plain, and respectful. It does not need to be perfectly warm. It does not need to be impressive. It needs to carry the truth without contempt.

The caregiver may also need to prepare for their own body's reaction. Boundary conversations can trigger a racing heart, trembling, tears, heat, numbness, or the urge to retreat. This does not mean the caregiver is weak or unready. It means the nervous system recognises risk: possible conflict, disapproval, guilt, or change in a close relationship. Before the conversation, it may help to breathe slowly, sit with both feet on the floor, keep the written sentence nearby, and decide not to answer immediately if overwhelmed.

During the conversation, a pause is allowed. The caregiver can say, "I need a moment." Or: "I am going to think before I answer." Or: "I do not want to respond from pressure." Pausing prevents old habits from taking over. It also models steadiness. The caregiver does not have to fill every silence simply because silence feels awkward.

After the conversation, documentation matters. A boundary spoken in an emotional setting can be misremembered, softened, or denied. A short written follow-up protects clarity: "Just to confirm, I will no longer take non-urgent calls after 8 p.m. I will call each morning at 9 unless there is an emergency." Or: "As agreed, I will book appointments, and Sam will handle transport for the next one." Or: "We agreed that paperwork needs to be sent to me by Thursday if I am expected to help with it." Written follow-up is not cold. It prevents future arguments about what was said.

Documentation is especially useful when several people are involved. Family care can become a tangle of good intentions, selective memory, and unspoken assumptions. A shared note, calendar entry, or task list can reduce emotional labour. It means the caregiver does not have to be the living archive of every decision. It makes responsibilities visible, which is often the only way to stop them drifting back to the most conscientious person.

A caregiver preparing for a boundary conversation should also define the minimum acceptable outcome. Sometimes the ideal outcome is broad understanding, sincere apology, and immediate cooperation. That may happen, but it should not be required. The minimum outcome might be that the boundary is clearly stated. Or that a specific request is made. Or that a task is assigned. Or that the caregiver stops accepting an assumed role. When expectations are realistic, the caregiver is less likely to view the conversation as a failure simply because it did not produce emotional harmony.

Some conversations will need to happen more than once. This is not always failure. People may need repetition. Old patterns may reappear. A person receiving care may test whether the new limit is firm. Relatives may agree in principle and then revert to convenience. The caregiver should not assume that one conversation will transform the system. Preparation includes accepting that boundaries become real through repetition and follow-through, not through one perfect speech.

There are also situations where a neutral third party may be needed. If conversations repeatedly become hostile, circular, manipulative, or impossible to hold safely, the caregiver may need support from someone outside the emotional pattern. This might be a trusted family mediator, counsellor, professional involved in care, adviser, or another appropriate support person. Involving someone else is not a sign of failure. It may be a sign that the current communication pattern cannot produce a workable agreement on its own.

The caregiver should be alert to conversations that are not safe or useful. If someone is shouting, threatening, insulting, or repeatedly using guilt to force compliance, the purpose shifts from discussion to protection. A prepared caregiver knows how to end the exchange: "I will not continue while I am being spoken to like this." "I am ending this call now." "We can speak when it is calmer." Not every conversation deserves to continue simply because the topic is important.

Preparing for boundary conversations is ultimately an act of respect for reality. It respects the caregiver's limits enough to name them. It respects the person receiving care enough to be honest rather than silently resentful. It respects relatives enough to make clear requests rather than vague accusations. It respects the care arrangement enough to move from assumption to agreement.

The conversation may still be uncomfortable. The other person may still resist. The caregiver may still feel guilt afterwards. But preparation changes the caregiver's position. They are no longer entering the room hoping their distress will be understood before they lose courage. They are entering with a clear outcome, a steady sentence, a realistic expectation of pushback, and a plan for what happens next.

A hard conversation does not have to be perfect to be useful.

It only has to be honest enough that the old pattern can no longer pretend nothing has been said.

Scripts for Common Conflicts

When caregivers hear the same objections again and again, the problem is not only the objection itself. It is the exhaustion of having to answer it while already tired. A familiar conflict can make the mind go blank. Someone says, "You are overreacting," and suddenly the caregiver is pulled into defending their judgement. Someone says, "You owe them," and the whole conversation shifts from practical care to moral accusation. Someone says, "You are the only one who can," and the caregiver feels the old pressure rise: if no one else will act, then perhaps the limit must collapse.

This is why scripts matter. Not because caregiving should become mechanical, and not because every conversation can be controlled by the perfect phrase. Scripts are not magic words. They are prepared language for predictable pressure. They reduce the burden of inventing a calm response when guilt, anger, fatigue, and family history are all speaking at once. They give the caregiver a sentence to hold when the conversation begins to pull them back into over-explaining, apologising, rescuing, or surrendering.

A good script does not try to win the argument. That is one of the most important principles. Many caregiving conflicts become exhausting because the caregiver enters them as though the goal is to make the other person finally understand. Understanding is welcome, but it cannot be required before a limit is allowed to stand. A script should therefore be clear rather than persuasive. It should state what is true, what is possible, what will happen next, or where the conversation must stop. The aim is not to defeat resistance. The aim is to prevent resistance from taking control.

The strongest scripts are brief. Under pressure, long sentences weaken. They invite debate, correction, interruption, and emotional appeal. A caregiver who says, "I cannot drive to every appointment because I have work and I am tired and I have already done so much and no one else helps" may be telling the truth, but every clause offers a point of attack. Someone can argue about work, minimise tiredness, mention what they have done, or accuse the caregiver of resentment. A cleaner script says, "I can coordinate appointments, but I cannot be the regular driver." It gives less for conflict to feed on.

Scripts work best when they are built around the caregiver's own actions. "You need to stop calling me so late" may be understandable, but it tries to control the other person. "I do not answer non-urgent calls after 8 p.m." is stronger because it defines the caregiver's behaviour. "You must stop criticising me" may lead to argument about what counts as criticism. "I will not stay in a conversation where I am being insulted" is clearer. A boundary script should return authority to the person who can actually carry it out.

One common conflict begins with the accusation: "You are overreacting." This phrase is powerful because it attacks the caregiver's interpretation of reality. The caregiver may immediately feel the need to prove the load, list examples, explain emotional strain, and justify the boundary. That is the trap. The response does not need to prove that the caregiver is right in every detail. It needs to keep the conversation attached to the limit.

A useful script is: "You may see it differently. This is still what I can do." The strength of this sentence is that it does not argue about perception. It allows disagreement without handing over the decision. Another version is: "I am not asking you to agree with my level of strain. I am telling you the arrangement I can sustain." This is especially useful with relatives who minimise because they do not see the daily work. The caregiver does not have to make them feel the burden before the boundary becomes valid.

Another common conflict is: "You owe them." Few statements strike deeper. It may refer to a parent's past sacrifices, a spouse's loyalty, a sibling bond, a cultural expectation, or a history of help received. The problem is not that gratitude has no place. Gratitude matters. Commitment matters. The danger comes when gratitude is used to erase capacity. A debt of love cannot reasonably become a demand for unlimited availability.

A grounded script is: "I am grateful for what they have done, and I still have limits." The word "and" matters. It refuses the false choice between gratitude and boundaries. Another version is: "I can honour the relationship without doing everything myself." This moves the conversation away from emotional debt and towards realistic care. If the accusation becomes sharper, the caregiver can say, "I am not debating whether I care. I am explaining what I can provide."

A third recurring conflict is: "You are the only one who can." Sometimes this is meant as praise. Sometimes it is panic. Sometimes it is pressure. It may even contain partial truth. The caregiver may indeed know the routines best, communicate most effectively, or have the strongest relationship with the person receiving care. But being capable does not mean being endlessly responsible. If every task stays with the person who does it best, no one else learns and the caregiver becomes trapped by competence.

A useful script is: "I may be the person most used to doing it, but that does not mean I can keep being the only person." Another is: "If I am the only one who knows how, then the next step is to share the information, not keep the task with me forever." This kind of script turns the pressure into a practical issue. It also exposes the weakness in the old arrangement: dependence on one caregiver is not proof of sustainability. It is a risk.

Sometimes the conflict is framed as helplessness: "No one else will help." This statement can be particularly difficult because it may be true. Other relatives may be absent. Friends may be unreliable. Paid support may be limited or unaffordable. The caregiver may feel that holding a boundary will simply leave the person receiving care without what they need. Yet if the caregiver cannot safely continue, pretending they can is not a plan.

A script for this moment is: "That is exactly why we need another plan. I cannot be the whole plan." Another is: "I understand the gap. I am not able to fill it in the same way anymore." These sentences are firm without pretending the situation is easy. They name the problem rather than allowing it to be solved invisibly through the caregiver's self-sacrifice. The caregiver may still help with a transition, but the old arrangement has been challenged.

Another conflict appears as emotional accusation: "So you are abandoning me." This can come from fear, grief, anger, or a genuine misunderstanding of what the boundary means. The caregiver may feel a strong urge to withdraw the limit in order to prove love. But the better response is to separate the relationship from the request.

A useful script is: "I am not abandoning you. I am changing what I can safely provide." Another is: "I care about you, and I am not available in that way." This language keeps connection present without surrendering the limit. It is especially helpful when the person receiving care interprets reduced availability as total rejection. The caregiver can repeat the distinction as often as needed: care remains, but the old pattern cannot.

Some conflicts involve comparison: "Your sister would do it," "Other people look after their parents," or "A good spouse would not need a break." Comparison is designed, intentionally or not, to shame the caregiver into compliance. It shifts attention away from the actual care load and towards an imagined moral standard. The caregiver does not need to defend themselves against every imaginary caregiver.

A strong script is: "I am making a decision based on my capacity and this care situation." Another is: "Comparing me with someone else does not change what I can do." These sentences return the conversation to reality. They prevent the caregiver from trying to prove they are good enough. The question is not whether some other person might do more. The question is what is sustainable, safe, and honest here.

Another familiar line is: "It will only take a minute." This is often used for small requests, but caregivers know that small tasks rarely arrive alone. A minute can interrupt work, reopen anxiety, create follow-up tasks, or become the first step in a much larger chain. The issue is not always the duration. It is timing, frequency, emotional cost, and the way small requests accumulate.

A useful response is: "It may be quick, but I am not available for it now." Another is: "Small tasks still need to fit within the care plan." If the request genuinely can wait, the caregiver might say, "Put it on the list for our planned call." This is a practical way to stop scattered demands from taking over the day. It teaches the system that not every small thing deserves immediate access.

Late-night calls deserve their own scripts because they so easily become hour-long crises. Evening and night-time conversations are emotionally risky. People are tired. Fear grows in the dark. Problems feel larger. The caregiver may be more vulnerable to guilt and less able to think clearly. A call that begins with a small worry can become a long loop of reassurance, complaint, panic, and exhaustion.

A calm closing line is essential: "This is not an emergency, so I am going to end the call and speak with you tomorrow." Another is: "I hear that you are upset. I cannot solve this tonight. We will talk at our usual time." If the person continues, the caregiver can repeat, "I am ending the call now. We will speak tomorrow." The point is not to sound uncaring. The point is to stop non-urgent distress from consuming the caregiver's sleep and turning every night into a crisis.

For circular debates, the caregiver needs scripts that close the loop. A circular debate is one in which nothing new is being said. The same objections return, the same explanations are demanded, and the caregiver feels worn down rather than heard. Many boundaries collapse in circular debates not because the other person offers a better argument, but because the caregiver becomes too tired to hold the line.

A useful script is: "We are repeating ourselves, so I am going to pause this conversation." Another is: "I have explained my decision. I am not going to keep discussing it tonight." If the topic must be revisited, the caregiver can add, "We can return to the practical details tomorrow." These scripts are especially important for caregivers who believe they must keep talking until the other person agrees. Agreement is not always available. Ending the conversation may be the boundary that protects every other boundary.

When someone cries, the caregiver may need a script that offers comfort without compliance. Tears are not automatically manipulation. They may be sincere distress. But sincere distress can still pull the caregiver into reversing a needed limit. The script should acknowledge the feeling and keep the boundary intact.

A useful response is: "I can see this is painful. I am still not able to do what you are asking." Another is: "I love you, and the answer is still no." Or: "I know this feels hard. I can stay with you for a few minutes, but I cannot change the arrangement." These sentences allow tenderness without abandoning reality. The caregiver is not rescuing the other person from every difficult feeling. They are staying present within a limit.

When someone becomes angry, the caregiver needs a different script. Anger can tempt a caregiver to defend, counterattack, appease, or retreat. None of those may serve the boundary. The first goal is to protect the conditions for respectful conversation.

A clear script is: "I will not continue while I am being shouted at." Another is: "I can talk about the plan, but not in this tone." If the anger continues: "I am ending this conversation now. We can try again when it is calmer." These lines do not require the caregiver to analyse the anger, soothe it, or win against it. They set the condition for continued contact.

When someone uses guilt directly, the caregiver can script a response that refuses the trial. For example, if someone says, "I thought you cared," the caregiver might respond, "I do care. I am not available for that task." If someone says, "You are being selfish," the caregiver might say, "You may feel that way. This is still my limit." If someone says, "After everything they did for you," the caregiver can say, "I am grateful, and I still cannot take this on." The caregiver does not need to argue their goodness. A script should not allow love to become the price of compliance.

There are also scripts for vague requests. "Can you help more?" may sound simple, but it can lead to undefined responsibility. "We all need to pull together" may feel inspiring and still produce no change. "Someone needs to sort this" often means the task will drift back to the main caregiver. Vague language creates future resentment because no one knows what has actually been agreed.

A useful script is: "What specific task are you asking me to take on?" Another is: "I can discuss a defined task, but I cannot agree to 'help more' without knowing what that means." Or: "Who is doing what, and by when?" These questions may sound plain, but they are powerful. They stop emotional language from pretending to be a plan.

Scripts for asking others for help should be specific and bounded. Instead of "I need more support," the caregiver can say, "Can you take over prescription collection every Friday?" Instead of "You need to visit more," they can say, "Can you visit for one hour on Sunday afternoons so I can have a break?" Instead of "I cannot manage all the admin," they can say, "Can you handle the bills and paperwork folder until the end of the month?" Specific requests reduce the other person's ability to offer sympathy without responsibility.

A caregiver may also need scripts for people who agree vaguely. If someone says, "Of course, just tell me what you need," the caregiver can respond, "Good. I need you to take this specific task." If someone says, "I will try," the caregiver can ask, "Can you confirm whether you can do it by tomorrow?" If someone says, "I am busy too," the caregiver can say, "I understand. What part can you realistically take?" These scripts keep the conversation from dissolving into mutual fatigue.

Another common conflict involves professional or family advice that ignores capacity. Someone may say, "You should just check on them every morning," or "You need to make sure they eat properly," or "You should keep a closer eye on things." The word "just" can conceal a large amount of labour. The caregiver needs language that brings capacity into the discussion.

A useful script is: "That recommendation requires time and availability I do not currently have. What is the realistic alternative?" Another is: "I can do part of that, but I cannot provide daily monitoring." Or: "If this needs to happen every day, it cannot depend only on me." These scripts prevent advice from turning into invisible assignment.

When the caregiver is asked to mediate between others, the script should return responsibility to the people involved. Many caregivers become family messengers because others prefer not to communicate directly. This role is exhausting and often thankless. It also places the caregiver in the centre of conflict that does not belong to them.

A script might be: "I am not going to be the messenger between you. Please speak to each other directly." Or: "I can share practical updates, but I will not carry complaints between family members." If someone insists, the caregiver can repeat, "That conversation needs to happen between you two." This protects the caregiver from becoming the emotional courier for the family system.

There are also scripts for when the caregiver needs time before answering. This is one of the most useful skills because guilt often pushes immediate agreement. A delayed response creates room for judgement.

The caregiver can say, "I need to check my capacity before I answer." Or: "I cannot decide that right now." Or: "I will reply tomorrow." Or: "I need to look at the week before committing." These sentences are simple but transformative. They stop the caregiver from making promises in the heat of pressure. They also teach others that access to the caregiver's time is not automatic.

Some scripts should be designed for self-talk, not for other people. Internal scripts matter because the caregiver's own guilt may be louder than anyone else. After saying no, the caregiver may need to say privately, "Feeling guilty does not mean I have done wrong." After holding a boundary, "This discomfort is part of changing the pattern." After someone reacts badly, "Their reaction is not the measure of my responsibility." After a difficult call, "I can be kind without being endlessly available."

These inner scripts are not sentimental affirmations. They are stabilising statements. They keep the caregiver from reopening a decision simply because the body is uncomfortable. They also reduce the tendency to over-repair after conflict. A caregiver who can speak steadily to themselves is less likely to surrender externally.

Scripts must sound like the caregiver. A phrase that feels too formal, too harsh, or too unlike the speaker may be hard to use under pressure. The caregiver should adapt language until it feels plain and believable. One person may say, "That does not work for me." Another may say, "I cannot take that on." Another may say, "I am not available for this." The exact wording matters less than the structure: clear limit, calm tone, no excessive defence.

It is useful to practise scripts aloud before they are needed. Words that look clear on a page can feel strange in the mouth. Practising helps the caregiver notice where they apologise unnecessarily, soften too much, or add explanations that weaken the boundary. Practice also builds familiarity. Under pressure, familiar words are easier to retrieve.

A caregiver should expect the first use of a script to feel uncomfortable. The discomfort does not mean the script is wrong. It may mean the caregiver is no longer playing their old role. If they have always over-explained, a brief sentence may feel rude. If they have always said yes quickly, a pause may feel selfish. If they have always soothed anger, ending a call may feel brutal. New boundaries often feel harsher internally than they sound externally.

Scripts should not become weapons. The aim is not to speak in cold formulas or shut down every emotional expression. The caregiver should remain human. They can listen. They can acknowledge. They can soften tone. They can offer realistic alternatives. But they should not abandon clarity in the name of warmth. A script is a support for honesty, not a replacement for compassion.

There is also a difference between repeating a script and becoming robotic. Repetition is necessary when someone keeps pushing. The caregiver can repeat the same message warmly: "I hear you. I am still not available tonight." "I know this is upsetting. The answer is still no." "I understand you want me to drive. I cannot be the regular driver." Repetition becomes cold only when contempt enters it. Without contempt, repetition is simply consistency.

Some situations will outgrow scripts. If a person repeatedly becomes abusive, threatening, manipulative, or unsafe, the caregiver may need stronger support, a changed contact pattern, or involvement from a neutral third party. Scripts are tools for common conflict, not substitutes for safety. A caregiver should not use prepared language to endure harm indefinitely. The script may be the first step in recognising that the communication pattern itself needs a different structure.

After a scripted conversation, it can help to document the agreement. "Just confirming: I will call at 6 p.m. on weekdays, not later, unless there is an emergency." "As agreed, you will collect the prescription this Friday." "I will coordinate appointments, but transport needs to be arranged separately." This follow-up prevents the conversation from being rewritten later. It also reduces the caregiver's mental load because the decision no longer lives only in memory.

The deeper value of scripts is that they protect the caregiver from the exhaustion of improvising under moral pressure. They make room for steadiness. They turn familiar conflict into a recognisable pattern with a prepared response. They help the caregiver stop treating every accusation as an emergency and every emotional reaction as a command.

A script will not make everyone reasonable. It will not guarantee approval. It will not remove guilt entirely. But it can keep the caregiver from being pulled into the same old theatre: defend, explain, apologise, surrender, resent, repeat. It can create a small firm place in the conversation where reality is allowed to stand.

The sentence may be simple.

"I care, and I cannot do that."

Sometimes that is enough to change the whole direction of the exchange.

Handling Anger, Tears, and Manipulation

The hardest boundary conversations are rarely hard because the words are complicated. They are hard because of what happens after the words are spoken. A caregiver may enter the conversation with a simple limit: I cannot answer non-urgent calls late at night. I cannot drive to every appointment. I cannot be shouted at. I cannot take on another task this week. The sentence itself may be reasonable, even modest. Yet the response can feel enormous. Anger rises. Tears appear. Silence stretches. Accusations begin. Suddenly the caregiver is no longer dealing only with a boundary; they are dealing with the emotional storm that the boundary has revealed.

This is where many caregivers lose their footing. They may have prepared the limit, but not the reaction. They may have expected discomfort, but not fury. They may have anticipated sadness, but not the feeling of being morally accused. They may have believed that if they spoke kindly enough, the other person would accept the limit with understanding. When that does not happen, they assume something has gone wrong. Perhaps the boundary was too harsh. Perhaps the timing was cruel. Perhaps they should soften it, explain again, make an exception, or take back the whole thing.

Emotional reactions are not proof that a boundary is wrong.

This sentence is simple, but it has to be learned deeply. Anger may mean the other person is frightened, ashamed, disappointed, accustomed to more access, or unhappy about losing a familiar pattern. Tears may mean grief, loneliness, fear, exhaustion, or genuine distress. Manipulation may mean the person has learned, consciously or unconsciously, that guilt and pressure are effective ways to regain control. These reactions deserve attention, but they do not automatically deserve obedience. A caregiver can respond with compassion without surrendering the limit that keeps care sustainable.

The first task is to stay regulated. This is not a fashionable phrase; it is a practical necessity. When another person becomes emotionally intense, the caregiver's body may react before their mind can think. The heart beats faster. The jaw tightens. The voice rises or disappears. The old family role wakes up: soothe, defend, apologise, explain, rescue, submit, escape. In that state, the caregiver may no longer be choosing from clarity. They may be choosing from threat, guilt, or the desperate desire to make the moment stop.

A pause is therefore not avoidance. It is protection for good judgement. The caregiver can take a breath before answering. They can place both feet on the floor. They can lower their voice deliberately. They can say, "I need a moment before I respond." They can refuse to answer a loaded question immediately. They can end a call and return later if the conversation has become too charged. These small pauses interrupt the automatic pattern in which emotional intensity becomes command.

Anger is often the reaction caregivers fear most because it can feel like danger, even when no physical danger is present. Anger may arrive as shouting, sharp criticism, sarcasm, accusation, blame, or a dramatic declaration that the caregiver has changed. The caregiver may feel pushed into defending their character rather than holding their boundary. "I am not selfish." "I have done so much." "You do not understand." "That is not fair." These statements may be true, but once the conversation becomes a contest over the caregiver's goodness, the boundary has already been pulled off centre.

A steadier response keeps the focus on conduct and limits. "I can talk about this, but not while I am being shouted at." "I hear that you are angry. I am still not available tonight." "I am not going to defend whether I care. I am telling you what I can do." "If the conversation continues like this, I will end the call and we can try again tomorrow." These sentences do not attack the angry person. They do not demand that anger disappear. They state the condition under which the caregiver will remain engaged.

The caregiver does not need to punish anger. They need to refuse to be governed by it. This distinction matters. Some people are frightened by boundaries and express fear as anger. Some feel powerless and try to recover power by becoming forceful. Some are used to the caregiver giving way when tension rises. The caregiver can understand all of this without making anger the steering wheel. Compassion explains behaviour; it does not excuse every behaviour or require the caregiver to absorb harm.

Tears require a different kind of steadiness. They often reach the caregiver's most tender places. A parent crying after being told that evening calls must stop. A spouse weeping because they feel alone. A sibling becoming tearful when asked to take on a task. A care recipient saying, "I did not think you would do this to me." The caregiver may feel the boundary dissolving before they have even answered. Tears can make a necessary limit feel cruel.

But tears are not always a request to reverse the boundary. Sometimes they are the other person's way of processing disappointment, grief, fear, or change. The caregiver can make space for the feeling without taking responsibility for removing it. "I can see this is upsetting." "I am sorry this feels painful." "I love you, and the boundary still stands." "This is difficult, and I am not able to go back to the old arrangement." These responses allow tenderness and firmness to exist together.

Many caregivers confuse comfort with compliance. They believe that if someone is distressed, the loving response is to take away the cause of distress. Sometimes that is appropriate. If the caregiver has been harsh, they can repair. If they have been unclear, they can explain. If the other person has misunderstood, they can clarify. But if the distress exists because a sustainable limit has been named, the caregiver does not have to remove the limit to prove love. Comfort can be presence, reassurance, patience, and repetition. It does not have to be surrender.

Manipulation is more complicated because it can be difficult to name, especially inside families. It may not look like a calculated scheme. It may appear as guilt, helplessness, comparison, exaggeration, silent treatment, sudden crisis language, emotional collapse, or affection withdrawn until the caregiver gives way. The person using these patterns may not think of themselves as manipulative. They may simply know, from long experience, that certain reactions get results. The caregiver does not have to diagnose motives in order to respond to the pattern.

A useful question is: does this reaction pressure me to abandon a reasonable limit without addressing the actual issue? If the answer is yes, the caregiver should slow down. Manipulation often creates urgency. It tries to make the caregiver act before thinking. "Fine, I will just be alone." "Do not bother then." "You clearly do not care." "Everyone else has abandoned me too." "I suppose I will just have to manage somehow." These statements are emotionally loaded because they turn the boundary into an accusation. They invite the caregiver to prove love by giving in.

The response should be calm and narrow. "I am sorry you feel alone. I am still not available tonight." "I do care, and I am not able to take this on." "I will not discuss my love for you as a condition of this boundary." "I can help with the agreed task, not with everything." "If this becomes a guilt conversation, I am going to pause it." The caregiver does not need to expose the manipulation dramatically. They need to refuse the invitation to make guilt the decision-maker.

One of the clearest signs of manipulation is repetition after clarity. The caregiver states the limit. The other person objects. The caregiver clarifies. The other person shifts the argument, intensifies emotion, brings up the past, compares the caregiver to someone else, suggests abandonment, or keeps the conversation going until the caregiver is worn down. This is no longer a discussion about understanding. It is pressure through endurance.

At that point, the caregiver needs a closing line. "I have explained what I can do. I am not going to keep discussing this tonight." "We are repeating ourselves, so I am ending the conversation now." "The answer is not changing because we continue talking." "I will speak with you tomorrow when we are both calmer." Closing the conversation may feel rude to a caregiver who has been trained to stay until the other person is satisfied. But satisfaction is not always available. Sometimes the healthier end point is clarity, not agreement.

The caregiver should also watch for the rescuer reflex. This reflex appears when another person's feeling becomes unbearable to witness. The caregiver rushes to fix, soften, reassure, apologise, offer extras, or reverse the boundary. It can feel loving, but it often prevents the other person from experiencing the natural adjustment that comes with a new limit. It also teaches the care system that sufficiently intense emotion will reopen the old arrangement.

Not every feeling needs rescuing. Some feelings need to be allowed. Disappointment can be allowed. Sadness can be allowed. Anger can be allowed, provided it is not expressed harmfully. Anxiety can be acknowledged without being allowed to dictate the caregiver's availability. The caregiver's role is not to create an emotional world in which no one feels discomfort. It is to act with care, honesty, and proportion.

This does not mean becoming indifferent. Indifference says, "Your feelings do not matter." Boundaried compassion says, "Your feelings matter, and they are not the only factor." That difference is crucial. The caregiver can listen for what is real in the reaction. Anger may contain fear. Tears may contain grief. Manipulation may contain desperation. The human need underneath may deserve a response, but the response must still fit reality. A person may need reassurance, but not unlimited calls. They may need company, but not the caregiver's entire weekend. They may need support, but not the collapse of every boundary.

Sometimes the caregiver should reflect back the feeling before restating the limit. "You sound frightened that I will not be there when you need me. I understand that fear. The plan is still that emergencies come through the agreed route, and routine calls happen tomorrow." Or: "I can hear that you feel let down. I am still not able to drive every week." Reflection can reduce escalation because it shows the person they have been heard. But reflection must not become a doorway into endless emotional processing that swallows the boundary.

A useful structure is: acknowledge, limit, next step. "I know you are upset. I am not able to continue this conversation while I am being shouted at. I will call tomorrow." "I hear that this feels lonely. I cannot come tonight. I can speak with you at our usual time in the morning." "I understand that transport is worrying. I cannot drive on Tuesdays. We need to use the agreed backup." This structure is simple enough to remember under pressure and strong enough to hold the line.

The caregiver should avoid arguing with distorted accusations. If someone says, "You never help," the caregiver may want to list every task they have done. If someone says, "You only care about yourself," the caregiver may want to prove devotion. If someone says, "You are abandoning me," the caregiver may rush into reassurance so extensive that the original limit disappears. These accusations are painful, but answering them literally often keeps the caregiver trapped.

A steadier response is to refuse the frame. "I am not going to debate whether I help. We are talking about tonight's boundary." "I care about you, and I will not accept being spoken to that way." "This is not abandonment. It is a change in what I can provide." The caregiver can correct the distortion without entering a long defence. The aim is not to win the accusation. The aim is to keep the conversation anchored.

There are times when anger, tears, or manipulation reveal that a neutral third party is needed. This is especially true when conversations repeatedly become hostile, circular, coercive, or emotionally unsafe. A caregiver may need another relative, a trusted friend, a counsellor, a mediator, a care professional, or another appropriate person to help structure the conversation. Involving a third party is not a failure. It is a recognition that some patterns cannot be changed by private willpower alone.

A neutral person can help keep the focus on practical agreements, reduce memory battles, interrupt escalation, and make responsibilities visible. They can also support the caregiver if the family system has a history of dismissing or pressuring them. The caregiver should not have to stand alone in every difficult conversation, especially when the conversation concerns shared care.

However, a third party should be chosen carefully. The aim is not to recruit someone to attack the other person. The aim is to create enough structure for truth to be spoken and decisions to be made. A poor third party can inflame the situation by taking sides, minimising the caregiver's limits, or turning the conversation into a moral judgement. A good third party helps everyone return to the care arrangement: what is needed, what is possible, who is responsible, what happens next.

When manipulation is persistent or severe, the caregiver may need stronger boundaries around contact. This might mean written communication instead of repeated calls, shorter conversations, scheduled check-ins, no discussion of certain topics without another person present, or ending conversations immediately when guilt tactics begin. These measures may feel harsh, but they can be necessary when ordinary conversation becomes a pathway for pressure.

The caregiver should not confuse access with care. Some relationships require less access in order to become safer. A caregiver may still provide practical support while reducing exposure to conversations that repeatedly damage them. They may still love someone while refusing to be available for emotional coercion. They may still act responsibly while changing the route through which communication happens.

It is also important to consider whether the person receiving care has changes in cognition, mood, pain, or distress that affect their reactions. Confusion, fear, frustration, dependency, and loss of control can intensify anger or tearfulness. This does not mean every behaviour must be tolerated, but it may shape the response. The caregiver may need simpler language, more predictable routines, fewer choices, calmer timing, or professional advice if behaviour changes suddenly or becomes difficult to manage safely.

Even then, the caregiver's wellbeing remains part of the care equation. Understanding why someone reacts strongly does not make the caregiver limitless. A person may not be fully responsible for every emotional reaction, and the caregiver may still need protection from the impact of those reactions. Compassion and boundaries are not enemies. In complex care, they often have to stand side by side.

The caregiver's own history also matters. Anger may trigger childhood fear. Tears may trigger a lifelong role of soothing a parent. Silence may trigger panic about rejection. Accusations may trigger shame learned long before caregiving began. These reactions are not weakness. They are old patterns being touched by present stress. The caregiver who understands their own triggers can prepare better. They can say, "This reaction makes me want to give in, but that does not mean giving in is right."

Self-regulation after the conversation is just as important as self-regulation during it. A difficult exchange can leave the caregiver shaking, guilty, angry, sad, or doubtful. They may replay every sentence and wonder whether they were too firm or too cold. This aftershock can undo the boundary if the caregiver immediately sends a softening message they do not mean. A pause after the conversation protects the boundary from emotional backlash.

The caregiver can ask: Was I clear? Was I respectful? Did I hold the limit? Did I respond to real risk? Did I avoid making promises from guilt? Did I need to repair anything about my tone, separate from the boundary itself? These questions create a balanced review. They allow accountability without collapse. If repair is needed, it can be specific: "I am sorry I raised my voice. The boundary about late calls still stands." Repair should not become surrender.

Documentation can help after an emotionally intense conversation. A brief message can confirm what was said: "Just to be clear, I will not be taking non-urgent calls after 8 p.m. I will call tomorrow morning." Or: "As discussed, I cannot continue appointment transport every week. We need to use another arrangement from next month." Written confirmation reduces the chance that anger, tears, or pressure will later rewrite the conversation. It gives everyone something steadier than memory.

The caregiver should be prepared for repeated testing. A boundary that has been held once may be tested again. This is not always deliberate; old habits are strong. The person may call late again. A relative may make another guilt-laden comment. Someone may cry the next time the limit appears. The caregiver should not treat each test as a new moral crisis. They can repeat the same response: "This is still the arrangement." "I know this is hard. The boundary remains." "We have discussed this, and I am not changing the plan tonight."

Consistency reduces emotional drama over time. It teaches that anger does not overturn the limit, tears do not erase the limit, and manipulation does not move the boundary. It also teaches the caregiver's own nervous system that they can survive another person's reaction without rushing to fix it. This is often the deeper healing: the caregiver learns that discomfort is not danger, and disapproval is not a command.

There will be times when the caregiver chooses flexibility. This is humane. A true emergency, a difficult transition, a rare crisis, or an unusual circumstance may justify bending a boundary. The key is to name the exception. "I am answering tonight because this is urgent, but routine calls still wait until morning." "I can help this once because the situation changed, but I cannot take this on regularly." Naming the exception prevents pressure from turning flexibility into a new expectation.

The caregiver must be especially careful with patterns that use crisis language to override limits. If everything is described as urgent, the boundary around urgency becomes meaningless. The care arrangement needs a shared understanding of what counts as a true emergency. Immediate safety, serious health change, urgent medication concern, or a situation requiring professional help may qualify. Loneliness, frustration, irritation, routine worry, or dislike of waiting may be real feelings, but they should not automatically become emergencies.

This distinction protects both people. The care recipient receives clearer support because true crises are not lost in a sea of emotional urgency. The caregiver preserves enough capacity to respond well when something genuinely serious happens. A person who is exhausted by repeated false alarms may be less able to meet a true alarm with steadiness.

Handling manipulation also requires refusing to manage other people's reputations or feelings at the cost of truth. A relative may become angry when asked to help because the request exposes their absence. A sibling may cry because they feel guilty. A care recipient may accuse because the boundary reveals dependence. The caregiver may be tempted to protect everyone from these uncomfortable truths. But if the caregiver continually absorbs the discomfort, the care system never matures.

Some discomfort belongs in the room. It belongs where responsibility has been avoided, where dependence has been hidden, where limits have been denied, where one person has carried more than is fair. The caregiver does not need to throw discomfort at others with cruelty. But they also do not need to swallow it all. A boundary conversation that leaves everyone mildly uncomfortable may be more honest than one that leaves the caregiver quietly broken.

The caregiver should also remember that emotional intensity can coexist with love. A person may be angry and still love the caregiver. A caregiver may hold a limit and still love the person receiving care. A relative may cry and still need to take responsibility. A conversation may be painful and still be necessary. Caregivers often interpret emotional pain as evidence that the relationship is breaking. Sometimes pain is evidence that the relationship is being asked to become more truthful.

There is no perfect way to handle anger, tears, and manipulation. Some conversations will go badly despite careful preparation. Some people will misunderstand. Some will push harder. Some will need time. Some will never respond as maturely as the caregiver hopes. The goal is not to create a reaction-free boundary. The goal is to become steady enough that another person's reaction does not automatically decide the caregiver's behaviour.

This steadiness is not cold. It is an active discipline. It requires the caregiver to keep breathing, keep listening, keep returning to the limit, and keep resisting the old invitation to make every feeling their responsibility. It requires knowing when to stay and when to end the conversation. It requires repair without self-erasure. It requires compassion that does not collapse.

A caregiver can say, "I see that you are angry."

They can say, "I am sorry this hurts."

They can say, "I care about you."

And they can still say, "The answer is no."

Documenting Agreements and Next Steps

A hard conversation is not finished when everyone stops talking. In caregiving, the end of a conversation is often the most fragile point. People may feel relieved that the tension has passed. Someone may say, "Yes, of course," or "We will sort it," or "I understand now." The caregiver may feel too tired to ask for precision. The room softens. The phone call ends. The messages go quiet. For a brief moment, it can seem as though progress has been made.

Then ordinary life returns, and the agreement begins to blur.

A sibling remembers the conversation differently. The person receiving care assumes the old arrangement still applies. A relative says they thought someone else was handling the task. A helper promises to visit "soon" but never chooses a day. A boundary around late calls is treated as flexible because it was spoken gently. A transport plan is discussed but not confirmed. The caregiver, who thought a responsibility had finally moved out of their hands, discovers that they are still expected to notice, remind, chase, correct, and rescue.

This is why documentation matters. It is not a cold administrative habit imposed on family life. It is a protective practice that turns fragile conversation into shared reference. It gives memory something to lean on. It reduces the chance that stress, guilt, convenience, or selective hearing will quietly rewrite what was agreed. In caregiving, where emotions are high and tasks have real consequences, a spoken agreement that is never captured can become another future crisis waiting for a date.

Many caregivers resist documenting agreements because it feels too formal. They worry it will make them seem controlling, mistrustful, or managerial. They may think, "Surely we are family. Surely we can remember what we said." But family memory is not neutral. It is shaped by habit, hope, anxiety, defensiveness, resentment, and the human tendency to remember the version that costs us least. A written note does not mean people are dishonest. It means the care arrangement is too important to be left entirely to mood and memory.

Documentation is especially useful because caregiving is full of invisible assumptions. One person hears, "I will help with appointments," and means they will make a few phone calls. Another hears the same sentence and assumes transport, reminders, attendance, note-taking, and follow-up. One person says they will "check in", meaning a short weekly call. Another believes this means daily monitoring. One person agrees to "sort the paperwork", then discovers that paperwork includes forms, bills, passwords, records, applications, letters, deadlines, and conversations with professionals. Vague language creates hidden labour. Documentation forces vague language to become practical.

A documented agreement should answer the questions that prevent future confusion: who is doing what, by when, how often, with what information, and what happens if they cannot do it. These questions may sound simple, but they expose the difference between goodwill and responsibility. "Everyone will help more" is goodwill. "You will collect the prescription every Friday before 4 p.m. and tell me if you cannot do it by Thursday evening" is responsibility. The first may comfort people emotionally. The second changes the care load.

The caregiver should not document everything in the life of care. That would become another impossible burden. The aim is not to create a bureaucratic empire. The aim is to capture the agreements that, if forgotten or blurred, will create stress, risk, resentment, or repeated conflict. The more a task affects safety, timing, emotional pressure, money, transport, medication, appointments, or the caregiver's boundaries, the more it deserves to be written down.

A simple written summary after a conversation can be enough. It might say, "Just confirming what we agreed: I will book the appointment, but I cannot drive. You will arrange transport by Wednesday and let us know once it is confirmed." Or: "To avoid confusion, non-urgent calls after 8 p.m. will wait until the next morning. Emergencies mean immediate health or safety concerns." Or: "From next week, I will send one family update on Sunday evenings. Please send questions before then unless something urgent changes." These notes are not elaborate. Their power lies in making the next step visible.

Tone matters. Documentation should be clear, but not punitive. The caregiver does not need to write as though preparing evidence for a trial. A good follow-up message is calm, brief, and practical. It should not reopen the argument or repeat every emotional detail of the conversation. It should not contain hidden sarcasm, accusation, or a list of past failures. It should simply confirm the arrangement. "Here is what we agreed" is stronger than "Since no one ever remembers anything, I am putting this in writing."

This distinction protects relationships. When documentation is used to shame people, it can create defensiveness. When it is used to clarify care, it reduces unnecessary friction. The caregiver can frame it as a support for everyone: "I am writing this down so we are all clear." Or: "This will help me not keep everything in my head." Or: "Let us keep the plan visible so no one has to guess." These sentences reduce the emotional charge around writing things down.

Documentation is also a way of moving responsibility out of the caregiver's memory. Many caregivers become the living archive of the care arrangement. They know the appointment dates, medication changes, preferred foods, passwords, family promises, professional names, warning signs, routines, and unresolved tasks. Others may believe they are helping, but the caregiver is still carrying the mental work of tracking whether help is happening. This is not true delegation. It is outsourced action with retained mental responsibility.

A written task list can change that, but only if responsibility is genuinely assigned. A list that the caregiver creates, updates, monitors, and chases alone may simply become another version of over-functioning. The purpose is not to make the caregiver a better manager of everyone. The purpose is to make the work visible enough that others can own their parts. A task with an owner should not require constant surveillance. If it does, either the task was not handed off clearly, the person is not reliable for that task, or the system needs a different backup.

Shared calendars can be valuable for appointments, visits, medication refills, supply checks, and family availability. Their usefulness is not in the technology itself, but in the principle: key information should not live only in one person's head. If appointment transport is needed, the date should be visible. If someone has agreed to visit, the time should be recorded. If a prescription needs collecting, the routine should be known. A calendar is not just a schedule; it is a boundary against constant last-minute remembering.

Task lists work best when they are specific. "Help Mum" is not a task. "Take Mum to the Tuesday appointment at 10 a.m." is a task. "Check food" is vague. "Check fridge on Friday and replace milk, bread, and ready meals if low" is usable. "Do paperwork" is too broad. "Open post, photograph urgent letters, and place bills in the folder every Thursday" is clearer. Specificity reduces the need for the caregiver to explain the same thing repeatedly.

Caregivers should include deadlines where timing matters. Without a deadline, a task can remain emotionally agreed but practically undone. "I will call the clinic" may drift for days. "I will call the clinic by Tuesday afternoon and send an update afterwards" has shape. Timing is especially important for tasks that prevent crises: medication refills, transport arrangements, bill payments, appointment confirmations, form submissions, supply checks, and follow-up calls. If the timing is not written down, the caregiver may remain anxious until they personally confirm it has happened.

Backups should also be documented. A care system without backups turns every forgotten task into a crisis. If the person responsible for transport becomes ill, who is next? If the caregiver cannot answer, what counts as an emergency and who else can be contacted? If a helper cannot visit, how soon must they say so? If medication collection fails, what is the next step? These questions are not pessimistic. They are realistic. Good documentation does not assume everything will go perfectly. It assumes ordinary human life will interfere.

The caregiver should be careful not to make backup planning another private burden. Where possible, the person taking responsibility for a task should also help define the backup. "If you cannot collect the prescription, who will you ask?" is more sustainable than the caregiver automatically becoming the fallback for every failure. Otherwise, the system remains secretly dependent on the caregiver, even when tasks appear to be shared.

Written agreements are also helpful after emotional conversations because emotions distort memory. A person may leave a conversation genuinely believing they agreed to less than they did. Another may focus on the part that hurt and forget the practical detail. A caregiver may soften their own memory because guilt rises afterwards. A short written summary gives everyone a stable version. It can prevent later arguments such as "You never said that," "I thought you meant only this week," or "No one told me it was urgent."

This is particularly important with boundaries. A boundary spoken once may be treated as a mood. A boundary written clearly becomes a policy. "As discussed, I do not take non-urgent calls after 8 p.m." is harder to reinterpret than a late-night conversation in which the caregiver sounded tired and upset. "I can coordinate appointments, but I cannot provide regular transport" makes the division visible. "I will not continue conversations where I am being shouted at" gives the caregiver a standard to return to.

Some caregivers worry that writing down boundaries will provoke conflict. It might, especially if others preferred the boundary to remain vague. But that reaction is itself information. A person who resists clarity may be benefiting from ambiguity. They may not mean harm, but vagueness gives them room to push, forget, minimise, or return tasks to the caregiver. Clarity can feel uncomfortable because it removes that room. Discomfort is not always a sign that documentation is wrong.

There is also value in documenting what was not agreed. This is often overlooked. If the caregiver says, "I can book appointments but not attend them," that limit should be visible. If a relative agrees to help with shopping but not personal care, that should be clear. If the person receiving care refuses a suggested support, the refusal may need noting in a simple, non-judgemental way. "We discussed a weekly visit from an outside helper, and you said you are not ready to try that yet." This prevents future confusion and helps the caregiver remember that some gaps remain because options were declined, not because the caregiver failed.

Documentation can protect against emotional revision. After a decision is made, someone may later say, "You never offered another option," or "No one asked me," or "I thought you would still do it if needed." A written note can reduce this kind of drift. It does not eliminate conflict, but it gives the caregiver something concrete to refer back to: "This is what we agreed." "This is the option that was discussed." "This is the task you said you would take." The conversation moves from memory battle to practical review.

For documentation to work, it must be accessible. A plan hidden in one person's notebook may help that person, but it does not create shared responsibility. Depending on the situation, accessibility might mean a group message, a shared calendar, a printed sheet on the fridge, a folder near the phone, a document shared with key relatives, or a note sent after each family discussion. The right format is the one that people involved can actually use. Sophisticated systems fail if they are too complicated for the people who need them.

The caregiver should favour simple tools over impressive ones. A plain calendar used consistently is better than a detailed app no one opens. A short weekly message is better than a colour-coded system that collapses after a fortnight. A visible folder with essential documents is better than a digital archive only one person understands. Caregiving systems must work when people are tired, worried, rushed, or resistant. If a system requires ideal behaviour, it will not survive real care.

A basic care documentation habit might include a weekly update, a shared task list, and a place for essential information. The weekly update can name upcoming appointments, supplies needed, current concerns, and who is responsible for what. The task list can show active responsibilities and deadlines. The essential information can include medication details, contact numbers, routines, preferences, emergency instructions, and relevant documents. The form can vary.

The principle is that the core facts should not have to be reconstructed during every problem.

It is important to keep documentation factual. Care notes should not become a diary of frustration. "Dad refused lunch again and was impossible" may express how the caregiver feels, but it is less useful than "Dad ate very little at lunch and became upset when offered several choices." The second version gives information that can guide care. It also reduces the risk that documentation becomes a record of resentment. Factual language protects dignity, especially if notes are shared.

This does not mean emotional cost should be ignored. There is room, in the caregiver's private record, to note that certain tasks are draining or that particular conversations leave them depleted. But shared documentation should generally separate practical facts from emotional processing. The family task list is not the place to punish people with the caregiver's accumulated pain. That pain may need another outlet: a trusted friend, counsellor, support group, journal, or direct conversation. Documentation should support care, not become a battlefield.

The caregiver should also decide how often agreements will be reviewed. Care needs change. A task that was manageable may become too large. A helper may prove unreliable. A boundary may need clearer wording. A routine may stop working because the person receiving care has changed. A monthly or regular review can prevent plans from becoming outdated. Without review, documentation can become a museum of old agreements that no longer match reality.

A review does not need to be lengthy. It can ask: What is working? What is being missed? Which tasks keep returning to the caregiver? Which agreement is unclear? What new pressure has appeared? What needs to be reassigned? This turns documentation into a living tool rather than a one-time effort. The care arrangement becomes something maintained, not merely endured.

When someone does not follow through, documentation helps the caregiver respond clearly rather than emotionally. Instead of saying,

"You never help," the caregiver can say, "You agreed to collect the prescription on Friday, and it was not done. Can you still take this task, or do we need another arrangement?" This is firmer and more useful. It names the behaviour, asks for reality, and avoids turning the moment into a global character judgement.

If the person repeatedly fails, the documentation provides evidence that the task is not safely assigned to them. The caregiver can then make a decision: simplify the task, provide clearer instructions, move it to someone else, create a backup, or acknowledge that this person cannot be relied upon for that responsibility. This may be disappointing, but it is better than living in a cycle of hope, failure, resentment, and rescue.

Documentation can also help the caregiver avoid becoming the family manager. This may sound contradictory. Does writing things down not make the caregiver more managerial? It depends on how it is used. If the caregiver keeps every list, sends every reminder, checks every task, and absorbs every failure, yes, documentation has become management. But if agreements are visible, assigned, and reviewed with shared accountability, documentation reduces the caregiver's centrality. It allows responsibility to sit with the person who accepted it.

A good phrase is: "The task is yours to manage, not mine to chase." This may be spoken gently but firmly when someone repeatedly expects the caregiver to remind them. Another phrase is: "Please put that in the shared calendar so everyone can see it." Or: "If you cannot do the task, please update the group by Thursday so another plan can be made." These sentences move responsibility outward. They also make the cost of unreliability visible.

The person receiving care may need documentation in a different form. Depending on their capacity and preferences, written routines, reminder cards, visible calendars, labelled folders, or simple daily notes may reduce anxiety and repeated questions. The goal is not to infantilise them, but to support independence and reduce reliance on the caregiver's constant verbal prompting. A written medication routine, a list of appointment dates, or a note about when the caregiver will call can provide reassurance without requiring repeated reassurance.

However, documentation should respect dignity. It should not turn the person's home into a wall of instructions unless that is genuinely helpful and acceptable. It should not broadcast private information unnecessarily. It should not be used to shame forgetfulness or resistance. The best documentation is quiet, useful, and proportionate. It supports care without making the person feel managed by paperwork.

Privacy and consent also matter. Not every detail should be shared with every relative. The person receiving care may have a right to decide who knows what, depending on their capacity and the nature of the information. The caregiver should distinguish between essential care information and private personal details. Sharing appointment times or medication instructions with a helper may be necessary. Sharing emotional disclosures, financial details, or sensitive health information more widely may not be. Good documentation is clear, but not careless.

The caregiver should also protect themselves in documentation. If they have stated a limit, it is worth confirming. If they have declined a task, it is worth noting. If they have handed over responsibility, it is worth recording. This is not paranoia. It is self-protection in a role where assumptions can become obligations. Written clarity prevents the caregiver from being quietly reabsorbed into tasks they had already released.

For example: "Just confirming that from next week, I will no longer be handling weekday transport. I will continue to coordinate appointment dates." This sentence prevents the old role from creeping back unnoticed. Or: "As agreed, I will not be the point of contact for routine updates during work hours. Please use the shared message thread." Again, the caregiver is not asking for permission. They are making the arrangement visible.

Documentation is also useful after conflict repair. If a conversation became heated but ended with a decision, a calm written note can separate the practical agreement from the emotional turbulence. "I am glad we were able to settle the next steps. To confirm, you will visit on Saturday, I will handle the medication list, and we will review the transport plan next week." This helps the relationship move forward. It prevents the conflict from swallowing the outcome.

Sometimes a person will object to written confirmation. They may say, "Why are you putting everything in writing?" or "Do you not trust me?" A calm response can be: "I am writing it down because there are too many details to keep in my head." Or: "This helps prevent misunderstandings." Or: "It is not about mistrust; it is about making the plan clear." The caregiver should not be drawn into a debate about whether documentation is insulting. The care load is complex enough to justify clarity.

There will be mistakes. A note may be incomplete. A calendar entry may be missed. A task may be written unclearly. Someone may not read the message. Documentation reduces confusion; it does not eliminate human fallibility. The caregiver should treat the system as adjustable rather than perfect. If people are not using the shared calendar, why? Is it too complicated? Are reminders needed? Is one person refusing responsibility? If the task list is ignored, does it need simplifying? A useful system is one that can be repaired.

The most important measure is whether documentation reduces crises and mental load. Are fewer appointments being forgotten? Are fewer tasks drifting back to the caregiver? Are relatives clearer about what they have agreed to do? Is the person receiving care less anxious because routines are visible? Is the caregiver spending less time reminding, explaining, and reconstructing decisions? If not, the documentation may be too vague, too hidden, too complicated, or too dependent on the caregiver maintaining it alone.

At its best, documentation protects relationships by reducing the number of arguments built from memory. It prevents "I thought you meant" from becoming a repeated source of conflict. It prevents vague help from masquerading as real support. It prevents the caregiver's mental load from remaining invisible. It gives everyone involved a fairer chance to act responsibly.

It also protects the caregiver's credibility with themselves. When agreements are written, the caregiver can see whether help is real or only promised. They can see whether a boundary is being respected or repeatedly tested. They can see whether the care arrangement is improving or merely producing better conversations without practical change. This evidence matters. Caregivers often doubt themselves. A written record can show what is actually happening.

Documenting agreements and next steps is not about turning love into paperwork. It is about refusing to make love depend on confusion. It is about acknowledging that care involves many moving parts and that goodwill alone cannot hold them all. It is about creating enough structure that people do not have to rely on guilt, memory, assumption, and last-minute rescue.

A clear note after a hard conversation may look small. A shared calendar entry may look ordinary. A task list may look unimpressive. But these small acts change the care arrangement from a collection of hopes into a set of visible commitments. They make it harder for responsibility to drift silently back to the person who is most likely to notice.

The question after any caregiving conversation should be plain: what has actually been agreed, who owns the next step, and where is that written so the caregiver does not have to carry it alone?

Chapter 6
Sharing Tasks Without Creating Chaos

How can getting help make caregiving feel heavier instead of lighter? The question sounds unreasonable until it happens. A relative offers to take over an appointment, then calls repeatedly for details the caregiver has already explained. A neighbour agrees to collect shopping, but buys the wrong things and leaves the caregiver managing the disappointment. A sibling promises to visit, arrives late, changes the routine, and leaves behind confusion that takes the rest of the day to settle. Help was given, technically. Relief did not follow.

This is one of the more frustrating discoveries of caregiving: support is not automatically supportive. A task handed over badly can return with interest. The caregiver may have to prepare the helper, reassure the person receiving care, write instructions, answer questions, monitor the outcome, correct mistakes, smooth hurt feelings, and then decide whether it would have been easier to do the task alone. After a few experiences like this, many caregivers stop asking. They become exhausted, not because no one could help, but because help has never been shaped into something reliable.

The support network may be larger than it first appears, but it is rarely organised by accident. Family may be part of it, but family alone is not the whole field. Friends, neighbours, community contacts, occasional visitors, practical acquaintances, and paid support where available may all have a place. The mistake is to look for one perfect substitute for the main caregiver. That person may not exist. A workable support system is often built from smaller contributions: one driver, one form-reader, one steady caller, one person who can sit for an hour, one person who can collect supplies, one person who can pay rather than attend.

The central tension is between sharing the care load and multiplying the caregiver's management load. Delegation is supposed to create space, but vague delegation creates supervision. A caregiver who asks for "more help" may receive sympathy, promises, or irregular bursts of effort, yet still remain responsible for the mental architecture of care. They are still the one who notices what needs doing, decides who might do it, explains the task, reminds the helper, checks whether it happened, and repairs what went wrong. The labour has changed shape, but it has not truly moved.

This matters because chaotic help can deepen resentment. The caregiver may feel angry at people who "help" in ways that create more work, then guilty for feeling ungrateful. Helpers may feel criticised when their contribution is corrected, then withdraw. The person receiving care may become unsettled by inconsistency, then cling more tightly to the main caregiver. Everyone may claim to want the burden shared, while the practical design of sharing remains too weak to hold. Good intentions, without structure, can become another source of strain.

The longer this continues, the more the care system becomes dependent on one person's private competence. The main caregiver knows the preferences, risks, routines, triggers, contacts, timings, and emotional shortcuts. Others do not learn because they are never given tasks in a way that makes learning possible, or because their first awkward attempts are so stressful that the caregiver takes everything back. This protects the short-term smoothness of care while making long-term stability more fragile. If only one person can do things properly, then every absence, illness, work demand, or emotional collapse becomes a threat to the whole arrangement.

A more durable approach begins by seeing support as a network to be mapped rather than a favour to be begged for. The question is not who cares most, but who can reliably do what. From there, requests must become specific enough that another person can say a real yes or a real no, not a vague promise that dissolves under pressure. And when help is accepted, the handoff must be designed so the caregiver is not left redoing the work in private while publicly pretending to be grateful.

This requires a sober definition of fairness. Fair does not always mean equal, and chasing equal shares can waste energy that care situations do not have. One person may have time but little emotional steadiness. Another may have money but no availability. Another may be poor at intimate care but excellent with forms. Another may not be suitable for sensitive conversations but can manage errands reliably. A workable team is built by matching tasks to capacity, not by forcing everyone into the same measure of contribution. The result may not satisfy every old family grievance, but it can reduce the load that is actually breaking the caregiver.

The next difficulty is precision. "Can you help more?" is emotionally honest but operationally weak. "Can you take Mum to the Tuesday 10 a.m. appointment once a month?" gives the other person something concrete to accept, decline, or negotiate. The difference is not merely wording. It is the difference between hope and responsibility. A clear request contains the task, timing, frequency, instructions, and limits. It reduces the back-and-forth that so often turns asking for help into another job.

Yet even a clear yes is not enough without a clean transfer. A task needs the right information, a simple standard, and a backup for when ordinary life interferes. Otherwise, the caregiver remains the hidden safety net beneath every helper's effort. The hard question is not simply, "Who can help?" It is sharper: "What would have to be true for someone else to help without everything still depending on me?"

Mapping the Support Network

A caregiver often discovers the limits of "I will just do it" long before anyone else sees the problem. The arrangement may still look workable from the outside. Appointments are attended. Shopping appears. Calls are answered. Forms are completed. The person receiving care is checked on, reassured, reminded, transported, and supported. But beneath that visible order sits a fragile truth: too much depends on one person noticing too much, remembering too much, and being available too often.

This is the point at which many caregivers are told to "ask for help", as though help were a single door waiting to be opened. The advice is well meant, but incomplete. Asking for help is not simple when the care load is complex, when family relationships are uneven, when previous offers have been vague, when people disappoint, when paid support may be limited, or when the caregiver has become so used to doing everything that explaining one task feels like another task. The problem is not only whether help exists. The problem is whether help can be shaped into something reliable.

A support network is not the same as a list of people who care. Many people may care emotionally while being unable, unwilling, or unsuited to provide practical help. Others may not be emotionally close but can offer something genuinely useful. A neighbour who can put bins out may be more helpful than a sibling who sends long messages about what should happen but never takes a task. A friend who can sit for an hour may provide more relief than a relative who arrives with criticism and creates emotional debris. Care support should be measured by usable contribution, not by sentimental closeness.

This is a difficult but liberating shift. Family may matter deeply, but family is not always the whole support system, and it is not always the most reliable part of it. Some relatives are too far away, too busy, too emotionally reactive, too unwell, too disorganised, or too entangled in old conflicts to be useful in every role. That does not mean they have no place. It means the caregiver must stop assuming that blood relationship automatically translates into practical capacity. A workable network is built from reality, not from what the family tree suggests should be possible.

Mapping the support network begins with widening the field. Possible helpers may include relatives, friends, neighbours, faith or community contacts, local groups, volunteer services, paid carers where available, cleaners, drivers, meal providers, gardeners, administrative helpers, professional advisers, or people who can offer occasional companionship. Some may help regularly. Some may be suitable only for one-off tasks. Some may be able to provide emotional support to the caregiver rather than direct care to the person receiving care. That still counts. A caregiver who is supported indirectly may have more capacity to provide direct care wisely.

The mistake is looking only for someone who can replace the main caregiver. That person may not exist. The more useful question is: what small pieces of the load could be carried by different people? One person may be able to collect prescriptions. Another may manage weekly shopping. Another may call on Sunday evenings. Another may handle paperwork. Another may drive to one appointment a month. Another may pay for a cleaner. Another may stay with the person receiving care while the caregiver attends their own appointment. No single contribution may look transformative, but together they can reduce the dangerous concentration of responsibility.

This is where caregivers must resist the trap of perfect fairness. Fairness matters, but perfect fairness is often impossible and can become a distraction from relief. Equal hours from every sibling may not be realistic. Equal emotional involvement may not happen. Equal competence is unlikely. One person may have money but not time. Another may have time but no transport. Another may be calm in practical situations but poor with emotional distress. Another may be willing but unreliable. Another may live nearby but have serious constraints of their own. If the caregiver waits for fairness in its purest form, they may remain unsupported while arguing with reality.

A better standard is workable contribution. What can this person actually do, consistently enough to be useful, without creating more work than they remove? This question cuts through fantasy. It prevents the caregiver from assigning delicate emotional tasks to someone impatient, complex paperwork to someone disorganised, personal care to someone the care recipient does not trust, or urgent transport to someone whose schedule is unpredictable. The goal is not to make everyone perform the same kind of care. The goal is to match real tasks to real capacity.

This matching process requires honesty about strengths. Some people are good with conversation. Some are better with errands. Some are calm with hospitals but useless with forms. Some can cook but cannot manage emotional conflict. Some are trustworthy with money but awkward with personal care. Some are practical, punctual, and emotionally limited. Some are warm, loving, and unreliable. A good support map does not shame these differences. It uses them. The wrong person in the wrong role creates chaos. The right person in a modest role can create genuine relief.

Availability must be treated just as seriously as willingness. Many people say they want to help. Fewer people can help at the required time, with the required frequency, and with enough follow-through to reduce the caregiver's load. A person who can help "whenever" may be less useful than someone who can commit to every second Tuesday. A person who offers broad support but never confirms dates may create more uncertainty. Availability should be concrete: days, times, frequency, notice required, transport limits, and what happens if they cannot attend.

Reliability is another category. A helper does not need to be perfect, but the caregiver must know what level of reliability they are dealing with. Someone who forgets often should not be assigned a task with serious consequences unless there is a backup. Someone who cancels frequently may still be useful for low-risk tasks. Someone who becomes defensive when corrected may not be suitable for tasks requiring careful instructions. Someone who is emotionally intense may be better away from the most sensitive conversations. Reliability is not a moral judgement; it is design information.

The caregiver should also consider the care recipient's experience. A helper may be willing, but not acceptable or calming to the person receiving care. There may be history, discomfort, embarrassment, preference, or fear involved. These feelings should not automatically veto every support option, especially if the current arrangement is unsustainable, but they should be taken seriously. A helper who increases distress may not reduce the overall load. Sometimes a gradual introduction, a smaller task, or a clearer explanation can help. Sometimes that person is simply not the right match.

Mapping support also means identifying people who support the caregiver rather than the care recipient. This is often overlooked. A friend who listens without judgement, a colleague who understands scheduling strain, a neighbour who notices when the caregiver is exhausted, or a counsellor who helps the caregiver think clearly may not directly reduce the shopping list or appointment schedule. Yet they may protect the caregiver from emotional isolation. A caregiver who has somewhere to tell the truth is less likely to pour all unspoken strain back into the care relationship.

The support map should include four broad kinds of help: practical, administrative, emotional, and respite. Practical help includes transport, shopping, meals, cleaning, gardening, household repairs, pet care, and errands. Administrative help includes forms, bills, appointment booking, calendars, phone calls, records, and paperwork. Emotional help includes companionship, regular calls, reassurance, family communication, and support for the caregiver. Respite includes anything that gives the caregiver protected time away from responsibility, even briefly. When these categories are visible, the caregiver can see where the network is strong and where it is dangerously thin.

Some caregivers discover that they have several people willing to visit, but no one willing to manage paperwork. Others have practical helpers but no emotional support. Some have relatives who will attend big appointments but no one to help with the weekly grind. Some have people who can respond to crises but not prevent them. This matters because not all help reduces the same pressure. A caregiver drowning in administration does not need only sympathetic visitors. A caregiver exhausted by constant companionship may not be relieved by another person offering to organise documents. The task must match the strain.

A useful support map should also separate one-off help from ongoing responsibility. A person who can help once may not be able to own a recurring task. Confusing the two leads to disappointment. "Can you take Mum to the appointment on Tuesday?" is different from "Can you be responsible for taking Mum to her appointments every month?" A one-off helper may still be valuable, but the caregiver should not mentally convert a single yes into a permanent solution. Hope is not a rota.

There is a particular danger in overvaluing dramatic help and undervaluing routine help. Someone who appears during a crisis may be praised, while the person who quietly performs weekly tasks remains unseen. Caregiving stability, however, is built largely from routine contribution. The prescription collected before it runs out. The weekly call that reduces anxiety. The transport confirmed before panic begins. The regular meal delivery. The scheduled visit that gives the caregiver time to rest. These acts may not look heroic, but they are the architecture of sustainable care.

When mapping the network, the caregiver should be careful not to edit people out too quickly because they cannot do the ideal task. Someone who cannot provide personal care may still do shopping. Someone who cannot visit during the week may manage weekend check-ins. Someone who lives far away may handle phone calls, forms, research, finances, scheduling, or emotional support. Someone who lacks money may have time. Someone who lacks time may contribute funds. The question is not, "Can they do everything I wish they would do?" It is, "Is there one useful thing they can reliably do?"

At the same time, the caregiver should not include people purely because they should help. A sibling who repeatedly refuses, forgets, criticises, or creates disruption may belong on a different kind of map: not the support network, but the source-of-strain list. This may sound blunt, but it is necessary. Not every person close to the situation is an asset. Some people increase the load through conflict, judgement, unreliability, or emotional pressure. Naming this privately can prevent the caregiver from continuing to seek help from places where help has repeatedly failed to become real.

The support map should be built from evidence, not longing. What has this person actually done? What have they done reliably? What have they promised but not delivered? What tasks suit their temperament? What tasks do they avoid? How much instruction do they need? Do they leave the person receiving care calmer or more unsettled? Do they communicate clearly? Do they respect boundaries? Do they create work before, during, or after their involvement? These questions may feel unsentimental, but they protect the care arrangement from wishful thinking.

A strong map also includes gaps. This is one of its most important functions. The caregiver may discover that no one is available for weekday transport, that paperwork has no owner, that emergency backup is weak, or that respite depends entirely on one unreliable person. Seeing the gap may be uncomfortable, but hidden gaps are more dangerous. A visible gap can be discussed, planned around, escalated, simplified, or used as evidence that the current arrangement needs more support. An invisible gap merely waits to become a crisis.

Gaps are not always personal failures. They may reflect limited resources, distance, illness, money, work patterns, family history, or the complexity of the care need. The caregiver should avoid turning every gap into self-blame. The point of mapping is not to prove that the caregiver has failed to build a perfect network. It is to show what the current network can and cannot carry. A bridge is not blamed for having a weight limit. It is designed around that limit.

The caregiver should also recognise hidden assets. Some people do not offer help because they do not know what would be useful. Others assume family has it covered. Some are afraid of intruding. Some feel awkward around illness or ageing but could manage practical tasks if asked clearly. Some people may be willing to provide narrow but dependable support. A support map can reveal who might be approached with a specific request, rather than waiting for vague offers to appear.

There is an emotional hurdle here: asking people outside the immediate family can feel exposing. Caregivers may fear judgement, pity, gossip, rejection, or the implication that the family is failing. Yet care has always been larger than the household that happens to be closest. Neighbours, friends, community connections, and paid support where possible can all form part of a humane care structure. Privacy matters, and dignity matters, but secrecy should not force one person to carry what a wider circle could safely share.

Not everyone needs to know everything. A neighbour who brings in bins does not need medical details. A friend who sits with the person receiving care for an hour does not need access to finances. A driver needs appointment timing and mobility information, not family history. Part of mapping support is deciding how much information each helper needs. This protects privacy while making help possible.

Too little information creates errors; too much information can feel intrusive or burdensome. The right amount is task-specific.

The caregiver should think of the support network as a set of roles rather than a set of personalities. Roles might include driver, shopper, caller, visitor, form-reader, meal organiser, medication collector, appointment companion, emergency contact, respite helper, household maintenance person, financial contributor, or emotional support for the caregiver. A person may fill more than one role, but the role should be named. Naming roles prevents the vague expectation that "help" means whatever the caregiver happens to need in the moment.

This role-based thinking also reduces conflict. Instead of saying, "You never help," the caregiver can say, "We need someone to own prescription collection." Instead of saying, "I am doing everything," they can say, "The unassigned roles are transport, paperwork, and Sunday companionship." This shifts the conversation from character accusation to practical design. People may still resist, but the issue becomes harder to dismiss.

Once possible helpers and roles are identified, the caregiver should classify tasks by sensitivity and risk. Some tasks are low-risk and easy to delegate: collecting groceries, dropping off supplies, putting bins out, mowing a lawn, delivering a meal. Others require more trust or skill: medication routines, financial paperwork, personal care, health conversations, emotional support during distress, transport for someone with mobility or cognitive challenges. High-risk tasks need clearer instructions, stronger reliability, and backups. Low-risk tasks can be useful entry points for new helpers.

Starting with lower-risk tasks can build confidence for everyone. The caregiver learns whether the helper follows through. The helper learns the rhythm of care without being overwhelmed. The person receiving care adjusts to receiving support from someone else. A small reliable task can become the foundation for larger involvement later. By contrast, throwing a new helper into a complicated task without preparation may confirm everyone's fear that only the main caregiver can do things properly.

The support map should also include backup capacity. Who can step in if the usual person cancels? Who can be contacted if the caregiver is unwell? Who knows where essential information is kept? Who can respond if transport fails? Who can cover a short visit at short notice? Many care systems appear to have support until the first helper becomes unavailable. Then everything returns to the main caregiver. A support network without backups is not a network; it is a chain with one weak link.

Backup planning does not require elaborate systems. It requires honest answers. If there is no backup, that should be known. If the backup is only available on weekends, that should be known. If the backup needs written instructions, those should exist before the crisis. If the caregiver is still the backup for every helper, the load has not truly shifted. The support map should show not only who helps, but what happens when help fails.

Caregivers must be careful with the phrase "I will just remind them." Reminder labour is still labour. If the caregiver has to remind every helper every time, they remain the manager of the entire system. Some reminders are normal during transition, but ongoing reminder dependence means the task has not been fully transferred. A good support arrangement should include the helper's responsibility to remember, confirm, and communicate. Otherwise, the caregiver may have delegated action but retained mental ownership.

A simple standard can help. For each helper, the caregiver might privately assess: Do they remember without repeated prompting? Do they communicate if they cannot do the task? Do they follow the agreed instructions? Do they leave the person receiving care settled? Do they reduce the caregiver's load? This standard is not about perfection. It is about whether the help is actually helpful. If the answer is repeatedly no, the role may need to change.

Mapping the network may bring grief. The caregiver may see clearly that someone they hoped would help is unlikely to do so. They may realise that support will not come in the form they wanted. They may feel abandoned by relatives, disappointed by friends, or embarrassed by the thinness of the available circle. This grief should not be brushed aside. It is painful to discover that love, history, or proximity do not automatically produce practical support.

But grief can sit beside strategy. The caregiver can mourn the help that did not arrive and still build with the help that is possible. They can stop asking an unreliable person for high-stakes tasks and start asking a modestly reliable person for one specific errand. They can stop waiting for ideal family fairness and begin creating workable distribution. This is not emotional defeat. It is adult realism.

The caregiver should also include themselves on the map, but not at the centre of everything. What roles are truly theirs? Which roles do they choose? Which roles are theirs only because no one else was asked? Which roles must remain with them because of trust, skill, or relationship? Which roles should move? This prevents the support map from becoming a decorative exercise while the caregiver continues carrying the bulk of the load by default.

A useful question is: "If I became unavailable for a week, what would fail first?" The answer reveals where the network is weakest. Medication? Transport? Meals? Emotional reassurance? Paperwork? Family communication? Safety checks? The point is not to frighten the caregiver. It is to expose the tasks most urgently needing shared knowledge, backup, or reassignment. A care system that cannot survive the caregiver being unavailable is too fragile.

The support map should be reviewed regularly because people and needs change. A helper's work schedule may shift. A neighbour may move. A relative may become more available or less reliable. The care recipient's needs may increase. A paid service may become possible or no longer affordable. A task that once took minutes may become complex. A support map is not a final document. It is a living picture of capacity around the care situation.

The caregiver should avoid making the map too complicated. A simple page may be enough: people, possible tasks, availability, reliability, limits, and backup options. The value lies not in beauty but in clarity. The map should help the caregiver think, ask, and decide. If maintaining it becomes another burden, it has missed its purpose.

The deeper purpose of mapping the support network is to break the illusion that care must move through one person or not at all. Even when the main caregiver remains central, they should not be the only route through which every task, feeling, and decision travels. A network gives care more than one path. It reduces dependence on private memory. It allows smaller contributions to become meaningful. It turns vague goodwill into visible capacity.

A workable support network will not remove every strain. Some people will disappoint. Some tasks will remain difficult. Some gaps will still require bigger decisions. But a mapped network gives the caregiver a clearer view of what is possible. It shows where to ask, where not to waste energy, where backup is missing, and where one modest contribution could make the week more liveable.

The question is not, "Who cares enough to save me?"

The better question is, "Who can carry which part of this load reliably enough that care no longer depends on me alone?"

Making Requests People Can Say Yes To

Many caregivers ask for help only after they have already reached the edge. By then, the request often comes out as a cry rather than a plan. "I cannot do everything." "Someone needs to help me." "I need more support." These sentences are honest. They may be the truest words the caregiver has spoken in months. But honesty alone does not make a request easy to answer.

The difficulty is that broad distress produces broad sympathy, not necessarily useful action. A relative may say, "Of course, just tell me what you need," and then wait. A friend may say, "I am here if you need anything," without knowing what that means. A sibling may agree that the situation is unfair, but no specific task moves from the caregiver's hands. Everyone feels concerned. Nothing changes. The caregiver then feels not only unsupported, but foolish for having asked.

A request people can say yes to is not vague. It is specific, bounded, and practical. It tells the other person what is needed, when it is needed, how often it is needed, what the task includes, and what the limits are. It does not require them to interpret the entire care situation before responding. It reduces the emotional and cognitive work required to help. In caregiving, a clear request is not merely polite communication; it is part of the care system.

"Can you help more?" is emotionally understandable, but operationally weak. "Can you take Mum to the Tuesday 10 a.m. appointment once a month?" is stronger. The other person can picture the task. They can check their calendar. They can say yes, no, or offer an alternative. The request has shape. It is no longer an atmosphere of need; it is a defined contribution.

This matters because many people do not refuse caregiving tasks directly. They drift. They agree in principle. They delay. They say they will "try". They wait for more information. They assume someone else will do it. They offer emotional support instead of practical responsibility. Sometimes this is avoidance. Sometimes it is incompetence. Sometimes it is genuine confusion. Specific requests do not eliminate all of this, but they reduce the hiding places.

A clear request begins with the task itself. Not the general area, but the actual action. "Help with transport" is still too broad. "Drive Dad to the clinic on the first Monday of each month, wait during the appointment, and bring him home" is a task. "Help with food" could mean shopping, cooking, planning, paying, checking expiry dates, encouraging eating, or cleaning up. "Bring three prepared meals every Friday afternoon and put them in the fridge" is clearer. "Help with paperwork" could mean anything from opening post to completing complex forms. "Open the post every Thursday, photograph anything urgent, and place bills in the red folder" gives the work a border.

A request also needs timing. Caregiving tasks are often time-sensitive, and without a time frame they become another source of uncertainty. "Can you visit sometime?" is weak because "sometime" is not a plan. "Can you visit on Sunday from 2 p.m. to 4 p.m. so I can have a break?" is usable. "Can you check in with him?" may be well meant but vague. "Can you call him every Wednesday evening at 6 p.m. for ten minutes?" is much easier to accept or decline.

Frequency must be stated as well. A one-off request and an ongoing responsibility are entirely different commitments. "Can you collect the prescription this Friday?" is not the same as "Can you collect the prescription every Friday?" Caregivers often become disappointed because they privately hope a one-off helper will become a regular helper, while the other person believes they only agreed to one task. Precision prevents this silent mismatch.

A request should also include the standard required. This does not mean micromanaging every detail. It means giving enough instruction that the helper can succeed without repeatedly returning to the caregiver for guidance. If someone is taking a person to an appointment, they may need to know where to park, whether mobility support is needed, what paperwork to bring, whether notes should be taken, and who should be updated afterwards. If someone is buying groceries, they may need to know preferred brands, dietary needs, spending limits, and what substitutions are acceptable. A task without standards often returns to the caregiver as correction work.

The caregiver should not confuse clarity with control. Some caregivers hesitate to give instructions because they fear sounding bossy. Others avoid details because they believe a willing helper should "just know". Both approaches create problems. A helper who lacks information may make mistakes. A caregiver who gives no standard but silently expects one may become resentful. Clear instructions are not an insult to the helper; they are a way of making success more likely.

At the same time, the caregiver must avoid turning every request into a training manual. Over-instruction can overwhelm people and make the task seem larger than it is. The art is to give the minimum information needed for the helper to complete the task safely and usefully. A prescription collection may require the pharmacy name, collection time, payment details if relevant, and what to do if there is a problem. It does not require a long speech about every previous prescription crisis unless that information changes the task.

A strong request has a defined end point. This is particularly important for helpers who are nervous about being pulled into endless responsibility. People are more likely to say yes when they understand the boundaries of the commitment. "Can you handle the paperwork?" may sound like a bottomless pit. "Can you help complete this form with me on Saturday morning?" is manageable. "Can you visit more often?" may feel indefinite. "Can you visit for one hour every other Sunday for the next two months?" gives the person a clear container.

The caregiver may feel embarrassed by such precision, but precision is kindness. It respects the other person's time and capacity. It also respects the caregiver's need for real help rather than vague goodwill. The purpose of asking is not to make everyone feel included; it is to move a specific part of the care load.

Many caregivers weaken requests by beginning with too much apology. "I am so sorry to ask, and I know you are busy, and please do not feel bad if you cannot, but I am really struggling and wondered whether maybe..." By the time the actual request arrives, the caregiver has already taught the other person that saying no is expected, perhaps even preferred. Warmth is fine. Apology is not necessary for making a legitimate request.

A clearer opening is: "I need to ask you about a specific care task." Or: "There is one thing that would make a real difference." Or: "Can you take on a defined task for the next month?" These openings are respectful without shrinking. The caregiver is not begging for a favour outside the bounds of ordinary decency. They are asking another person to consider a practical role in a care arrangement.

A request should allow a real yes and a real no. This may seem obvious, but many caregiving requests are emotionally loaded in a way that makes refusal feel forbidden. "You have to help me" may express desperation, but it can trigger defensiveness. "Can you take Dad to the appointment next Tuesday?" gives the other person room to answer. If they say no, the caregiver has information. If they say yes, there is a commitment. A coerced yes is rarely reliable. A clear no is more useful than a vague yes that collapses later.

This does not mean the caregiver must accept every no silently or without consequence. If a sibling repeatedly refuses to help, that may need a harder conversation. If someone agrees in principle but never follows through, that is information about reliability. But the first request should still be shaped so that the answer can be clear. A person who cannot say no clearly often cannot say yes clearly either.

The best requests match the person's strengths and availability. Asking a disorganised person to manage complex paperwork may create more strain. Asking an emotionally volatile relative to handle delicate reassurance may unsettle the person receiving care. Asking someone with a rigid work schedule to provide weekday transport may invite repeated failure. A well-chosen request increases the chance of follow-through because it fits the helper's real life, not the caregiver's fantasy of what they should be able to do.

This is where the support map becomes practical. The caregiver can look at each possible helper and ask: what can this person realistically do well? What have they done reliably before? What kind of task suits their temperament? How much notice do they need? Do they prefer one-off tasks or regular duties? Are they better with errands, money, forms, visits, calls, transport, meals, or companionship? A request built on this knowledge is far more likely to succeed.

For example, a sibling who avoids emotional conversations but is punctual and practical may be ideal for prescription collection. A friend who cannot provide transport but enjoys cooking may be able to deliver freezer meals. A neighbour who is not close enough for personal care may still put bins out, check the post, or sit with the person receiving care while the caregiver runs an errand. A relative who lives far away may not visit often, but may handle phone calls, online orders, research, appointment scheduling, or family updates.

The request should not carry an entire history of resentment. This is difficult, especially when the caregiver has felt unsupported for a long time. They may want to say, "You have never helped, and I am exhausted, and it is unfair that everything falls on me." That may be true, and it may need to be said in a different conversation. But if the immediate goal is to secure a task, the request should stay close to the task. "Can you collect the prescription every Friday for the next month?" is more likely to produce practical movement than a speech about years of unequal labour.

There is a place for naming unfairness. Caregivers should not be expected to swallow all resentment. But task requests work best when they are not overloaded with the entire emotional case. The other person may become defensive and miss the practical point. The caregiver may become so upset that they accept a vague apology instead of a concrete commitment. If the aim is help, the request must be specific enough to survive emotion.

A helpful formula is: task, time, frequency, instructions, confirmation. For example: "Can you take Mum to her physiotherapy appointment on Tuesday at 10 a.m., pick her up at 9.15, wait during the appointment, and text me when she is home?" Another example: "Can you call Dad every Sunday at 5 p.m. for the next month and ask whether he has eaten, taken his evening tablets, and checked the heating?" Another: "Can you handle the electricity bill this week? The letter is in the folder. It needs paying by Friday. Please send a message when it is done."

These requests may feel plain, but plainness is their strength. They leave little room for misunderstanding. They also make it easier to evaluate follow-through. Either the appointment was handled or it was not. Either the call happened or it did not. Either the bill was paid or it was not. Caregivers often suffer because support remains too vague to assess. Clear requests turn support into visible action.

The caregiver should also ask for confirmation. "Can you do that?" is not always enough if the person replies with "I will try" or "Should be fine." A firmer follow-up is: "Can you confirm by tonight?" Or: "Please let me know by Friday whether you can take this on." Or: "I need a definite yes or no so I can make another plan." This may feel uncomfortable, but it prevents the caregiver from waiting in uncertainty. Uncertainty is itself a burden.

A helper's "I will try" should be treated as a maybe, not a yes. This is not harsh. It is practical. A maybe is not reliable enough for essential tasks unless there is a backup. The caregiver can respond, "Thank you. I need a definite answer by tomorrow because the appointment is time-sensitive." Or: "If you are not sure, I will ask someone else." This protects the care plan from drifting on good intentions.

Requests should also make cancellation expectations clear. Helpers will sometimes become unavailable. Work changes. Illness happens. Cars break down. Children need attention. The issue is not whether cancellation is allowed; it is whether cancellation throws the whole task back at the caregiver without notice. A good request includes: "If you cannot do it, please tell me by Thursday so we can arrange backup." Or: "If something changes, please update the group rather than messaging only me." This prevents the caregiver from remaining the hidden emergency manager.

Caregivers often ask in ways that keep themselves at the centre. "Let me know if you cannot do it and I will sort something." This may sound efficient, but it preserves the caregiver as the default fallback. A better version is: "If you cannot do it, please contact the backup person and update the group." Of course, this requires a backup to exist where possible. The principle is that the person accepting a task should carry some responsibility for what happens if their plan changes.

The caregiver should avoid asking several people the same vague question at once: "Can anyone help with transport?" In many groups, this produces silence because each person assumes someone else will answer. It also allows responsibility to dissolve into the crowd. Direct requests are stronger. "Sam, can you take the Tuesday appointment?" "Rina, can you cover the Friday prescription?" "James, can you do the Sunday call?" Naming a person may feel more exposed, but it prevents group vagueness.

A group message can still be useful when tasks are clearly assigned. "There are three tasks this week: Tuesday transport, Friday prescription, and Sunday visit. Please choose one by tonight, or I will assign based on availability." This is more structured than a general plea. The caregiver should use judgement; not every family will respond well to this level of directness. But if vague group appeals have failed repeatedly, the problem may be the vagueness, not the people's alleged inability to help.

Some requests should be made in writing. Written requests are useful for tasks with details, deadlines, addresses, medication names, appointment times, or multiple steps. They reduce memory errors and stop the caregiver from having to repeat instructions. A written request also gives the helper something to refer back to. This is particularly helpful when the caregiver is tired of being the source of every detail.

A written request might say: "Could you please collect the prescription from the pharmacy on Friday before 5 p.m.? The prescription is for Mum. Bring her date of birth if asked. Please check there are two items in the bag before leaving. Text the group when it is dropped off." This may feel overly detailed, but if those details prevent a mistake, they reduce work later. The caregiver can adjust the level of detail according to the helper's experience.

For emotionally sensitive tasks, the request should include relational guidance. If someone is visiting a person who becomes anxious, the helper may need to know not to discuss certain topics, not to promise changes, not to argue about food, or not to raise future care plans without preparation. This is not controlling. It is protecting the care recipient and the caregiver from avoidable fallout.

For example: "Can you visit on Saturday for an hour? Please keep it to companionship and a cup of tea. Do not discuss moving house or care changes, as that tends to make her anxious afterwards." This kind of instruction can prevent a well-meaning visit from creating emotional work for the caregiver later. Helpers often need to understand not only what to do, but what not to disturb.

The caregiver should also be honest about the task's emotional difficulty. If a helper is likely to encounter resistance, confusion, sadness, or anger, they should know enough to prepare. A request that hides the difficulty may secure a yes but produce a failed handoff. "Can you help Dad with his bills?" may sound simple. "Can you sit with Dad while he opens the bills? He may become embarrassed and irritable, so keep it calm and only sort the urgent letters" is more realistic. The helper can then decide whether they are suited to the task.

There is a balance, however. Overdescribing difficulty can scare people away. The caregiver should provide enough information to support success, not so much that the task sounds impossible. A useful standard is: what would I need to know if I were doing this for the first time? That question keeps instructions practical rather than emotionally overloaded.

Some people will say no. This is not automatically failure. A clear no gives the caregiver accurate information about the support network. It may be disappointing, but it is better than an unreliable yes. The caregiver can respond simply: "Thank you for letting me know." If appropriate, they can ask, "Is there a smaller task you could take on?" Or: "Would another time work?" But they should not turn every no into a persuasion campaign. Chasing unwilling helpers can consume more energy than it saves.

Some people will say yes and then fail. This, too, is information. The caregiver should address it clearly rather than quietly absorbing the task. "You agreed to collect the prescription on Friday, and it was not done. Can you still own this task, or do we need to move it?" This sentence is direct without being dramatic. If the person makes excuses but the pattern continues, the caregiver should reassign the task or create a backup. Hope should not keep an unreliable person in a high-risk role.

The caregiver may feel guilty making precise requests because precision exposes other people's choices. A vague plea allows others to remain comforted by their own goodwill. A precise request requires them to decide. They may have to admit they cannot help, will not help, or can only help in a small way. That discomfort can feel harsh, but it is necessary. Care cannot be shared on imagined generosity. It must be shared through actual commitments.

A request people can say yes to also protects the helper. It prevents them from accidentally agreeing to more than they can manage. It allows them to contribute without fear of being swallowed by the whole care situation. Many people avoid helping because they sense that once they step in, the need may become endless. A bounded request reassures them: this is the task, this is the time, this is the frequency, this is where it ends.

This is why modest requests often work better than sweeping ones. "Can you take over Sunday evenings forever?" may be too much. "Can you visit for one hour this Sunday?" is easier. Once trust is built, a recurring role may become possible. The caregiver should not mistake a small yes for insignificance. Small reliable yeses are the foundation of a functioning support network.

The caregiver should express appreciation for real follow-through, but not in a way that makes help seem heroic for being minimal. "Thank you for collecting the prescription; that helped" is enough. Overpraise can be understandable when the caregiver is desperate for support, but it may also reinforce the idea that ordinary shared responsibility is extraordinary generosity. Gratitude is healthy. Grovelling is not required.

The caregiver should also avoid rescuing helpers from their own responsibility. If a helper asks a question they can answer from the information provided, it may be tempting to respond immediately. But if the caregiver remains instantly available for every minor uncertainty, the handoff does not mature. A better response may be: "The details are in the message I sent." Or: "Please check the folder." Or: "Use the contact number on the appointment letter." This encourages helpers to use the system rather than the caregiver as the system.

Of course, support should be given when a helper genuinely needs clarification, especially early on or for higher-risk tasks. The point is not to be unhelpful. The point is to avoid turning delegation into constant live supervision. If a task requires repeated questions every time, the instructions may need improving, the task may need simplifying, or the helper may not be the right fit.

Requests should be reviewed after they are tried. Did the helper understand? Did the task get done? Did it reduce the caregiver's load? Did it unsettle the person receiving care? Was the timing realistic? Were the instructions clear? Did the helper need too much chasing? Did the task need a backup? This review should not be treated as failure. It is how support becomes reliable. The first version of a request may need adjustment.

For example, a caregiver may ask a sibling to visit for two hours, only to discover that the visit is too long and leads to emotional agitation afterwards. A better request may be a shorter visit with a defined activity. Another helper may manage shopping well but not communicate when it is done, leaving the caregiver anxious. The request can be adjusted: "Please send a photo of the receipt and message when the shopping is in the kitchen." Small refinements prevent resentment from returning.

The caregiver should also protect their own boundaries when making requests. Asking for help should not become another occasion for over-explaining, apologising, or accepting criticism. If someone responds with advice rather than commitment, the caregiver can say, "I am not asking for advice right now. I am asking whether you can take this task." If someone minimises the workload, the caregiver can say, "You may see it differently. The request is still this." If someone turns the conversation into a debate, the caregiver can say, "I need a yes or no by tomorrow."

This clarity may feel uncomfortable at first, especially for caregivers accustomed to softening every need. But unclear requests have a cost. They produce unclear help. They leave the caregiver chasing, interpreting, and correcting. They allow others to feel involved without carrying responsibility. Precision is not rudeness. It is a refusal to let support remain theatrical.

A strong request also includes what the caregiver will not do. For example: "Can you handle the appointment transport? I will send the appointment details, but I will not be available during work to answer routine questions." Or: "Can you manage the bill payment? I can show you where the documents are, but I cannot keep reminding you." This prevents the hidden work from remaining with the caregiver. The task should move, not merely acquire an assistant.

The caregiver should be especially clear when asking for respite. Many people misunderstand respite as optional leisure rather than essential recovery. A vague request such as "I need a break" may be met with sympathy but no cover. A clear request is: "Can you stay with Dad from 1 p.m. to 4 p.m. on Saturday so I can be completely unavailable during that time?" The words "completely unavailable" matter if the caregiver is not to spend the break answering questions, checking messages, and remaining mentally on call.

Respite requests should include what the helper should do if something minor arises. Otherwise, the caregiver's break becomes a remote management shift. "If he asks about dinner, the meal is in the fridge. If he asks when I am back, tell him 4 p.m. If something non-urgent comes up, write it down for me. Call only if there is a safety concern." This kind of instruction protects the break from being pierced by every ordinary question.

Caregivers should also ask for help before collapse where possible. Requests made at the point of breakdown may be urgent, emotional, and harder to organise. Earlier requests can be calmer and more specific. "I need someone to take over pharmacy collection from next month" is easier to plan than "I cannot do this anymore" after the medication has nearly run out. Prevention applies to support as much as to care tasks.

There may be times when the caregiver needs to make the same request to several people before someone says yes. This can feel humiliating. It can also feel enraging, especially when the need is obvious. The caregiver should remember that asking clearly is not begging. It is an attempt to build a care system around reality. A refusal may reveal limits in the network, but it does not diminish the legitimacy of the request.

When help is accepted, the caregiver should capture the agreement in writing. "Thank you. Just confirming: you will take Mum to the Tuesday 10 a.m. appointment once a month, starting next week. I will send the details by Sunday. Please let us know by Monday morning if you cannot make it." This follow-up prevents the request from becoming a memory contest. It also establishes the standard for future communication.

The deeper purpose of making requests people can say yes to is not merely efficiency. It is dignity. The caregiver's dignity is protected because they stop pleading in vague distress and begin naming real needs. The helper's dignity is protected because they receive a clear opportunity to contribute within their capacity. The person receiving care is protected because support becomes more reliable and less dependent on one exhausted person's improvisation.

A vague request asks others to enter the fog and somehow know what to carry.

A clear request places one handle on one part of the load and says, "Can you take this?"

Designing Handoffs and Backups

Help only becomes helpful when the task actually leaves the caregiver's hands. This sounds obvious, yet it is where many attempts to share care fail. Someone offers to step in, the caregiver gratefully agrees, and then the hidden work begins. The caregiver explains the routine, answers questions, sends reminders, worries about whether the task has been done, checks the outcome, corrects errors, soothes the person receiving care, and quietly repairs anything that went wrong. On paper, the task was shared. In reality, the caregiver became the supervisor of the task, and sometimes the cleaner-up afterwards.

This is why handoffs matter. A handoff is not simply telling someone else what to do. It is the transfer of a defined responsibility with enough information, authority, and clarity for the other person to carry it without constant dependence on the main caregiver. A poor handoff moves only the visible action. A good handoff moves the mental load as well. The difference is enormous. If someone collects a prescription but the caregiver still has to remember the date, remind the helper, check the collection, confirm the medicine, and update the list, the caregiver has not handed off the task. They have merely outsourced one errand.

Caregivers often accept poor handoffs because they are desperate for relief and reluctant to seem ungrateful. When someone finally helps, it can feel rude to be precise. The caregiver may avoid giving instructions because they do not want to sound controlling. They may say, "Do not worry, it is simple," even when the task carries details that matter. They may believe that a willing helper should be able to work it out. Then, when the helper misses something, the caregiver feels frustrated, the helper feels criticised, and the person receiving care may experience the consequences. Everyone ends up more tense than before.

A well-designed handoff prevents this. It treats care tasks as real work with real standards. Not complicated for the sake of complication, but clear enough that another person can succeed. The task should have a beginning, an end, a purpose, a standard, and a way to report completion. If the helper is driving to an appointment, they need the time, location, parking or access details where relevant, mobility needs, what to bring, whether to wait, whether notes should be taken, and who should be updated afterwards. If they are managing groceries, they need the list, preferred alternatives, payment arrangement, delivery place, and what counts as complete. If they are making a check-in call, they need to know what to ask, what to ignore, what to record, and what should be escalated.

This does not mean every task needs a manual. Overdesign can become its own burden. The aim is the minimum useful structure. Low-risk tasks need light instructions. Higher-risk tasks need more care. Putting the bins out may require little more than the day and location. Medication collection may require clear timing, pharmacy details, checks, and a backup if there is a problem. Appointment support may require more context than a social visit. The seriousness of the handoff should match the consequence of failure.

A useful handoff begins with one plain question: what would this person need to know to complete the task without coming back to me for ordinary decisions? The answer will usually reveal what has been living invisibly in the caregiver's head. The pharmacy closes early on Fridays. The person receiving care becomes anxious if appointment details are discussed too far in advance. The front door key sticks. The preferred soup is the plain one, not the spicy one. The doctor's letters are kept in the blue folder. The person may say they have taken their tablets when they has only moved the box. These details may seem small, but small details often determine whether help reduces strain or creates more of it.

The handoff should also define the helper's authority. This is often missed. Can the helper make substitutions at the shop? Can they rearrange an appointment if the time is unsuitable? Can they speak to a receptionist? Can they spend up to a certain amount? Can they decide whether a concern can wait, or must they always contact the caregiver? When authority is unclear, helpers either over-contact the caregiver for every small decision or make decisions that cause problems later. Both outcomes keep the caregiver tethered to the task.

A clear handoff might say, "If the exact meals are unavailable, choose similar plain options and keep within the agreed amount." Or: "If the appointment time changes, message the shared group before confirming." Or: "If the pharmacy says an item is missing, ask when it will be ready and update the group; do not leave it for me to chase unless it becomes urgent." Such statements may feel ordinary, but they turn the helper from a messenger into a responsible participant.

Completion must be defined. In caregiving, a task is often not complete when the visible action ends. A prescription collection is not complete until the medicine is checked and delivered to the correct place. An appointment trip is not complete until the person is safely home and any important information is passed on. A grocery run is not complete until perishables are put away and missing items are noted. A paperwork task is not complete until the form is submitted, copied where needed, and the next step is known. Without a completion standard, the caregiver may remain uncertain and anxious.

This is where a simple completion message is powerful. "Prescription collected and placed on the kitchen table." "Mum is home from the appointment; doctor advised a follow-up call next week." "Shopping done; milk was unavailable, so I bought the usual alternative." "Bill paid; confirmation saved in the folder." These messages stop the caregiver from having to chase, guess, or mentally hold the task open. A task that remains open in the mind is still part of the caregiver's load.

Checklists can support handoffs, especially for repeated tasks. The word checklist may sound formal, but in care it can be a quiet act of mercy. A checklist prevents the caregiver from re-explaining the same details. It prevents the helper from relying on memory. It makes the standard visible. It also reduces the emotional sting of correction, because the issue becomes "follow the list" rather than "you did it wrong". The caregiver is not being fussy. They are building a way for someone else to help without needing the caregiver as a live instruction service.

A checklist should be short enough to use. A long, anxious document may overwhelm helpers and reinforce the belief that only the main caregiver can manage. The best checklists are plain, task-specific, and practical. For an appointment, the list might include time, transport, documents, mobility aids, questions to ask, note-taking, and update afterwards. For a visit, it might include checking food, heating, post, mood, and any urgent concerns. For a meal drop-off, it might include storage, heating instructions, dietary needs, and what to do if the person refuses food. The checklist should remove uncertainty, not create a new administrative burden.

Information packets can be useful for bigger handoffs. These do not need to be elaborate folders filled with everything ever known about the care situation. They should contain the essentials: key contacts, medication list, appointment information, routines, preferences, access instructions, emergency guidance, and any important risks. The goal is not to make every helper an expert. The goal is to prevent the entire care arrangement from depending on the main caregiver's memory.

The caregiver should be careful with privacy. Helpers need information relevant to their task, not unrestricted access to sensitive details. A neighbour collecting groceries does not need a full medical history. A sibling handling bills may need financial information that a casual visitor does not. A respite helper may need more detail about routines and safety. Good handoffs respect both usefulness and dignity. The right information goes to the right person for the right purpose.

Handoffs should be designed with the person receiving care in mind. A helper may understand the task, but the person receiving care may feel anxious, embarrassed, resistant, or unsettled by someone else doing what the main caregiver usually does. A transfer that looks efficient to the family may feel like loss of control to the care recipient. This does not mean the handoff should be abandoned. It means the transition may need preparation. The person may need to know who is coming, when, for what purpose, and what will stay the same. Familiarity reduces friction.

Sometimes the caregiver has to avoid apologising for the handoff. "I am so sorry, but Sam will have to take you this time" can make the change sound like a failure or rejection. A steadier phrasing is: "Sam is taking you to the appointment on Tuesday. I have given him the details, and he will bring you home afterwards." The tone communicates confidence. The person receiving care may still prefer the main caregiver, but the arrangement is presented as normal support, not a regrettable downgrade.

The caregiver also needs to tolerate imperfect help. This is difficult. Helpers may not do things exactly as the caregiver would. They may take a different route, use different words, buy a different brand, or handle a minor issue in a less polished way. If the outcome is safe, respectful, and good enough, the caregiver may need to let it stand. Otherwise, every handoff becomes impossible because the standard is not care, but replication of the caregiver. The aim is not identical performance. The aim is reliable support.

That said, "good enough" does not mean careless. Some standards matter. Medication must be handled accurately. Safety concerns must be taken seriously. Privacy must be respected. The person receiving care should not be belittled, confused by unnecessary changes, or left without essential follow-up. The caregiver should distinguish between personal preference and necessary standard. Correct the necessary. Release the merely different.

A handoff should include a feedback loop. After the task is done, especially the first time, the caregiver may ask: What worked? What was unclear? What did the helper need that they did not have? Was the person receiving care settled? Did the task actually reduce the caregiver's load? Did anything come back to the caregiver that should have stayed with the helper? This is not an interrogation. It is maintenance. A care system improves by learning from use.

However, the feedback loop should not become the caregiver's permanent monitoring role. Early support may require more checking. Over time, a recurring task should need less. If the caregiver has to keep inspecting every detail indefinitely, the task may not be properly transferred. Either the helper needs better instructions, the task needs simplifying, another helper is needed, or the caregiver must accept that this person is not reliable for that role.

Backups are the other half of sustainable handoffs. Without backups, every delegated task remains fragile. A helper may become ill, forget, face work pressure, have transport problems, or cancel at the last moment. If the main caregiver is always the automatic fallback, the load has not truly been shared. It has been placed on a temporary shelf, with the caregiver standing underneath ready to catch it.

A backup plan answers the question: what happens when the first plan fails? For transport, who is the second driver or alternative service? For medication collection, what happens if the helper cannot go? For visits, who should be informed if the visit is cancelled? For meals, what is the emergency food option? For paperwork, what is the deadline by which a missed task must be escalated? For a check-in call, what should happen if the person does not answer? Backups are not pessimism. They are respect for ordinary life.

The caregiver should insist that helpers participate in backup thinking. If someone accepts a recurring task, they should know what to do if they cannot complete it. "Please tell the group by Thursday if you cannot do the Friday prescription collection" is better than "Let me know and I will sort it." The second sentence quietly returns responsibility to the caregiver. The first creates shared accountability. Where possible, the helper who cancels should activate the backup, not simply drop the task back into the caregiver's lap.

There will be cases where the caregiver remains the only safe backup for a certain task. That may be reality for now. But it should be named honestly, not hidden. If every backup route leads back to the caregiver, the support system is still weak. Naming this allows the caregiver to make decisions with open eyes. They may choose to accept the risk temporarily, seek another helper, simplify the task, reduce the frequency, or escalate the need for more support. What they should not do is pretend the task has been fully shared when it has not.

Backups should be proportionate. A low-risk task may need a loose backup. If a social visit is missed, perhaps it can be rearranged. If a prescription collection fails, the backup needs to be clearer. If a safety check is missed, the response must be defined. Not every task needs the same level of contingency. The care arrangement becomes overwhelming when everything is treated as equally critical. The purpose of backup planning is to reduce panic, not create a new universe of anxiety.

One of the most useful tools is a simple escalation rule. This tells helpers when to act, when to wait, and when to contact someone else. For example: "If she does not answer the phone, try once more after ten minutes. If there is still no answer and you are concerned, call the neighbour. If there is an immediate safety concern, use the emergency route." Or: "If the prescription is incomplete, ask when it will be ready and post the update in the group. If it cannot be ready before the current supply runs out, contact me and the backup collector." These rules prevent helpers from either panicking too soon or delaying too long.

Escalation rules also reduce the caregiver's fear of letting go. Many caregivers hold tasks tightly because they fear others will not know when something matters. Clear rules make the invisible judgement visible. The caregiver does not have to remain constantly available for every uncertainty. The helper has a path.

For recurring handoffs, rhythm matters. A task done at the same time, in the same way, by the same person where possible, is easier to remember and easier for the care recipient to accept. Irregular help may still be valuable, but stable routines reduce the management burden. "Every Friday before 4 p.m." is better than "whenever you can." "First Sunday of each month" is better than "occasionally." Predictability turns help from a favour into infrastructure.

The caregiver should be wary of help that depends entirely on enthusiasm. Enthusiasm is pleasant, but it can fade. A person may offer grand help in an emotional moment and then disappear when the routine begins. A smaller commitment made clearly is usually more valuable than a dramatic promise made under guilt. A sustainable handoff is not built on intensity. It is built on repeatability.

Some helpers will resist structure. They may say, "Just tell me what needs doing," but dislike specific instructions. They may offer help but become irritated when asked for confirmation. They may want appreciation without accountability. This kind of help may still have a place, but it should be assigned carefully. A person who resists clarity is not suitable for high-risk or time-sensitive tasks. The caregiver can say, "For this task, I need someone who can confirm and follow the steps. If that does not suit you, I can ask you for something else."

This is not rejection. It is role matching. Not every helper belongs in every role.

The caregiver should also consider emotional backups. What happens if the person receiving care becomes distressed during a helper visit? What should the helper say if they are asked why the main caregiver is not there? What if the person becomes angry, tearful, or refuses the task? Without guidance, the helper may either overreact, make promises, call the caregiver immediately, or leave the person more unsettled. A few prepared phrases can help: "She will call you at the usual time." "I am here to take you today." "Let us do this one step at a time." "I cannot change the plan, but I can help with this task."

Emotional guidance is especially important when the person receiving care uses pressure to pull the main caregiver back in. A helper may hear, "I only want her," or "He always does this for me," or "Call her now." The helper should know the boundary: when to contact the caregiver and when to reassure without calling. Otherwise, every delegated task can become a route back to the caregiver's phone.

A well-designed handoff also protects the helper from being overwhelmed. Helpers who are given vague, expanding tasks may withdraw. A person who agrees to visit may find themselves expected to clean, cook, manage paperwork, and handle emotional distress. If they did not agree to that, they may avoid future involvement. Clear task boundaries help helpers remain willing. They know what they are saying yes to and where it ends.

This is one reason caregivers should avoid the temptation to load too much onto a new helper at once. Start with a contained task. Let the helper succeed. Let the person receiving care adjust. Let the caregiver test whether the handoff truly reduces load. Then consider expansion if appropriate. Sustainable support is often built through gradual trust rather than sudden transfer.

The caregiver may need to accept a transition period. At first, handing off may feel like more work. Instructions need writing. Helpers need orientation. The person receiving care may resist. Mistakes may be corrected. This can make the caregiver think, "It is easier to do it myself." Sometimes that is true in the short term. But if the task is recurring, the short-term effort of designing the handoff may prevent months of future overload. The question is not whether it is easier today. The question is whether it will reduce dependence over time.

Still, not every task is worth handing off. Some tasks are so sensitive, rare, or relationship-specific that transferring them creates more strain than relief. Others may be better simplified or stopped rather than delegated. A caregiver should ask: does this task need doing? Does it need doing by me? Does it need doing in this way? Could it be reduced, automated, batched, or reassigned? Handoffs are one tool, not the only tool.

When a handoff fails, the caregiver should avoid turning immediately to blame. Failure may mean the instructions were unclear, the task was mismatched, the helper overestimated their capacity, the person receiving care resisted, the backup was weak, or the standard was too complicated. A calm review is more useful than a burst of resentment. The caregiver can say, "This did not work as planned. Let us identify what failed." That sentence keeps the focus on design.

If the same helper repeatedly fails despite clarity, the conclusion may be simple: they are not reliable for that task. This can be disappointing, especially if the person is a close relative who "should" be able to help. But care systems must be built on evidence. An unreliable helper in a crucial role creates more stress than no helper, because the caregiver is left both hoping and preparing to rescue. Move the person to a lower-risk task if possible, or stop relying on them for that category.

Reliable systems prevent resentment from returning because they reduce the number of hidden disappointments. Resentment often grows when the caregiver believes a task has been shared but still carries the anxiety, reminders, and consequences. A proper handoff makes ownership visible. A backup plan makes failure less frightening. Completion messages close the mental loop. Checklists reduce repeated explanation. Standards prevent arguments about what "done" means. Together, these structures turn help from a favour into a functioning part of care.

The caregiver should not underestimate the emotional change required to let others help. If they have been the central person for a long time, letting go may feel like risk. They may worry that others will not do it properly, that the care recipient will be upset, that they will be judged for stepping back, or that a mistake will prove they should have kept the task. These fears may be understandable. But the alternative is a care system that can only function when one person remains endlessly available. That is not safety. It is fragility wearing the costume of control.

A handoff is therefore both practical and psychological. It asks the caregiver to make knowledge shareable. It asks helpers to accept responsibility rather than merely offer goodwill. It asks the person receiving care to adapt, where possible, to a broader circle of support. It asks the care system to stop depending on one person's private competence as the hidden engine.

The best handoffs are calm, specific, and unglamorous. They do not need dramatic family speeches. They need clear tasks, clear information, clear standards, clear completion, and clear backups. The caregiver should be able to step away from the task without holding it mentally the whole time. That is the test.

If the caregiver still has to remember it, chase it, check it, and rescue it, the handoff is unfinished.

If the helper knows what to do, does it, communicates completion, and knows what happens if the plan fails, the care load has genuinely begun to move.

Chapter 7
Routines That Reduce Crisis Care

How can something as small as a repeated check-in, a fixed call time, or a familiar meal reduce the emotional weight of caregiving? The answer seems too modest at first. When the care load feels heavy, caregivers often look for large solutions: more people, more time, more certainty, more control. Yet much of the daily strain comes not only from the size of the needs, but from the constant need to decide, remember, improvise, and respond as though every ordinary task has become freshly urgent.

Crisis care thrives where there is no rhythm. The morning begins without a clear sequence, so medication, breakfast, washing, mood, transport, and messages collide. Appointments appear as isolated events rather than part of a weekly pattern, so every one requires a new burst of organisation. Supplies run low because no one checks them until they are needed. Paperwork waits in a pile until a deadline gives it teeth. Family communication arrives in scattered messages, each one asking the caregiver to stop, think, answer, reassure, correct, or coordinate. Nothing may be catastrophic on its own, but the day becomes a series of small alarms.

The paradox is that routines can feel restrictive while actually creating freedom. A caregiver may resist them because life already feels controlled by care, and another structure sounds like another demand. But a good routine is not a cage. It is a handrail. It reduces the number of decisions that have to be made under pressure. It gives the person receiving care a more predictable world. It gives helpers a clearer way to step in. It gives the caregiver fewer moments of wondering, "What am I forgetting?" Stability does not come from perfect control. It comes from fewer avoidable surprises.

The central tension is between care that is constantly invented in the moment and care that has enough repeated structure to hold under strain. Improvisation will always be part of caregiving. People have difficult days. Bodies change. Feelings rise. Plans fail. Yet when everything is improvised, the caregiver becomes the only system. Their memory becomes the calendar. Their attention becomes the warning light. Their availability becomes the backup plan. Their nervous system becomes the place where all unfinished tasks wait.

This matters because repeated decision-making is its own form of depletion. Choosing what to do, when to do it, how to phrase it, whether to answer now, whether something can wait, who needs updating, what must be checked, and what should be postponed consumes energy that many caregivers do not have to spare. A routine removes some of that demand. It does not make care easy, but it makes parts of care less negotiable, less dramatic, and less dependent on the caregiver's mood or stamina on a particular day.

There is also a relational cost when routines are missing. The person receiving care may become more anxious because they do not know when contact will come, what will happen next, or who is responsible for what. Relatives may become more critical because they see gaps but not the workload behind them. Helpers may hesitate because they do not know the standard. The caregiver may become sharper because every interruption feels like an invasion. A routine can soften this atmosphere. It turns some moments from personal negotiations into known arrangements.

The work begins with daily stability: small repeatable actions that prevent ordinary care from spiralling into emergency, including check-ins, medication cues, meal defaults, and protected pauses. The rhythm then widens into weekly coordination, where appointments, supplies, communication, and planning are gathered into a predictable pattern instead of scattered across the caregiver's attention. Beneath both sits the practical discipline of information: keeping essential details clear enough that panic does not become the filing system and the caregiver's memory is not the only place the care plan exists.

The standard is not an ideal schedule. Ideal schedules often collapse because they are designed for calm people, cooperative days, and uninterrupted time. Caregiving requires something sturdier and less impressive: the minimum viable routine. A morning pattern that still works when everyone is tired. A meal option that can be repeated without debate. A weekly planning habit short enough to survive resistance. A paperwork system simple enough to use when the caregiver is already worn thin. The best routine is not the one that looks most organised; it is the one that still functions on a bad day.

The question, then, is not how to turn caregiving into a perfectly ordered life. That would be fantasy. The sharper question is where the same avoidable crises keep appearing because no repeatable structure has been allowed to take root. Which part of the day is still being reinvented every time it arrives?

Daily Stability Routines That Work

Daily caregiving can become unstable not because every day contains a major crisis, but because too many ordinary tasks are left to chance. A tablet is remembered only when someone mentions it. Breakfast depends on mood, timing, appetite, and whatever happens to be in the fridge. A morning call drifts later because work intrudes. A visit begins without a plan and ends with new worries scattered through the caregiver's mind. None of this looks dramatic. Yet this is often where crisis care is born: in repeated small uncertainties that quietly gather force.

A daily stability routine is not an attempt to make life rigid. It is a way of giving the day a few reliable anchors. Caregiving already contains enough unpredictability: pain, confusion, fatigue, resistance, mood changes, appointments, messages, and sudden practical problems. A routine does not remove these. It gives both the caregiver and the person receiving care a more predictable way to meet them. Without a routine, every need can feel new. With a routine, some parts of care become familiar enough that they no longer require negotiation each time.

The best routines are modest. This is where many caregivers go wrong. They imagine a complete schedule: perfect wake-up time, ideal meals, planned exercise, medication taken without resistance, calm communication, tidy rooms, restful breaks, and a peaceful evening. It looks sensible on paper and collapses by Wednesday. Then the caregiver feels defeated and concludes that routines do not work. The problem is not routine itself. The problem is designing for an imaginary day instead of the day that actually exists.

A routine that survives a bad day is more valuable than a beautiful plan that depends on everyone being rested, cooperative, and uninterrupted. Caregiving routines must be built for friction. They need to work when the person receiving care is irritable, when the caregiver is tired, when the appointment runs late, when the weather is poor, when a helper cancels, when the morning begins badly, or when a small problem interrupts the expected sequence. The routine should not be so delicate that one disruption destroys it.

This is why the starting point is the minimum viable routine. Not the best possible routine. Not the most complete routine. The smallest repeatable pattern that reduces avoidable stress. A minimum viable routine might be one morning check-in at the same time each day. It might be a visible medication cue. It might be three default lunches that remove daily decision-making. It might be a five-minute evening reset. It might be a protected pause for the caregiver after a difficult call. The routine begins where repetition can realistically hold.

Daily stability depends less on ambition than on repetition. A small action repeated consistently teaches the care system what to expect. The person receiving care begins to know when contact will come. The caregiver begins to know when certain checks happen. Helpers can be told the pattern. Problems become easier to spot because there is a normal rhythm against which change becomes visible. A routine is not merely a task; it is a way of reducing uncertainty.

Morning routines are often the first place to look because mornings set the emotional temperature of the day. A chaotic morning can leave everyone unsettled for hours. The person receiving care may wake anxious, stiff, confused, hungry, or unsure what is happening. The caregiver may already be watching the clock, thinking about work, transport, medication, breakfast, washing, messages, and whether another family member will interfere with advice but not help. Without structure, the morning becomes a collision of needs.

A morning check-in should be simple enough to repeat. It might ask the same few questions: How did you sleep? Have you taken your morning tablets? Have you eaten or planned breakfast? Is there pain, dizziness, distress, or anything unusual? What is happening today? The purpose is not to conduct a full assessment every morning. The purpose is to create a predictable point of contact where essential information is gathered before the day begins to unravel.

The check-in should also have a boundary. A morning call that turns into an open-ended emotional session may exhaust the caregiver before the day has started. A good check-in has a clear shape: a time, a purpose, and a natural ending. "I will call at 9 to check tablets, breakfast, and today's plan" is different from "Call me whenever you need me." The first creates stability. The second creates constant alert.

Medication routines are another key stability point because missed, delayed, duplicated, or confused medicines can quickly create stress. The caregiver should avoid relying solely on memory, especially when several people are involved. A cue can be physical, visual, or linked to an existing habit. Tablets might be associated with breakfast, a visible chart, a labelled organiser, a phone alarm, or a written tick-off sheet, depending on the person's capacity and the safety needs involved. The exact tool matters less than the principle: the routine should not depend entirely on someone remembering perfectly at the right moment.

Medication cues also reduce repeated questioning. Instead of the caregiver asking anxiously, "Did you take them?" and the person receiving care feeling monitored or accused, the cue becomes part of the environment. A ticked chart, an empty section in a tablet organiser, or a repeated habit can lower the emotional charge. The task becomes less about trust and more about routine. That shift can protect dignity as well as safety.

Meal routines can reduce another daily spiral. Food can become surprisingly difficult in caregiving because it touches appetite, health, independence, memory, taste, money, shopping, cooking ability, loneliness, and control. Asking "What do you want to eat?" every day may seem respectful, but for some care situations it creates too much decision-making. The person may become overwhelmed, refuse everything, choose impractically, or say they are not hungry when the real issue is fatigue, confusion, low mood, or lack of easy options.

Meal defaults are not about removing choice. They are about reducing repeated negotiation. A few reliable breakfasts, lunches, or dinners can make the day easier. The caregiver might know that soup and toast works when appetite is low, that porridge is accepted in the morning, that a particular ready meal is tolerated, that sandwiches are easiest after appointments, or that the person eats better when the choice is between two options rather than six. A default meal is a fallback, not a prison. It says, "When the day is difficult, we already know what can happen next."

This kind of routine also helps helpers. If another person is covering lunch, they should not have to discover the entire food history from scratch. A short note with acceptable meals, dislikes, allergies or dietary needs where relevant, heating instructions, and what to do if food is refused can prevent a simple task from becoming complicated. The caregiver should not remain the only person who knows what "something easy" actually means.

Daily routines should include the caregiver's rest, not as an afterthought but as part of the care structure. This is where many care plans are dishonest. They contain medication times, appointment times, meal times, and visit times, but no recovery time for the person holding it all together. The caregiver is expected to absorb the emotional and practical impact of care, then immediately return to work, family, errands, or another task. That may be possible occasionally. It is not stable as a daily pattern.

A rest break does not have to be long to be real. Ten minutes after a difficult call. A quiet cup of tea after a visit before driving home. A walk around the block before re-entering the household. A no-message period after an appointment. A fixed evening cut-off for non-urgent care matters. The break should be protected enough that the caregiver's body begins to recognise it as recovery, not merely a pause before the next interruption.

The difficulty is that caregivers often treat rest as negotiable. If someone calls, the break disappears. If a relative sends a message, the break is interrupted. If guilt rises, the break is abandoned. A rest routine must therefore have a boundary around it. "I will respond after 6." "I am unavailable for the next half-hour." "I do not take non-urgent calls during this time." Without such limits, rest becomes theoretical. It exists only until someone else wants something.

Daily routines should be built around existing habits wherever possible. A routine is more likely to survive when it attaches to something already happening. Medication after brushing teeth. A check-in after breakfast. A supply note written after lunch. A short walk after a visit. A paperwork basket checked after opening the post. A person is more likely to repeat a routine when it does not require the day to be completely redesigned around it. The aim is to make the desired action easier to remember than to forget.

The routine must also respect the person receiving care. A daily structure that feels imposed may create resistance, especially if the person is already grieving lost independence. Where possible, routines should be explained as supports, not controls. "This helps us avoid last-minute stress." "This means you do not have to keep everything in your head." "This helps me know what has been done without asking you repeatedly." "This makes it easier for someone else to help if I am not here." The language matters because dignity matters.

Resistance should not automatically defeat the routine, but it should inform the design. If the person refuses a chart because it feels childish, perhaps a discreet notebook is better. If they dislike being asked questions in the morning, perhaps the check-in begins with ordinary conversation and moves gently to practical points. If too many reminders cause irritation, fewer, clearer cues may work better. A routine that ignores the person's temperament will require constant enforcement. A routine that fits them well has a better chance of becoming normal.

The caregiver should also avoid building routines that depend entirely on their presence. If the routine only works when the main caregiver performs every step, it may reduce some daily chaos but deepen dependence. A better routine is shareable. Another helper should be able to understand it. The person receiving care may be able to participate in part of it. The steps should be visible enough that the caregiver is not always the interpreter. A routine locked inside one person's memory is not yet a system.

This is why written cues can be helpful. A short morning note. A small medication checklist. A simple meal list. A visible weekly pattern. A folder with current details. These are not signs that the family has become cold or bureaucratic. They are signs that the caregiver is no longer willing to let care depend entirely on their private mental load. Written cues allow repetition to continue even when the caregiver is tired or absent.

The routine should be tested against the bad-day question: what happens when this goes wrong? If the person misses the morning check-in, what is the next step? If tablets are not taken, who needs to know? If the default meal is refused, what is the fallback? If the caregiver cannot make the usual call, who covers it or how is the person informed? A routine without a fallback can become another source of panic. A routine with a simple backup becomes sturdier.

Backups do not need to be complicated. If the morning call is missed, a text may be sent. If there is no reply, a neighbour or helper may check in, depending on the level of risk. If the preferred lunch is unavailable, the second default is used. If a rest break is interrupted by a non-urgent matter, it is resumed rather than abandoned. The purpose is to prevent one disruption from destroying the entire day.

Daily stability also requires reducing unnecessary choice. Modern life often treats choice as freedom, but in caregiving too much choice can become strain. What should be eaten? When should the call happen? Which task matters first? Who should be updated? Should the caregiver go now or later? Should the person receiving care bathe today or tomorrow? Which errand can wait? Every question consumes energy. A routine answers some questions in advance.

This does not mean life becomes inflexible. It means ordinary decisions do not have to be remade every day. The check-in happens at the usual time unless there is a reason to change it. Meals come from the default list when energy is low. Medication follows the cue. Non-urgent messages wait until the communication window. The caregiver takes the rest break after the visit. Predictability creates room for real flexibility because the whole system is not already exhausted by avoidable decisions.

A daily routine should be visible but not oppressive. Too many reminders, alarms, notes, and instructions can make life feel dominated by care. The caregiver may become more anxious, not less. The person receiving care may feel managed rather than supported. The best daily routines are often almost quiet. They sit beneath the day, reducing friction without drawing constant attention to themselves. They create a familiar path rather than a strict regime.

The caregiver should introduce one routine at a time where possible. Trying to add morning check-ins, meal planning, medication charts, exercise, paperwork review, rest breaks, and family updates all at once can overwhelm everyone. Start with the routine that addresses the most repeated daily pressure. Let it settle. Then adjust or add another. Stability is not built through a grand launch. It is built by repeating one useful thing until it becomes ordinary.

Choosing the first routine should be guided by safety, frequency, and emotional cost. If medication uncertainty creates risk and anxiety every day, begin there. If mornings regularly unravel, begin with the morning sequence. If meals are a daily battleground, begin with defaults. If the caregiver is emotionally depleted after every visit, begin with a recovery routine. The first routine should relieve a real pressure, not merely make the care plan look more organised.

It is also important to measure whether the routine works. A routine that looks good but increases conflict needs revision. A check-in that always turns into an hour-long conversation may need a clearer ending. A meal plan that is repeatedly refused may be too ambitious or mismatched to appetite. A medication chart that no one uses may be in the wrong place or too complicated. A rest break that is always interrupted may need stronger boundaries. The question is not, "Did we follow the plan perfectly?" The question is, "Did this routine reduce crisis, confusion, or strain?"

Routines should be adjusted without shame. Care needs change. A person who once managed breakfast may need more support later. A medication routine may need revision after a change in prescription. A caregiver's work hours may shift. A helper may become available or unavailable. A routine is not a moral contract.

It is a practical tool. When it stops helping, it should be repaired, simplified, or replaced.

The caregiver should beware of perfectionism disguised as care. Perfectionism says the routine must be complete, elegant, consistent, and universally approved. Sustainable care says the routine must be useful. A useful routine may be a little untidy. It may involve repeated meals, basic notes, imperfect checklists, and ordinary reminders. That is fine. Caregiving is not improved by making the caregiver responsible for an impressive system. It is improved by reducing avoidable strain.

There is also a psychological benefit to routine: it reduces the caregiver's sense of constant alert. When key tasks have a known place, the mind can release them more easily. The caregiver does not have to wonder all day whether tablets were taken, whether food was planned, whether someone has checked in, whether the next issue will arrive as a surprise. Not every thought disappears, but fewer tasks remain open loops. A routine closes some of those loops before they become worry.

The person receiving care may also feel safer inside a routine, even if they resist it at first. Predictable contact can reduce the fear of being forgotten. Familiar meals can reduce decision fatigue. Medication cues can reduce anxiety about mistakes. Regular rest breaks for the caregiver can make interactions calmer. A routine communicates, quietly, that care is not dependent only on mood or emergency. It has shape.

Helpers benefit too. When routines exist, help becomes easier to accept because the task is easier to understand. A helper can step into a morning check-in, a meal routine, or a medication cue more readily than into a vague instruction to "make sure everything is okay". Good routines make care less mysterious. They reduce the caregiver's role as translator of every preference, risk, and habit. They allow support to become practical rather than symbolic.

Daily routines cannot solve every problem. They will not remove grief, cure illness, make relatives fair, or guarantee cooperation. They should not be used to pretend that a care situation needing more support can be fixed with a chart. If the needs have grown beyond what home routines can safely manage, that truth must be faced. A routine is a tool for stability, not a substitute for adequate care.

Yet for many caregivers, daily instability is worsened by the absence of small repeatable anchors. The same tasks are rediscovered each day. The same decisions are remade. The same confusion returns. The same distress builds from the same preventable gaps. In that situation, routine is not a small matter. It is the beginning of a different rhythm.

A daily stability routine should make care less dependent on emergency energy. It should reduce the number of times the caregiver has to improvise. It should make the person receiving care feel less adrift. It should create clearer openings for help. It should protect at least one small space in which the caregiver can breathe.

The question is not, "What perfect schedule would make this care situation look well managed?"

The question is, "What small repeated pattern would prevent tomorrow from becoming the same crisis in a slightly different form?"

Weekly Planning and Coordination

Daily routines keep ordinary care from becoming a string of avoidable alarms. Weekly planning does something different: it gives the whole care arrangement a wider rhythm. It creates a place where appointments, supplies, communication, responsibilities, and concerns can be gathered before they scatter across the week. Without that rhythm, the caregiver is forced to manage care in fragments. A message here. A phone call there. A prescription remembered too late. A relative asking for an update during work. A letter found the night before it matters. Each piece may seem small, but together they create a life of constant interruption.

A weekly planning routine is not about becoming more organised for the sake of appearance. It is about reducing the number of decisions that have to be made in a state of urgency. Caregiving becomes heavier when every question arrives separately: Who is taking them to the appointment? Are there enough tablets? Has the shopping been done? Did anyone update the family? Is the bill urgent? Who is visiting this weekend? Can this wait? Should I call now? The caregiver may spend more energy switching between these questions than actually completing the tasks. Weekly planning gathers the questions into one place, where they can be handled with less panic and more judgement.

The central principle is batching. Instead of allowing care to interrupt the day repeatedly, the caregiver creates planned windows for certain kinds of thinking. Appointment review happens at a chosen time. Supply checks happen before things run out. Family updates happen in one agreed communication window rather than through scattered daily texts. Decisions are grouped. Questions are collected. Small issues are noticed early. The caregiver stops being dragged into care administration whenever another person feels anxious, forgetful, or unsure.

This does not mean every care need can be contained neatly inside a weekly plan. Emergencies will still happen. Moods will shift. Health can change. Helpers may cancel. The person receiving care may have a difficult day that no planning could prevent. But a weekly rhythm reduces the avoidable emergencies, the ones created by late noticing, unclear roles, missing information, and decision-making left until the last possible moment. It makes the unpredictable easier to face because the predictable is no longer being handled as though it were a surprise.

A useful weekly planning routine begins with appointments. Appointments are rarely just appointments. They carry transport, preparation, paperwork, medication questions, clothing, mobility, emotional reassurance, waiting time, follow-up, and family communication. If they are not reviewed ahead of time, they become pressure points. The caregiver may find themselves trying to arrange a lift, locate a letter, calm anxiety, and update relatives all in the same morning. A weekly appointment review prevents the appointment from ambushing the household.

The review should ask plain questions. What appointments are coming? Who is attending? Who is driving or arranging transport? What papers, questions, or medication details are needed? Does the person receiving care know enough to feel prepared, but not so much that they become overwhelmed too early? Who needs an update afterwards? What follow-up is likely? These questions turn an appointment from a vague event into a sequence. Once the sequence is visible, it becomes easier to share, adjust, or simplify.

Supply checks are another essential part of the weekly rhythm. Many caregiving crises begin with ordinary items running out: medication, food, continence products, cleaning supplies, batteries, toiletries, pet food, hearing aid supplies, or household basics. The problem is not the item itself; it is the timing. A missing item discovered at the wrong moment can consume an afternoon. A weekly supply check prevents the caregiver from living in a state of discovery-by-crisis.

The supply check should be simple enough to survive tiredness. It does not need to become a grand inventory. The caregiver or assigned helper looks for what tends to run low and what would cause stress if it disappeared suddenly. Medication should usually be treated with particular seriousness because delay can create real risk. Food defaults matter because mealtimes become harder when there is no easy fallback. Household essentials matter because a small missing item can become another errand the caregiver did not have capacity to absorb. The point is not perfection. The point is to reduce the number of avoidable scrambles.

Weekly communication is equally important. Many caregivers are exhausted not only by tasks, but by being constantly available for updates, opinions, questions, and emotional reactions. A sibling texts during work. Another relative asks whether an appointment happened. Someone wants reassurance. Someone else sends advice. The caregiver becomes the communication hub, not because this is efficient, but because no other rhythm exists. A weekly update can reduce this burden dramatically.

One planned communication window is often stronger than many reactive messages. A weekly call or written update can gather the main points: appointments, current concerns, tasks needed, changes in routine, and who is responsible for what. Relatives who want to be informed know when information is coming. The caregiver is less pressured to respond to every scattered enquiry. Questions can be saved for the agreed time unless something truly urgent changes. The tone of care becomes less frantic because communication has a container.

This is especially useful with siblings or wider family. Daily texts can create the illusion of involvement while increasing the caregiver's workload. Every message requires reading, interpreting, deciding, answering, sometimes soothing, sometimes correcting. A weekly alignment call or update shifts the family from constant commentary to clearer coordination. It also makes responsibility harder to evade. Instead of everyone vaguely "keeping in touch", one person may be assigned transport, another prescriptions, another paperwork, another a visit. Coordination becomes visible.

The weekly planning session itself should be short and practical. If it becomes too long, too emotional, or too complex, people will avoid it. The aim is not to hold a family summit every week. The aim is to create a reliable checkpoint. What is coming up? What is missing? What needs doing? Who is doing it? What might go wrong? What can wait? What has changed since last week? These questions are enough to move care from anxiety into logistics.

The caregiver should resist turning the planning session into a place where every unresolved family grievance is reopened. There may be real resentment, unfairness, and history. Those matters may need conversation. But the weekly planning rhythm has a narrower purpose: to keep the care arrangement functioning. If it becomes a battlefield, it will stop being used. The caregiver may need a separate time for harder relational issues. The planning routine should protect the week, not become another emotional storm.

A weekly rhythm should also include the caregiver's own commitments. This is often forgotten. The care calendar may contain the recipient's appointments, visits, prescriptions, and support needs, but not the caregiver's work deadlines, medical appointments, parenting duties, rest periods, or protected time. When the caregiver's life is invisible in the plan, it is easily overwritten. Weekly planning must ask not only what the person receiving care needs, but what capacity the caregiver actually has that week.

This is not selfish. It is accuracy. A week with a major work deadline, school commitments, poor sleep, or the caregiver's own health appointment is not the same as a quieter week. The care plan must reflect that. If the caregiver has less capacity, tasks may need to be reassigned, simplified, postponed, or handled differently. Pretending every week is the same only makes the caregiver's strain invisible until it breaks through as resentment or collapse.

The weekly plan should identify one or two pressure points in advance. Perhaps an appointment is likely to be emotionally difficult. Perhaps a supply is running low. Perhaps a family visit may unsettle the person receiving care. Perhaps paperwork is due. Perhaps the caregiver has a demanding workday and cannot take calls. Naming these pressure points early allows the system to prepare. It also reduces the sense that the caregiver must be ready for everything at all times.

One of the most useful outcomes of weekly planning is deciding what does not need attention yet. Caregiving creates endless possible tasks. There is always something that could be improved, cleaned, chased, reviewed, organised, discussed, or worried about. Without a planning rhythm, everything can feel active in the caregiver's mind. A weekly session allows some matters to be parked deliberately. Not ignored. Parked. "This is not urgent this week." "This can wait until the monthly review." "This is a preference, not a priority." Such decisions free mental space.

Weekly coordination also helps protect boundaries. If the caregiver has already stated that non-urgent calls happen during certain times, the weekly plan can reinforce that. If family updates are batched, the caregiver is less vulnerable to scattered demands. If tasks are assigned ahead of time, fewer people can assume the caregiver will fill the gap at the last moment. Planning turns boundaries from isolated statements into operating principles.

The plan should be written somewhere accessible to the relevant people. A plan that lives only in the caregiver's head has not become a system. It remains a private mental burden. The format can be simple: a shared message, a calendar, a notebook, a printed sheet, or a shared document. What matters is that the key information is visible: appointments, tasks, owners, deadlines, supplies, concerns, and communication windows. The caregiver should not have to act as the living noticeboard.

Caregivers should be wary of tools that look impressive but are not used. A complicated digital system may appeal during a moment of desperation, but if helpers do not open it, it will fail. A plain weekly message that everyone reads is better than an elegant platform that becomes another thing for the caregiver to maintain. The right tool is the one that reduces work, not the one that gives the appearance of control.

A weekly rhythm should include confirmation, not assumption. If someone has agreed to take a person to an appointment, the plan should show that they have confirmed. If a prescription is being collected, the person responsible should send a completion message. If a family member is visiting, the time should be clear. Confirmation closes mental loops. Without it, the caregiver may remain anxious even when someone else supposedly owns the task.

When confirmation is missing, the caregiver should not automatically rescue the task in silence. They can ask directly: "Can you confirm by this evening whether transport is covered?" Or: "Please update the group once the prescription is collected." Or: "If you cannot do the visit, please say so by Thursday so another plan can be made." These sentences may feel firm, but they prevent the caregiver from carrying uncertainty as a private burden.

Weekly planning can also expose recurring failures. If the same task is unassigned every week, the support network has a gap. If the same helper cancels repeatedly, the role may need to move. If the same appointment preparation causes stress, the routine needs redesign. If the same family argument appears in every planning conversation, communication may need stricter structure. The weekly plan becomes a diagnostic tool. It shows not only what needs doing, but where the care system is weak.

This is where honesty matters. The caregiver should not use the plan to pretend things are more stable than they are. If there is no transport, write that there is no transport. If no one has taken the paperwork, name the gap. If the caregiver is still the fallback for every failed task, acknowledge it. Hidden instability does not become safer because it is politely unnamed. A visible gap may be uncomfortable, but it is actionable.

At the same time, weekly planning should not become a forum for self-criticism. If something was missed, the question is not, "Who is a bad caregiver?" The question is, "What made this easy to miss, and how do we prevent that next time?" Was there no reminder? No owner? Too little notice? Too much information in one message? A task assigned to the wrong person? A deadline unclear? This design-based approach reduces shame and improves the system.

The person receiving care may be involved in weekly planning where appropriate. Their involvement can protect dignity and reduce resistance. They may know their preferences, worries, energy patterns, and social needs. They may want a say in visits, meals, appointments, or routines. However, their involvement should match their capacity and the emotional reality of the situation. Some people may feel overwhelmed by too much information. Others may become anxious if appointments are discussed too far ahead. Planning should support them, not flood them.

Where the person receiving care cannot participate fully, the plan should still preserve respect. It should not become a document that treats them as a project rather than a person. Preferences matter. Familiar routines matter. Privacy matters. The plan should make care easier without stripping away dignity. A good weekly rhythm makes life feel more supported, not more managed.

The caregiver should also build in a brief review of their own recovery. What space exists this week for rest? After which appointment will recovery be needed? Which evening is protected from care administration? Who can cover a short break? If recovery is not placed in the week, the week will usually consume it. Caregiving tasks expand naturally. Rest has to be defended deliberately.

This is one reason weekly planning should happen before the caregiver is already depleted. If planning is left until the pressure is high, it becomes another crisis response. A regular planning time, however modest, allows the caregiver to approach the week with more steadiness. The planning itself may take little time, but it changes the emotional position from "What is coming at me?" to "What can be seen and arranged?"

Some weeks will not go to plan. This is not failure. A weekly plan is not a promise that life will behave. It is a preparation for handling what can be known. If an appointment changes, the plan is updated. If a helper cancels, the backup is activated. If a new concern appears, it is placed in the next appropriate decision window unless it is urgent. The routine survives by adapting, not by pretending nothing will disrupt it.

The caregiver should distinguish between a plan that fails because life changed and a plan that fails because it was unrealistic. Life changes are unavoidable. Unrealistic plans need redesign. If the weekly planning session is too long, shorten it. If people ignore the written update, make it clearer or move to a better format. If tasks keep returning to the caregiver, assign ownership more explicitly. If the plan depends on someone unreliable, change the role. The plan should serve the care arrangement, not become another standard the caregiver fails to meet.

There is a quieter benefit to weekly planning: it gives the caregiver evidence of work done. Caregiving can feel like endless motion without progress. A weekly plan shows what was handled, what was prevented, what was shared, and what remains unresolved. This can reduce the corrosive feeling that nothing is ever enough. It also helps when asking for more support because the caregiver can point to real tasks rather than general exhaustion.

Weekly coordination can transform family conversations. Instead of scattered emotional check-ins, the conversation begins to ask practical questions. Who is taking this? When will it be done? What information is needed? What is the backup? What can wait? This does not remove emotion from caregiving, nor should it. But it prevents emotion from being the only organising force. Planning turns stress into logistics, and logistics can be changed more easily than vague distress.

The caregiver should remember that a weekly rhythm does not need everyone's enthusiasm to be useful. Some relatives may resist. Some may ignore updates. Some may prefer the old pattern where the caregiver handled everything and they could comment from the side. The caregiver can still use the weekly plan for their own clarity and for the people who will engage. Over time, the written rhythm may make it harder for others to claim they did not know what was needed.

If family involvement is limited, weekly planning is still valuable. The caregiver can use it alone or with one trusted helper. They can review appointments, supplies, risk points, rest, and paperwork. They can decide which tasks to simplify and which requests to make. They can identify the one change that would reduce the week's pressure. Even when support is thin, planning gives the caregiver a clearer relationship with reality.

A good weekly rhythm should leave the caregiver feeling less scattered, not more burdened. If the planning routine becomes another heavy obligation, it should be simplified. The minimum version might be ten minutes with a calendar and a short list: appointments, supplies, tasks, calls, rest. That may be enough. The purpose is not to produce a flawless care management system. The purpose is to prevent the same avoidable pressures from arriving unannounced.

Weekly planning and coordination are acts of quiet prevention. They lack the drama of last-minute rescue, but they reduce the need for it. They make responsibilities visible. They protect the caregiver's attention. They give helpers clearer entry points. They reduce family confusion. They allow the person receiving care to move through the week with fewer surprises. They create a rhythm in which care is not constantly invented under stress.

The question for the caregiver is simple: what keeps interrupting the week because it has no proper place in the week?

Managing Information and Paperwork

Caregiving creates paper even when most of life seems to have moved onto screens. Letters arrive. Appointment cards are placed somewhere "safe" and then vanish. Medication changes are mentioned in a conversation and later half-remembered. Forms ask for details no one has gathered. Passwords sit in different notebooks. Phone numbers live in old messages. Receipts, bills, care notes, prescriptions, discharge summaries, insurance documents, mobility information, benefit letters, and instructions from professionals collect in drawers, handbags, inboxes, kitchen counters, and the caregiver's tired mind.

This flood of information can become its own form of caregiving. It is not enough to care, comfort, visit, cook, drive, call, and reassure. Someone must also know. Know which medicine changed. Know who to ring. Know where the letter is. Know what the professional said. Know which relative has been updated. Know whether the bill was paid. Know what the person receiving care prefers, refuses, forgets, worries about, and needs in a difficult moment. Information becomes a second care load, one that often remains invisible until something goes missing.

The problem is not only the amount of information. It is the way information becomes scattered. One detail sits in a text message, another in a paper letter, another in the caregiver's memory, another in the person's home, another with a sibling who may or may not remember to pass it on. When care is calm, this fragmentation may seem inconvenient but manageable. When care becomes urgent, fragmentation becomes panic. The caregiver wastes precious energy searching, asking, guessing, reconstructing, and apologising for not having what should have been easy to find.

Good information management is not about becoming perfectly organised. Perfection is the wrong standard. Caregivers do not need a beautiful filing system that impresses anyone. They need a system that works when they are tired, when a helper steps in, when an appointment is moved, when a call comes at an awkward time, when someone asks for a medication name, when a letter must be found quickly, or when the caregiver is not available and another person needs to act. The system must be simple enough to survive real life.

The guiding question is plain: what information would someone need if I were not here to explain everything?

That question can feel unsettling because it exposes how much of the care arrangement may live inside one person's head. Many caregivers have become the unofficial archive of another person's life. They remember the professional's name, the date of the last appointment, the best way to calm anxiety before a visit, the phrase that triggers resistance, the food that is usually accepted, the neighbour with the spare key, the pharmacy opening pattern, the document that must be brought, the relative who must not be told sensitive details, and the sign that a mood change is unusual. This knowledge is valuable. It is also dangerous when it has no backup.

A practical information system begins with essentials, not everything. Caregiving paperwork can easily become overwhelming if the caregiver tries to organise every document from every year. The first task is to identify the information that prevents panic and mistakes. This usually includes key contacts, current medication details, appointment information, essential health notes, routines, preferences, access arrangements, emergency instructions, financial or administrative deadlines, and the tasks different people have agreed to handle. These are the facts that help care continue when pressure rises.

A key contacts list should be easy to find and easy to understand. It might include close relatives, neighbours, regular helpers, professionals involved in care, transport contacts, pharmacy details, and anyone who should be reached in a problem. The point is not to create an elaborate directory. The point is to prevent the caregiver from being the only person who knows whom to call. A contact list buried in an old notebook or hidden inside a phone only the caregiver can unlock is not truly accessible. The right people need the right information in the right place.

Medication information deserves particular care. Confusion around medicines can create unnecessary risk, anxiety, and arguments. A current medication list should be kept somewhere reliable, with names, doses, timing, purpose where useful, allergies or known sensitivities if relevant, and the pharmacy or prescribing contact. The caregiver should also know when the list was last updated. Old medication information can be worse than none because it gives false confidence. If a medicine changes, the list must change. This sounds simple, but many care systems fail at exactly this point.

The medication list should not depend on memory or casual conversation. "They changed the small white tablet" is not enough. "The doctor said something about stopping one of them" is not enough. Details need to be written clearly and checked where necessary. If several helpers are involved, everyone should know where the current list is kept and who is responsible for updating it. Otherwise, the caregiver may remain the only person capable of answering every medicine-related question, which keeps the mental load firmly attached to them.

Routines and preferences also belong in the information system. These may seem less official than medication or appointments, but they often determine whether care feels smooth or stressful. What time does the person usually prefer a morning call? Which foods are accepted when appetite is low? What topics cause anxiety? Which phrases help during resistance? Where are spare glasses kept? Does the person become unsettled if appointments are discussed too early? Are there mobility issues around steps, bathrooms, or getting in and out of cars? This practical knowledge helps others provide support without accidentally creating extra distress.

Preferences should be recorded with dignity. The person receiving care is not a set of instructions. They are a person with habits, dislikes, history, pride, and rights. A note that says "likes tea in the blue mug and becomes anxious if rushed" is different in tone from "difficult in mornings". The first helps a helper approach the situation wisely. The second labels the person and may harden resentment. Information should support humane care, not reduce someone to their most inconvenient moments.

Paperwork needs a home. Not a perfect home, but a consistent one. If letters are left in several places, the caregiver will eventually lose time and patience trying to reconstruct what matters. A simple current folder can hold active paperwork: appointment letters, recent professional notes, forms not yet completed, bills needing action, and documents that must be taken somewhere. Completed or older documents can go elsewhere, but the current folder should be the place where active matters live. The caregiver should not have to search the entire house for the one letter that suddenly matters.

The word "current" is important. Many filing systems fail because they mix urgent documents with old paperwork. The caregiver opens a folder and finds years of letters, outdated instructions, expired cards, receipts, leaflets, and forms that may or may not matter. The system becomes a paper swamp. A current folder reduces this. It says: these are the documents that may affect decisions now. Everything else can be archived, boxed, scanned, or left for a less pressured time.

A simple colour or label system can help if it remains easy. For example, one folder for health, one for money and bills, one for current appointments, and one for household or practical matters. But the caregiver should avoid building a system that only they understand. If a helper cannot find a letter without calling the caregiver, the system is not yet doing its job. The test of a paperwork system is not whether it looks tidy. The test is whether the right person can find the right document quickly enough.

Digital information can be just as scattered as paper. Emails, text messages, appointment reminders, photos of letters, online accounts, saved documents, and app notifications may all contain important details. Caregivers often take photographs of letters or screenshots of messages, intending to sort them later. Later rarely comes. The phone becomes a filing cabinet with no drawers. When the detail is needed, the caregiver scrolls through old messages while becoming increasingly tense.

Digital simplicity matters. Important documents can be saved in one named folder, shared where appropriate, or printed if paper is more reliable for the people involved. Photos of letters should be named or moved to a place where they can be found. If a key appointment detail is sent in a message, it should be added to the calendar or current folder, not left buried in the message thread. The aim is not technological sophistication. The aim is to stop important information from hiding in places where only one person knows to look.

Passwords and access details require careful handling. Many caregivers struggle because bills, appointments, services, or accounts are locked behind information only the person receiving care knows, half-remembers, or has written somewhere obscure. This can create serious stress when action is needed. Where appropriate and lawful, access arrangements should be clarified before crisis. Who can speak on behalf of the person? What permissions are needed? Where are account details stored? What should happen if the person cannot manage a call or form? These questions may feel awkward, but avoiding them often creates greater distress later.

Privacy must be respected. Managing information does not mean sharing everything with everyone. A neighbour helping with bins does not need health details. A sibling arranging transport needs appointment time and mobility information, not every emotional conversation. A helper preparing meals may need dietary information, not financial paperwork. Caregivers should think in terms of need-to-know. The right information should reach the right person for the task, without turning the care recipient's private life into open family property.

Emergency information should be especially accessible. In a crisis, no one should have to search through piles of paper or call the main caregiver repeatedly for basic facts. A concise emergency sheet might include the person's full name, key contacts, current medicines, allergies or important medical information, usual professionals or services, access instructions, and any essential communication needs. It should be kept somewhere appropriate and known to the right people. This is not alarmism. It is a way of reducing panic if something happens when the usual caregiver is not present.

Information management also supports handoffs. If another person is taking over a task, they need the relevant details without requiring a long briefing each time. A transport helper needs appointment information, mobility notes, parking or access details where relevant, and what to do afterwards. A shopping helper needs the list, preferences, substitutions, and payment arrangement. A paperwork helper needs the active documents, deadlines, and authority to act. The more usable the information, the less the caregiver remains the live control centre.

Caregivers should be wary of becoming the interpreter of every document. It is easy to fall into the pattern where all letters are sent to the caregiver, all professional instructions are explained by the caregiver, and all forms are completed by the caregiver because they are "better at it". Competence can become captivity. If paperwork is a recurring task, another person may need to learn part of it, or a system may need to make it easier to share. The caregiver should not be the only person who understands the administrative side of care unless there is no other safe option.

A regular paperwork time can prevent administrative ambush. Instead of opening letters only when anxiety spikes, the caregiver or assigned helper can review current paperwork at the same time each week. What arrived? What needs action? What can be filed? What has a deadline? What requires a call? What should be photographed or shared? This routine turns paperwork from a lurking threat into a manageable checkpoint. It also reduces the chance that a letter sits unopened until it becomes urgent.

The paperwork routine should be short enough to repeat. A caregiver who tries to process every document perfectly may avoid the task entirely. Better to spend a small regular block sorting current items than to wait for the mythical clear afternoon when everything will finally be organised. Caregiving administration rewards consistency more than intensity. Small repeated sorting prevents large desperate searching.

There should also be a way to capture new information immediately. After an appointment, a conversation, or a phone call, the caregiver may think they will remember the details. Often they will not, especially if they are tired or emotionally stirred. A simple note made at the time can prevent confusion later. What changed? What was agreed? What needs doing? Who is responsible? When is the next step? These questions are more useful than a long narrative. The goal is to capture action, not compose a report.

After appointments, information often needs translation into tasks. A professional may give advice, change a medicine, request monitoring, schedule a follow-up, or suggest a referral. If this information remains as a memory of "they said we should keep an eye on it", the caregiver carries anxiety without a clear plan. It is better to write: what should be watched, how often, what counts as concerning, who should be contacted, and when review is needed. Vague instructions create mental load. Specific information creates action.

Family updates should also be handled carefully. Information shared badly can create more work. If every relative receives partial updates in different messages, the caregiver may spend the week repeating themselves. If too much detail is shared, relatives may respond with opinions and anxiety. If too little is shared, they may claim they were not informed. A regular, concise update can reduce this: what happened, what matters, what tasks are needed, and what is not yet decided. Information should serve coordination, not feed commentary.

The caregiver should avoid using paperwork as a hiding place for anxiety. Sometimes, when care feels emotionally difficult, organising papers can feel like control. There is nothing wrong with creating order, but it should not displace more important care decisions. A perfectly arranged folder will not solve an unsafe routine, an unshared workload, or a boundary that keeps being crossed. Information management should reduce burden and clarify action. If it becomes a way to avoid harder conversations, it may be offering the illusion of progress.

At the same time, neglected information can make every other problem worse. Without clear records, the caregiver may not know whether a task has been done. Without a medication list, helpers may hesitate or make mistakes. Without current appointment details, transport becomes uncertain. Without paperwork deadlines, administration becomes a crisis. Without routines written down, no one else can step in. Information is not glamorous care, but it is one of the foundations that allows care to function.

A useful standard is "findable by someone tired". If the system only works when the caregiver is calm, well-rested, and present, it is too fragile. A helper should be able to find the appointment letter. The medication list should be obvious. The current folder should be named. The emergency information should not require detective work. Instructions should be plain enough to use under pressure. Caregiving systems must be designed for tired people because caregiving often makes people tired.

Another useful standard is "updated enough to trust". A document does not need to be perfect, but it must not be dangerously outdated. Old medicine lists, old contact numbers, old routines, old preferences, and old task assignments can create confusion. If a document is kept, someone should know when it was last reviewed. A simple date at the top can help. "Updated this month" gives confidence. A note with no date invites doubt.

Caregivers should decide who owns each information category. Who updates the medication list? Who keeps appointment details current? Who opens post? Who manages bills? Who maintains the shared calendar? Who sends family updates? If the answer to every question is the main caregiver, the information system may be neat but the load is still concentrated. Even if the caregiver remains responsible for some categories, others may be moved. Information work is work, and it should be visible enough to share.

This is where paperwork connects directly to resentment. A caregiver may not resent the person receiving care for needing help; they may resent being the only person who knows what is going on. They resent being asked for every detail. They resent correcting relatives who did not read the update. They resent searching for documents others misplaced. They resent carrying deadlines in their head. They resent being blamed when information no one helped manage is missing. A better system does not remove all resentment, but it reduces one of its fuel sources.

Managing information should also make it easier for the caregiver to be absent. This is a crucial test. Can the caregiver go to work, sleep, attend their own appointment, visit a friend, or take a break without being the only source of essential information? If not, the system needs attention. A caregiver who cannot be unavailable because all knowledge routes through them is not merely busy. They are structurally trapped.

A simple "if I am unavailable" note can be valuable. It might say who to contact, where key information is kept, what counts as urgent, what can wait, and which tasks are already assigned. This does not mean the caregiver expects disaster. It means they have stopped treating their own constant availability as the only emergency plan. Such a note can be especially useful for helpers who want to do the right thing but panic when the main caregiver does not answer.

Information systems should be reviewed as care changes. A new diagnosis, medicine change, mobility issue, professional contact, financial arrangement, or routine shift can quickly make old information unreliable. The caregiver should not wait until confusion reveals the problem. A brief regular review, perhaps attached to the weekly planning routine, can keep the essentials current. What has changed? What needs updating? What can be removed? What does someone else need to know? Small reviews prevent major confusion.

There is also a dignity in order. Not showy order, but humane order. When information is clear, the person receiving care is less likely to be asked the same distressing questions repeatedly. Helpers are less likely to make avoidable mistakes. Relatives are less likely to create confusion through partial knowledge. The caregiver is less likely to sound irritated because they have explained the same detail too many times. Good information reduces friction in the emotional atmosphere of care.

Still, the caregiver should not turn information management into another standard of perfection. There will be messy weeks. Papers will pile up. Notes will be incomplete. Someone will forget to update the calendar. A helper will ask a question already answered. The aim is not flawless administration. The aim is to reduce avoidable panic and make the essential things easier to find, share, and act upon. Good enough, maintained consistently, is stronger than perfect, abandoned quickly.

The most useful information system is often modest: a current folder, a key contacts sheet, a medication list, a simple calendar, a place for active paperwork, and a short note on routines and preferences. These basics can do more than an elaborate archive if they are actually used. The caregiver should build from the pressure points, not from an abstract idea of organisation. What information do people keep asking for? What documents keep getting lost? What details cause panic when missing? Start there.

Managing information and paperwork is not separate from care. It is part of making care safer, calmer, and shareable. It turns private knowledge into usable structure. It reduces the caregiver's role as the sole memory of the system. It allows helpers to help without constant dependence. It gives urgent moments a better chance of being handled with clarity rather than panic.

The question is not, "How do I organise every piece of paper perfectly?"

The question is, "What information must be findable, current, and shareable so care does not collapse into confusion when I am tired, busy, or unavailable?"

Chapter 8
Burnout Signals and Recovery Practices

How can a caregiver be exhausted and still not recognise burnout when it arrives? The answer is uncomfortable: burnout does not always enter dramatically. It may not announce itself as collapse. It may appear as the moment you feel nothing when the phone rings. It may appear as irritation at a harmless question, forgetfulness around a task you would once have handled easily, or a heaviness in the morning before the day has even begun. It may look less like breaking down and more like slowly becoming someone you do not quite recognise.

This is why burnout is so easily misread. A caregiver may call it impatience, poor attitude, weakness, laziness, selfishness, or lack of gratitude. They may decide they need to try harder, organise better, sleep less, feel kinder, or stop complaining. They may look at the person receiving care and think, "They have it worse, so I have no right to struggle." The signal is then buried under shame, and the arrangement continues unchanged. The body has raised its hand, but the caregiver has mistaken the warning for a personal defect.

The paradox is that caregivers often wait for collapse before they believe their strain is serious, yet collapse is precisely what sustainable care is meant to prevent. A warning light on a dashboard is useful because it appears before the engine fails. No one praises the driver for covering it with tape and carrying on until smoke appears. Yet caregivers do this to themselves constantly. They ignore numbness, dread, forgetfulness, resentment, sleep disruption, emotional flatness, and a growing sense of being trapped because the tasks still have to be done and someone else's need looks more urgent.

The central tension is between endurance and maintenance. Endurance can be necessary in short bursts. There are difficult days, emergencies, painful transitions, and seasons when the caregiver has to stretch further than they would choose. But endurance cannot become the operating model. A care arrangement that relies on the caregiver continually overriding their own warning signs is not stable; it is postponing the bill. Maintenance asks a different question: what must be repaired, restored, reduced, shared, or escalated before the caregiver becomes part of the crisis?

The stakes are practical as well as emotional. Burnout changes care. It narrows patience, makes decisions more reactive, reduces attention to detail, and turns ordinary requests into threats. It can make the caregiver avoid calls, rush visits, resent the person receiving care, or swing between over-functioning and withdrawal. The person receiving care may sense the strain and become more anxious, demanding, guilty, or resistant. The relationship begins to carry an extra burden: not only the original need, but the damage caused by trying to meet that need without adequate recovery.

There is also a future cost. If early signals are ignored, the range of choices shrinks. A caregiver who notices strain early may still be able to adjust routines, ask for help, protect sleep, renegotiate tasks, or build recovery into the week. A caregiver who waits until they are brittle, numb, or constantly overwhelmed may need more drastic intervention because the system has been allowed to run too hot for too long. Early recognition creates options. Late recognition often creates emergencies.

The work begins by treating burnout signals as information rather than indictment: not "What is wrong with me?" but "What is this telling me about the load?" From there, recovery has to move out of the realm of hopeful leftovers and into the structure of the week, through small pauses that interrupt depletion and larger blocks that allow real restoration. Then comes the harder discernment: knowing when the current arrangement has crossed a threshold and needs more support, a different design, or professional input before crisis forces the decision.

This requires abandoning the fantasy that recovery must wait until everything else is settled. Everything else will not be settled. Care produces another call, another form, another worry, another appointment, another emotional aftershock. Recovery cannot be something the caregiver earns after the queue is empty. It has to be built into the care plan as deliberately as medication, transport, meals, and appointments. A protected walk after a difficult visit, a short period without messages, a regular evening off, or a genuine block of respite is not an indulgence. It is part of keeping the caregiver usable, humane, and present.

The question now is not whether you are strong enough to keep going. Strength has probably carried you further than many people realise. The more important question is sharper: which warning signs have you been explaining away because admitting them would mean the care arrangement has to change?

Recognising Burnout Early

Burnout in caregiving rarely begins with a dramatic collapse. More often, it arrives quietly, disguised as ordinary tiredness, impatience, forgetfulness, or a dull reluctance to answer the phone. The caregiver keeps moving because the tasks keep coming. There is another appointment, another message, another prescription, another emotional conversation, another small problem that needs to be prevented from becoming a larger one. From the outside, the arrangement may still appear functional. The caregiver is still doing what needs doing. That is precisely why the warning signs are so easy to miss.

Many caregivers expect burnout to look like complete exhaustion, as though the body will one day simply refuse to continue. Exhaustion can be part of it, but burnout often has more subtle faces. It can look like numbness when you used to feel concerned. It can look like irritation at questions you once answered gently. It can look like dread before a visit, resentment after a call, or an inability to concentrate on anything that is not care-related. It can look like losing your place in a conversation, forgetting a simple task, or feeling strangely detached from your own life.

This is why early recognition matters. If burnout is noticed only when the caregiver can no longer function, the care arrangement has already been allowed to run beyond its safe limits. The aim is not to wait until the warning signs become undeniable. The aim is to treat them as information while there are still choices available. A warning sign is not a confession of weakness. It is data from a system under strain.

The first shift is to stop asking, "What is wrong with me?" and begin asking, "What is this telling me about the load?" That one change alters the meaning of burnout signals. Irritability becomes a clue about depleted patience, not proof of cruelty. Forgetfulness becomes a sign that the mental load may be too high, not evidence of incompetence. Dread becomes a message that something about the routine, relationship, task, or timing needs attention, not a moral failure. Numbness becomes a serious signal that the caregiver may be protecting themselves by feeling less.

Burnout is often misunderstood because caregivers are good at functioning through distress. They learn to keep going while tired, to sound calm while anxious, to reassure others while privately uncertain, and to complete tasks even when their own reserves are low. This skill can be useful in short bursts. It becomes dangerous when it convinces everyone, including the caregiver, that functioning equals wellbeing. A person can still function and be burning out. They can still meet obligations while losing warmth, steadiness, and the ability to recover.

One of the earliest signs is irritability. Not the occasional frustration that belongs to ordinary life, but a sharper, more frequent impatience that seems out of proportion to the immediate situation. A repeated question feels unbearable. A minor delay provokes anger. A relative's message causes an instant surge of resentment. The caregiver may then feel ashamed and try to compensate by being extra patient, which only consumes more energy. The better response is not self-punishment. It is curiosity. What is repeatedly scraping against the edge of capacity?

Irritability often points to a boundary problem. The caregiver may be receiving too many interruptions, absorbing too much emotional pressure, working without recovery, or handling tasks that should have been shared. It may also point to hunger, poor sleep, pain, overstimulation, or decision fatigue. The immediate feeling may appear during one small interaction, but the cause may be cumulative. A caregiver who snaps at a harmless question may not be reacting only to that question. They may be reacting to a whole week with no protected space.

Another common signal is numbness. This can frighten caregivers because it feels like a loss of love. They may notice that they are no longer moved by distress in the same way. They hear worry and feel blank. They perform the task but cannot access tenderness. They sit beside someone they care about and feel emotionally far away. This does not automatically mean love has disappeared. It may mean the caregiver's system has reduced feeling in order to keep functioning. Numbness can be a form of emotional insulation when the full weight of the situation has become too much to feel continuously.

Numbness deserves attention because it can quietly change the care relationship. The caregiver may become efficient but less present. They may avoid deeper conversations because they cannot bear more feeling. They may become detached from their own needs as well as the care recipient's. The danger is not only emotional coldness; it is the loss of feedback. Feelings often tell us when a boundary is crossed, when grief needs tending, when rest is overdue, or when a task has become too costly. When everything goes flat, the caregiver may stop receiving those signals clearly.

Dread is another important warning sign. It may appear before a visit, before opening a message, before a family conversation, before a night-time call, or before a particular task. Dread is more than reluctance. It is the body anticipating strain. A caregiver may minimise it because the task itself seems ordinary: a short visit, a quick phone call, a routine errand. Yet the body may understand the hidden cost. Perhaps the visit includes criticism, resistance, grief, or emotional labour. Perhaps the call rarely stays brief. Perhaps the errand has become symbolic of being taken for granted. Dread asks the caregiver to look beyond the task and examine the pattern around it.

Forgetfulness can also signal overload. Caregiving requires memory not only for facts, but for future actions, emotional details, risks, preferences, deadlines, and other people's expectations. The caregiver remembers appointments, medicines, supplies, conversations, promises, symptoms, bills, family updates, and the small adjustments that make care go more smoothly. When the mental load becomes too high, things begin to slip. The caregiver may forget a call, misplace a letter, miss a detail, or feel unable to hold one more instruction. This is not always carelessness. It may be a sign that too much information is living in one person's head.

A useful response to forgetfulness is not shame, but system design. What can be written down? What can be moved to a shared calendar? What task needs an owner? What information keeps being requested because it is not accessible? What reminder would reduce mental load? The warning sign points towards a practical correction. If the caregiver simply tries to "be more careful", the underlying overload remains.

Burnout can also appear as constant alertness. The caregiver may find it hard to relax even when nothing is happening. The phone is silent, but part of the mind waits for it. A visit has ended, but the caregiver replays what was said. A quiet evening is interrupted by imagined problems: Did they take the tablets? Was that comment a sign of decline? Should I have stayed longer? What if something happens tonight? This state of readiness is exhausting because the body never fully stands down. Rest becomes shallow because vigilance keeps watch.

Constant alertness often means the care system lacks reliable boundaries, routines, or backups. If the caregiver is the only person who knows what to do, if every call might be urgent, if no one else can step in, or if there is no agreed response plan, the mind tries to compensate by staying on duty. The solution is not simply to relax. The solution is to make the arrangement less dependent on continuous private vigilance.

Another signal is loss of perspective. Under burnout pressure, every request can feel enormous, every problem personal, and every criticism like confirmation of failure. The caregiver may struggle to distinguish urgent from merely loud, important from emotionally charged, or their own responsibility from someone else's. Small decisions become heavy because the mind is already overloaded. The caregiver may swing between saying yes too quickly and wanting to refuse everything. This is not a character flaw. It is what happens when decision-making has been overused without recovery.

A further warning sign is resentment that becomes a constant background tone. Occasional resentment can be useful information. It may reveal unfairness, invisibility, or a boundary that has been crossed. But when resentment becomes the emotional climate of care, it is a serious signal. The caregiver may begin keeping a private ledger: what they did, who failed to notice, who did not help, who criticised, who asked again. The ledger may be accurate, but living inside it is corrosive. It turns every new request into evidence of an old wound.

Resentment should not be treated as proof that the caregiver is a bad person. It should be treated as a message about repeated imbalance. What has become unseen? Which task has become too much? Where has help failed to become real? Which boundary is being crossed again and again? Which choice no longer feels like a choice? Resentment often points to the place where the care arrangement needs redesign.

Burnout may also show up in avoidance. The caregiver delays calling back. They leave messages unread. They postpone paperwork. They take longer to arrange appointments. They sit in the car before going inside. They find reasons not to begin tasks they once handled promptly. Avoidance is often misread as laziness, but it can be a protective response to overwhelm. The mind steps away from what it no longer has capacity to meet.

Avoidance becomes dangerous when it increases risk or creates more pressure later. The caregiver then feels guilty, rushes to repair, and may over-function to compensate. The better approach is to ask what the avoidance is protecting against. Is the task too vague? Too emotionally loaded? Too large? Too frequent? Too likely to trigger conflict? Does it require information that is hard to find? Is the caregiver avoiding the task itself, or the conversation attached to it? Once the real obstacle is named, the task can often be reduced, shared, scheduled, or bounded.

Physical signals matter as well. Caregivers may notice headaches, digestive problems, muscle tension, sleep disruption, recurring minor illness, changes in appetite, or a general heaviness that does not lift with one quiet evening. These signs should not be dismissed as "just stress". The body often speaks before the caregiver is ready to admit that the load is too high. A care arrangement that repeatedly affects the caregiver's body is not only emotionally difficult; it is demanding attention at a basic level of functioning.

Sleep deserves particular seriousness. A caregiver who cannot fall asleep, wakes during the night, dreams about care tasks, or rises already tired may be losing one of the main foundations of stability. Poor sleep affects patience, memory, judgement, and emotional control. It makes guilt louder and boundaries harder to hold. If care regularly interrupts sleep through late calls, worry, night-time tasks, or emotional aftershocks, that is not a minor inconvenience. It is a sign that the care plan is drawing from reserves it cannot safely keep spending.

Burnout signals are highly personal. One caregiver becomes snappish. Another becomes silent. One starts forgetting details. Another starts doing everything with rigid control because they fear one missed task will bring disaster. One cries often. Another cannot cry at all. One eats constantly. Another loses interest in food. One over-functions. Another avoids. The point is not to match a perfect description of burnout. The point is to recognise your own pattern of depletion.

To identify that pattern, the caregiver can ask: What changes in me when I am overloaded? What do other people notice before I do? What tasks or conversations leave me unusually drained? What time of day is hardest? Which person, message, or responsibility makes my body tense before anything has happened? What do I begin to neglect when capacity is shrinking? What do I tell myself to keep going? These questions turn vague distress into usable information.

The situations that trigger burnout signals should be tracked as carefully as the signals themselves. A caregiver may feel fine after practical tasks but depleted after emotional conversations. They may cope with visits but struggle with family messages afterwards. They may manage appointments but dread the paperwork that follows. They may handle daily routines until a helper cancels, then feel disproportionately angry because the cancellation exposes the absence of backup. Burnout is not only about total workload. It is about the specific points where workload, emotion, responsibility, and lack of recovery collide.

For example, the caregiver who becomes irritable every Sunday evening may discover that the problem is not Sunday itself, but the weekly family update that invites questions, criticism, and vague advice. The caregiver who feels dread before every morning call may discover that the call has no boundary and often becomes an hour of reassurance. The caregiver who forgets details after appointments may realise they are leaving appointments emotionally flooded and without time to write notes. These patterns are not personal failures. They are design clues.

Treating burnout signals as operational data changes the next step. Instead of asking, "How do I stop being like this?" the caregiver asks, "What part of the care system is producing this response?" That question points towards practical adjustments: shorter calls, clearer handoffs, protected recovery after visits, written notes after appointments, fewer scattered messages, a defined emergency plan, a shared medication list, a helper for transport, or a boundary around late-night contact. The signal becomes a guide.

This does not mean every feeling must be converted into a productivity exercise. Some burnout signals carry grief and need tenderness. If the caregiver feels numb after witnessing decline, the response may include rest, conversation, emotional support, or space to mourn. If they dread visits because the person they love has changed, the problem is not only routine design. It is sorrow. Operational thinking and emotional care can coexist. The signal may point to both a practical burden and an unprocessed loss.

Early recognition also requires honesty about what caregivers often hide. Many caregivers do not admit burnout signals because they fear judgement. They worry that saying "I dread visits" will sound cruel, that saying "I feel numb" will sound unloving, or that saying "I resent my sibling" will sound petty. But hidden signals do not become less real. They simply influence behaviour from the shadows. A caregiver who cannot speak honestly anywhere may eventually speak through irritability, avoidance, or collapse.

A safe place to name the truth is therefore part of early recognition. This may be a trusted friend, counsellor, support group, journal, or private conversation with someone who will not immediately minimise, shame, or problem-solve. The point is not to complain endlessly. The point is to hear oneself say the truth before the truth turns into an outburst. Language can prevent escalation. "I am starting to dread the calls" is easier to respond to than a sudden decision never to answer again.

The caregiver should also notice when they begin to lose themselves outside care. Burnout is not only about how care feels. It is also about what remains of the caregiver's own life. Are friendships fading? Are hobbies abandoned? Is every conversation about care? Has the caregiver stopped making plans because they assume care will interrupt them? Do they feel guilty when they enjoy something? Do they struggle to remember what they want beyond the next task? These are serious signals. They show that care is no longer one part of life; it is consuming the available space.

Loss of identity can make burnout harder to reverse because the caregiver has fewer sources of restoration. If there is no place where they are known beyond usefulness, no activity that returns them to themselves, and no future that belongs to them, care becomes emotionally total. Early recognition should therefore include noticing not only distress, but disappearance. What part of the caregiver's life has quietly gone missing?

It is important to distinguish normal tiredness from burnout signals, although the boundary is not always neat. Normal tiredness usually improves with rest, a quiet day, or a completed task. Burnout-related depletion often persists, returns quickly, or changes the caregiver's relationship to care. The caregiver may rest briefly and still feel dread. They may sleep and still wake heavy. They may complete tasks and feel no relief. They may find that even enjoyable things no longer restore them. This persistence is worth taking seriously.

Another marker is loss of recovery. If the caregiver cannot return to baseline after difficult moments, the system may be overloaded. A hard appointment leaves them unsettled for days. A family argument ruins sleep. A routine visit drains the whole weekend. A short call creates hours of rumination. Recovery time lengthens while available recovery space shrinks. That mismatch is a warning. The caregiver is spending more than the week is replenishing.

Burnout recognition should lead to early adjustment, not merely self-observation. Naming signals without changing anything can become another burden. If the caregiver identifies dread, they need to ask what boundary, support, or routine might reduce it. If they identify forgetfulness, what system can carry memory? If they identify irritability, where is recovery missing? If they identify numbness, what emotional support or respite is needed? If they identify constant alertness, what backup or emergency plan would allow the body to stand down?

The caregiver should avoid waiting for permission. Others may not notice early burnout, especially if the caregiver is still performing well. They may even resist the idea because recognising the caregiver's strain means recognising the need for change. If the caregiver waits until everyone agrees that the situation is serious, the warning signs may deepen. Early recognition requires trusting the evidence of one's own functioning.

There is no need to dramatise the signs, but there is also no need to minimise them. A calm statement is enough: "I am noticing that I am becoming irritable and forgetful. The current setup needs adjustment." Or: "I am dreading evening calls, so we need a different communication rhythm." Or: "I am not recovering after visits, so I need protected time afterwards." These statements treat the signal as relevant care information. They do not ask others to decide whether the caregiver deserves relief.

Burnout signals should be reviewed alongside the care load. What has changed recently? Has the care recipient's need increased? Are appointments more frequent? Has a helper become less reliable? Has the caregiver's work intensified? Has sleep worsened? Has family conflict increased? Has paperwork multiplied? Has the caregiver taken on a "temporary" task that became permanent? Burnout often reflects a mismatch between old arrangements and new demands. The caregiver may be trying to operate with a care plan that belongs to an earlier, easier stage.

This is why early recognition can prevent crisis. It creates a chance to adjust before the caregiver becomes too depleted to think clearly. It allows small changes before large ones become unavoidable. It makes it possible to ask for help, simplify routines, document tasks, schedule recovery, or escalate support while there is still some energy to act. Waiting until collapse may feel more legitimate, but it leaves fewer choices.

The caregiver should remember that burnout signals are not accusations against love. You can love someone and dread the next call. You can be devoted and irritable. You can be responsible and forgetful when overloaded. You can be compassionate and numb after too much exposure to distress. These signals do not prove that care has failed morally. They prove that care is being delivered through a human being with limits.

Recognising burnout early is an act of care for everyone involved. It protects the caregiver from becoming damaged by the role. It protects the person receiving care from the effects of a depleted caregiver. It protects the relationship from resentment, sharpness, withdrawal, and silent emotional distance. It protects the care system from pretending it is stable simply because one person has not yet fallen apart.

The question to ask is not, "Am I burned out enough to justify change?"

That question keeps the caregiver trapped in proving suffering.

The better question is, "What signs are already telling me that this care arrangement is spending capacity faster than it is restoring it?"

Building Recovery into the Week

Recovery is often treated as the thing a caregiver will do when everything else is finished. When the appointment has been attended, the prescription collected, the meals arranged, the forms completed, the phone calls returned, the family updated, the kitchen restored, the person reassured, and the next concern placed neatly somewhere manageable, then the caregiver will rest. This sounds reasonable until the caregiver notices the truth: everything else is never finished.

Care produces more care. A completed task often reveals the next task. A difficult visit leaves emotional residue. A phone call creates a follow-up. A form generates another question. A relative's message requires clarification. A medical appointment leads to new instructions. Even an apparently calm day may still contain the mental hum of monitoring, wondering, remembering, and preparing. If recovery must wait until the care queue is empty, recovery will remain theoretical. The caregiver will live on leftovers and call it devotion.

This is one of the quietest ways burnout becomes normal. The caregiver does not decide to abandon themselves in one dramatic act. They postpone themselves in small, reasonable increments. Not today, because there is too much to do. Not this evening, because someone might call. Not this weekend, because the family visit will be complicated. Not this month, because the situation is unsettled. Eventually, the caregiver's own restoration becomes the first thing removed from the week and the last thing defended.

Recovery must be moved from the margins into the care plan itself. Not as a luxury. Not as a reward. Not as something earned by being sufficiently selfless first. Recovery is part of what makes care sustainable. A caregiver who never recovers does not become more loving; they become more depleted. A caregiver who is permanently depleted may still perform tasks, but patience narrows, judgement becomes more reactive, resentment grows faster, and the relationship becomes strained by the very care meant to protect it.

The first step is to understand what recovery actually means. It is not always a holiday, a spa day, or a full afternoon of uninterrupted peace, though longer rest matters when it is possible. Recovery is any protected experience that allows the caregiver's body and mind to stand down from care mode. It may be brief or extended. Quiet or active. Alone or with someone safe. What matters is that it interrupts the state of constant readiness. It tells the nervous system, for a defined period, that it does not have to monitor, answer, soothe, plan, or prevent.

There are two forms of recovery that caregivers need to take seriously: micro-recovery and macro-recovery. Micro-recovery is small enough to fit into an imperfect day. Ten minutes after a difficult phone call. A short walk after a visit. Sitting in the car before driving home. Drinking tea without answering messages. Breathing quietly before opening a care-related letter. Standing outside for a few minutes after an emotionally heavy conversation. These moments will not solve a broken care arrangement, but they can prevent strain from stacking without interruption.

Micro-recovery works because caregiving stress often arrives in small surges. A tense message. A repeated question. A rushed errand. A conversation that requires restraint. A worry that appears during work. Each surge asks the caregiver to regulate themselves and continue. Without small recovery moments, the body carries every surge into the next task. By evening, the caregiver may feel inexplicably raw, not because one event was unbearable, but because no event was followed by release.

A micro-recovery practice should be specific enough to happen automatically. "I need to relax more" is too vague. "After a difficult visit, I will sit quietly for ten minutes before checking my phone" is usable. "After a hospital appointment, I will not schedule another demanding task immediately afterwards" is a recovery policy. "After an evening care call, I will write down any next step and then stop thinking about it until morning" gives the mind a boundary. Recovery begins to work when it becomes a repeated habit, not a desperate improvisation.

The caregiver may feel guilty protecting even ten minutes. This guilt is worth noticing, because it reveals how deeply the care role has colonised the week. If a caregiver feels unable to claim a brief pause after giving emotional or practical support, the problem is not the pause. The problem is the belief that their body should be available without maintenance. A short recovery moment is not a withdrawal of care. It is the reset that makes the next act of care less likely to be sharp, resentful, or automatic.

Macro-recovery is different. It is a real block of time, long enough for the caregiver to experience themselves outside the care role. An evening off. A regular morning protected from care tasks. A few hours when someone else is responsible. A weekend afternoon with the phone boundary clearly set. A planned period of respite. Macro-recovery matters because the caregiver needs more than small breathers. They need time in which their attention can belong to their own life.

This kind of recovery often meets more resistance because it disrupts the care system more visibly. A ten-minute pause can be hidden. An evening off must be planned. Someone else may need to cover a task. The person receiving care may need reassurance. Relatives may need to be told the caregiver is unavailable. Boundaries may be tested. Yet this visibility is part of the point. A care arrangement that cannot tolerate the caregiver being unavailable for any meaningful block of time is not stable. It is dependent on constant access.

A macro-recovery block should be placed in the week before the week consumes it. Caregivers often wait to see when they can "fit it in", but care tasks expand into unprotected space. A regular evening off, even if imperfect, is stronger than a vague hope for rest. A planned walk after the weekly visit is stronger than promising to decompress later. A protected Sunday morning is stronger than waiting for a quiet moment that never arrives. Recovery needs a place on the calendar because invisible intentions are easily overridden by visible demands.

The recovery block should also have a clear access rule. If the caregiver is technically resting but still monitoring the phone, answering routine questions, coordinating helpers, or mentally managing the care situation, the block is not fully recovery. It is remote duty. The caregiver may need to define what counts as urgent, who is responsible during that period, and when they will return to messages. "I am unavailable between 6 p.m. and 9 p.m. unless there is a true emergency" is different from "I will try to rest tonight." The first can be defended. The second can be dissolved.

Recovery should be matched to the kind of depletion the caregiver is experiencing. If the caregiver is physically exhausted, recovery may require sleep, stillness, nourishment, warmth, or gentle movement. If they are mentally overloaded, recovery may require quiet, fewer decisions, a written brain-dump, or time away from screens and messages. If they are emotionally raw, recovery may require solitude, supportive conversation, tears, music, prayer, reflection, or simply not being needed for a while. If they feel trapped, recovery may require movement, fresh air, novelty, or contact with a part of life not organised around care.

This matters because caregivers sometimes choose recovery activities that look restorative but do not restore the actual depleted system. Scrolling through messages may feel like a break but keep the mind stimulated and alert. Watching a programme while half-expecting a call may pass time but not create release. Meeting a friend who only asks for care updates may not return the caregiver to themselves. True recovery should leave some trace of restoration, even if small: a softened body, a quieter mind, a less clenched mood, a sense of being a person rather than only a function.

The caregiver should not wait to feel deserving before building recovery into the week. Deserving is a poor gatekeeper. It asks whether the caregiver has suffered enough, done enough, sacrificed enough, and proven enough. Sustainable care asks a better question: what level of recovery is necessary for this caregiver to remain functional, humane, and well enough to continue? That question removes the performance of worthiness. A car does not need to deserve fuel. A body does not need to deserve rest.

Recovery also needs protection from care-related rumination. Many caregivers step away physically but continue rehearsing conversations, imagining disasters, judging themselves, or planning the next task. Rumination can make a rest block feel useless because the caregiver has not truly left the care field. A simple closing ritual can help. Write down the next action. Put the paper in a visible place. Send the necessary message. Set the alarm or reminder. Then say, internally, "This is held until the next care time." The mind may return to it, but the caregiver has given the worry a container.

It can also help to create a transition between care and recovery. Caregiving often has no natural end point. A visit ends, but the caregiver carries the mood home. A call ends, but the body remains tense. A planning session ends, but the mind keeps sorting. A transition tells the body that one mode is ending and another is beginning. It might be a short walk, washing hands slowly, changing clothes, sitting in silence before entering the house, stretching, writing three notes, or making a cup of tea without multitasking. The act itself can be simple. Its purpose is to mark the boundary.

Recovery should not depend entirely on the caregiver escaping the care situation. Sometimes escape is necessary and healthy, but everyday recovery also has to exist within imperfect conditions. A caregiver may not be able to take a full day away, but they may be able to protect twenty minutes after lunch. They may not have reliable respite yet, but they can stop answering routine evening messages. They may not be able to travel, but they can reclaim one weekly activity that has nothing to do with care. The absence of ideal recovery should not prevent the use of available recovery.

At the same time, micro-recovery should not be used to justify an impossible load. Ten minutes of breathing will not fix a care arrangement that requires night-time vigilance, daily emotional crisis management, all transport, all administration, and no meaningful support. Small recovery practices can keep the caregiver steadier, but they cannot make an unsustainable system fair. If recovery moments are constantly overwhelmed by the scale of the load, the signal is not that the caregiver is bad at resting. The signal is that more structural change is needed.

A weekly recovery plan should include both immediate and protected forms. Immediate recovery answers, "What helps me reset after a difficult care moment?" Protected recovery answers, "Where in the week do I have a real break from responsibility?" The caregiver needs both. Without immediate recovery, stress accumulates throughout the day. Without protected recovery, the caregiver never fully leaves the role. One keeps the pressure from spiking. The other prevents care from becoming total.

The caregiver may need to communicate recovery as a policy rather than a plea. "I need some time to myself" may be emotionally true, but it can invite minimisation or negotiation. "I am unavailable for routine care matters on Thursday evenings" is clearer. "After hospital appointments, I do not take on additional care tasks that evening" is a policy. "I take a walk after Sunday visits before responding to messages" is a policy. Policies reduce the number of times the caregiver must justify basic maintenance.

When other people resist, the caregiver can keep the explanation short. "This helps me stay well enough to keep supporting care." "This is part of the plan now." "Routine matters can wait until tomorrow." The caregiver does not need to prove that they are exhausted enough. They do not need to convince everyone that recovery is pleasant, deserved, or convenient. They need to make it real enough that the week begins to respect it.

Recovery is also easier when it is linked to handoffs and backups. A caregiver cannot rest properly if everything still depends on them. Who covers the regular call? Who handles transport if an appointment falls during the recovery block? What happens if the person receiving care feels anxious? Who is contacted for a true emergency? What is allowed to wait? Without these answers, the caregiver's body may remain on alert even during protected time. Recovery requires not only permission, but design.

There is a particular skill in allowing others to do enough. Helpers may not perform tasks exactly as the caregiver would. They may use different words, take a different route, or handle a minor issue less elegantly. If the outcome is safe and acceptable, the caregiver may need to let it stand so that recovery can happen. Perfectionism can become a thief of rest. If the caregiver must supervise every detail from a distance, they have not truly stepped away.

Recovery also includes emotional nourishment, not merely absence of tasks. A caregiver may need contact with people who do not treat them only as the responsible one. They may need laughter, beauty, faith, music, movement, books, nature, creativity, or ordinary conversation. These things are not decorative. They help restore identity. Burnout is not only the result of too much work; it is also the result of too little life returning to the person doing the work.

This is why joy can feel uncomfortable and still be necessary. A caregiver may feel guilty enjoying an evening while the person receiving care is lonely or unwell. They may feel disloyal laughing, eating well, seeing friends, or looking forward to something. But another person's suffering does not require the caregiver to surrender every source of aliveness. Joy is not betrayal. It is one of the things that keeps care from becoming a prison.

The caregiver should track what genuinely restores them. Not what sounds virtuous. Not what other people recommend. What actually helps? A walk may restore one person and bore another. Social time may energise one caregiver and drain another. Quiet may be medicine for one and loneliness for another. Movement, music, prayer, gardening, reading, cooking, sitting in silence, meeting a friend, or doing something with the hands may each have different effects. Recovery should be personal enough to work.

A simple weekly review can help. What drained me most this week? What helped even a little? Where did I feel most like myself? Which care task required recovery afterwards but did not receive it? Which boundary protected me? Which one failed? What recovery block needs to be placed before the next pressure point? These questions keep recovery connected to real conditions rather than abstract self-care ideals.

The caregiver should also notice whether they are confusing distraction with recovery. Distraction can be useful. It gives the mind a break from constant concern. But not all distraction restores. Some forms leave the caregiver more numb, tense, or avoidant. True recovery does not always feel easy at first, especially if the body is used to constant alert, but over time it should return some capacity.

If an activity helps the caregiver avoid feeling for a while but leaves them more depleted, it may not be enough.

Recovery may include processing emotion, not only escaping it. After a hard visit, the caregiver may need to acknowledge sadness. After an argument, they may need to name anger. After witnessing decline, they may need to grieve. If every recovery block is used to suppress feeling, the feeling may return as irritability, dread, or numbness. Sometimes restoration requires a safe place to tell the truth: "That was painful." "I hated how I felt." "I am scared." "I miss who they were." Honest feeling can be part of recovery when it is held in a safe enough container.

Caregivers who have been over-functioning for a long time may find rest unsettling. Stillness can reveal exhaustion that busyness has hidden. The first quiet evening may bring tears rather than peace. The first walk after a difficult visit may bring anger. The first real break may feel empty because the caregiver has forgotten how to want anything. This does not mean recovery is failing. It may mean the body is finally safe enough to report what it has been carrying.

In such moments, the caregiver should not rush back into tasks just to avoid the discomfort of rest. Recovery sometimes begins as withdrawal from constant urgency, and withdrawal can feel strange. The nervous system may keep looking for the next demand. The caregiver may feel guilty, restless, or suspicious of quiet. Repetition matters. The body learns through repeated proof that protected time does not always lead to disaster.

Recovery should be built around predictable pressure points. If Wednesday appointments always drain the caregiver, Wednesday evening should not be filled with difficult calls. If Sunday visits stir grief, Sunday night may need quiet. If family updates create tension, they should not be scheduled immediately before sleep. If morning routines are demanding, the caregiver may need a pause before beginning paid work where possible. Recovery works best when placed where strain actually occurs.

This is where the weekly care plan becomes useful. Recovery should sit beside appointments, visits, calls, and administrative tasks. Not hidden beneath them. A calendar that includes only care duties tells a false story about capacity. A truthful calendar shows the recovery required to make those duties sustainable. The caregiver's walk, rest block, therapy appointment, exercise class, quiet evening, or time with a friend belongs in the same planning reality as the prescription collection and appointment review.

Some caregivers will need to negotiate recovery with others. This can be uncomfortable, especially if relatives are used to the caregiver being constantly available. The request should be specific. "I need a break" is easier to sympathise with than to implement. "Can you sit with Dad from 2 p.m. to 5 p.m. on Saturday so I can be unavailable?" is actionable. "Can you handle Sunday evening calls for the next month?" is clearer than "I need people to step up." Recovery becomes possible when cover is defined.

Paid help, where available, may also be part of recovery. This does not mean the caregiver has failed. It means some tasks may need support beyond the informal network. A cleaner, driver, respite worker, meal service, administrative help, or another paid arrangement may reduce the pressure enough to protect the caregiver's capacity. Not everyone will have access to paid help, and cost may be a serious barrier. But where it is possible, it should not be dismissed as indulgence. It may be a structural support.

Recovery must also include boundaries around information. A caregiver who receives constant updates, questions, and alerts may never recover because the care system keeps entering their attention. Communication windows, shared calendars, written task lists, and clear emergency criteria are recovery tools as much as organisational tools. They prevent the caregiver's mind from being permanently available. Sometimes the most restorative practice is not a bath or a walk, but the absence of non-urgent messages during a protected evening.

The caregiver should be prepared for recovery to expose the need for escalation. If a regular evening off is impossible because the person receiving care is unsafe, the issue is not merely scheduling. If no one can cover even a short break, the support network is too thin. If the caregiver cannot sleep because night-time care is constant, micro-recovery will not be enough. If every attempt at rest is interrupted by genuine risk, the care arrangement may require more help, different routines, or a higher level of support. Recovery is not only restorative; it is diagnostic.

This is a powerful point. If recovery cannot be built into the week at all, the care plan is sending a message. It may be saying that tasks are too concentrated, risks are too high, support is too unreliable, or the caregiver is being treated as the emergency infrastructure. Instead of concluding, "I am bad at taking breaks," the caregiver can ask, "What is preventing recovery, and what does that reveal about the care arrangement?"

The caregiver should start small but not stay small if small is not enough. A ten-minute walk may be a beginning. A protected cup of tea may be a first boundary. A no-message window may create breathing space. But if the load continues to produce burnout signals, the recovery plan must grow. A person cannot survive indefinitely on scraps of restoration. Micro-recovery is valuable. Macro-recovery is necessary. Structural relief may become essential.

There is no single recovery pattern that suits every caregiver. A caregiver supporting a parent from a distance will need different recovery from a spouse providing daily physical care. A caregiver with children at home will face different constraints from someone living alone. A caregiver with a demanding job, financial pressure, complicated family history, or their own health concerns will need a plan that reflects those realities. The principle remains constant: recovery must be designed around the actual life being lived, not an idealised schedule.

The deeper shift is moral. The caregiver must stop treating recovery as evidence that they are less committed. Recovery is evidence that they understand the seriousness of the role. Serious roles require maintenance. No responsible system runs on depletion as its main fuel. A caregiver who builds recovery into the week is not stepping away from care; they are refusing to let care become dependent on their silent deterioration.

A week without recovery teaches the caregiver that their life is the flexible part of the care system.

A week with recovery begins to teach something different: the caregiver's stability is part of the plan.

That lesson may feel unfamiliar at first. It may even feel selfish. But the care arrangement will become more honest when the caregiver stops asking, "When will I be allowed to recover?" and begins asking, "Where must recovery go so this care can continue without destroying me?"

Knowing When to Escalate Support

There comes a point in caregiving when the familiar arrangement no longer fits the reality in front of you. The visits that used to be enough are no longer enough. The phone calls that once reassured now multiply into repeated distress. The medication routine that seemed manageable begins to produce worry. The person receiving care needs more supervision, more help, more emotional containment, or more physical support than the current system can reliably provide. The caregiver may feel this change before they can explain it. Something has shifted.

The difficulty is that caregivers often respond to this shift by trying harder. They visit more often, answer faster, sleep less, postpone their own needs, smooth over more conflicts, and stretch the old routine as far as it will go. This is understandable. Escalating support can feel like admitting failure, betraying a promise, inviting judgement, or opening a door to decisions no one feels ready to face. So the caregiver keeps patching the system. Another reminder. Another favour. Another late call. Another emergency errand. Another "just for now" that quietly becomes the new normal.

But escalation is not failure. It is recognition. It means the care need, the caregiver's capacity, or the surrounding support has changed enough that the old arrangement must be reconsidered. A setup that once worked can become unsafe or unviable without anyone having done anything wrong. Illness can progress. Mobility can decline.

Memory can change. Anxiety can intensify. The caregiver's own health, work, family responsibilities, or emotional reserves can shift. Sustainability is not a permanent status. It has to be reviewed against reality.

The first sign that support may need to escalate is repeated crisis. Not one difficult day. Not an unusual week. Repetition. The same problem returns in slightly different clothing: missed medicines, unsafe movement, distressing calls, food not being eaten, bills missed, appointments becoming chaotic, night-time disruption, falls or near-falls, family conflict, or the caregiver repeatedly needing to drop everything to prevent harm. When the same crisis keeps returning, the question should no longer be, "How do I fix this again?" The question should be, "What level of support would prevent this from needing rescue so often?"

Another threshold appears when the caregiver becomes the only functioning safety net. If the person receiving care would be at serious risk whenever the caregiver is ill, at work, asleep, travelling, emotionally depleted, or simply unavailable, the arrangement is too fragile. A care plan that depends on one person never being absent is not a plan; it is an accident waiting for the wrong day. This is especially important where there are health, safety, medication, mobility, confusion, or supervision concerns. The issue is not whether the caregiver loves enough. The issue is whether the system has enough depth.

Escalation may also be needed when the caregiver's burnout signals become persistent despite reasonable adjustments. A difficult season may require extra effort, but if numbness, dread, irritability, poor sleep, forgetfulness, resentment, or emotional collapse continue after boundaries, routines, and recovery practices have been attempted, the care load may exceed the current structure. The caregiver should not treat their own deterioration as an acceptable price of keeping things unchanged. Their condition is part of the condition of care. If the arrangement is damaging the person providing care, the arrangement needs attention.

There is a particular danger in normalising the unacceptable because it happened gradually. A caregiver may not notice how much the baseline has shifted. The first night-time call felt exceptional; now it happens regularly. The first missed meal was worrying; now the caregiver expects it. The first time a relative cancelled transport was frustrating; now the caregiver assumes they must be ready to rescue. The first time paperwork created panic seemed unusual; now administration is always urgent. Gradual decline is still decline. Repetition turns warning signs into evidence.

The caregiver should pay close attention to safety signals. Safety is broader than dramatic emergency. It includes whether the person can manage essential medicines, food, hydration, hygiene, mobility, heating, money, appointments, communication, and urgent help in a reasonably reliable way. It includes whether the home environment has become risky, whether confusion or distress is increasing, whether the person is making decisions that repeatedly place them at risk, and whether the caregiver is being asked to compensate through constant vigilance. A care arrangement that relies on hope rather than safeguards needs review.

Emotional safety counts too. If the caregiver is regularly exposed to shouting, insults, manipulation, intense distress, or conversations that leave them unable to recover, support may need to change. This does not mean abandoning the person receiving care. It means recognising that emotional strain can make a care role unsafe in a different way. A caregiver should not be expected to absorb ongoing harm because the other person is vulnerable. Vulnerability explains some behaviour; it does not erase the caregiver's need for protection.

Escalation does not always mean one dramatic decision. It may mean adding a helper, increasing visits, involving another relative more specifically, using paid support where available, arranging respite, changing transport, seeking professional assessment, simplifying the care plan, reviewing living arrangements, or creating a stronger emergency structure. Sometimes escalation is practical and modest. Sometimes it is serious and life-changing. The common thread is that the old level of support is no longer treated as sacred simply because it is familiar.

The caregiver should avoid one-size-fits-all thinking. More support does not look the same in every situation. For one family, the crucial change may be weekly help with bathing or meals. For another, it may be medication oversight. For another, it may be respite for the caregiver. For another, it may be a professional review because the person's needs have become too complex for informal care alone. The correct escalation is the one that responds to the actual pressure point, not the one that satisfies someone else's idea of what care should look like.

Decision signals are more useful than emotional ultimatums. A caregiver does not have to wait until they say, "I cannot take this anymore." They can act when certain thresholds appear: repeated safety concerns, no reliable backup, the caregiver losing sleep regularly, essential tasks being missed, the person receiving care needing more than the current routine can provide, helpers failing in high-risk roles, or the caregiver's health beginning to suffer. These signals should be written down if necessary. Written signals help the caregiver make decisions from evidence rather than guilt.

It can be helpful to separate inconvenience from unsustainability. Some care tasks are inconvenient but manageable. Others are no longer viable. A long appointment may be tiring but possible if it happens rarely and recovery follows. Weekly appointments that repeatedly disrupt work, sleep, family life, and emotional stability may require a different transport or attendance plan. A difficult conversation may be unpleasant but survivable. Daily distress calls that leave the caregiver unable to function are a different matter. The issue is not whether care is ever hard. Care is often hard. The issue is whether the hardness has exceeded what the current system can carry.

Escalation often brings grief. It may mean admitting that the person receiving care has changed. It may mean facing the limits of family help. It may mean accepting that a promise made in an earlier stage of life cannot be kept in the same form. It may mean disappointing someone who wanted everything to remain private, familiar, or centred on one caregiver. This grief is real. It deserves tenderness. But grief should not be allowed to disguise danger. Feeling sad about change does not mean change is wrong.

Guilt will almost certainly appear. The caregiver may think, "I should be able to manage," "They will feel abandoned," "Other people will judge me," or "If I ask for more help, I am admitting I have failed." These thoughts are common, but they are not reliable decision-makers. A more grounded question is: what happens if nothing changes? If the honest answer includes increasing risk, worsening burnout, repeated crises, emotional harm, or practical failure, then guilt is not protecting care. It is protecting an outdated arrangement.

The person receiving care may resist escalation. They may fear loss of independence, privacy, control, or dignity. They may dislike outsiders. They may believe accepting more help means admitting decline. Their feelings matter and should be treated with respect. But resistance cannot be the only factor, especially when safety or caregiver viability is at stake. A humane escalation explains as much as appropriate, preserves choice where possible, and avoids unnecessary forcefulness, but it still takes reality seriously.

Relatives may also resist. Some may minimise the situation because admitting the need for more support would require them to contribute. Others may criticise from a distance. Some may prefer the main caregiver to continue because that arrangement is convenient. Some may argue about cost, roles, pride, or family reputation. The caregiver should listen for useful information, but not allow resistance to erase the decision signals. A care system should not be held hostage by the comfort of people who are not carrying its daily weight.

Escalating support requires clear language. "Things are getting too much" may be true, but it can be dismissed as emotion. "There have been repeated medication problems, I am no longer sleeping properly, and there is no backup when I am unavailable" is harder to ignore. "Mum needs more help" is vague. "Mum is missing meals, becoming distressed in the evenings, and I cannot safely cover daily checks alone" is more precise. Clear language turns private worry into shared reality.

Documentation matters here. Patterns are easier to address when they have been recorded. Not in a dramatic or accusatory way, but plainly. What happened? When? What was the risk? Who responded? What was the effect on the caregiver? What keeps repeating? A short record can show whether a situation is changing. It can also help in conversations with relatives or professionals because the caregiver is not relying only on memory or emotion. Evidence reduces the chance that serious concerns are minimised.

Escalation should be framed around fit, not blame. "This arrangement no longer fits the need" is more useful than "No one is helping" or "They are impossible." Blame may be understandable, especially when the caregiver has been unsupported, but blame often triggers defensiveness. Fit is harder to argue with. It acknowledges that needs and capacity must match. When they do not, the plan must change. This language can protect dignity for everyone involved while still refusing denial.

Sometimes the first escalation is asking for a review of the care plan with the people already involved. What has changed? Which tasks are failing? Which risks are increasing? What support is missing? What can be simplified? What must no longer depend on the main caregiver? Sometimes this conversation reveals practical changes that can be made quickly. At other times, it reveals that the family system is not enough. Both outcomes are useful because they replace vague strain with a clearer assessment.

The caregiver should also examine whether support needs to escalate for them, not only for the person receiving care. They may need counselling, respite, peer support, medical attention, a break from certain tasks, paid help where possible, or a firmer redistribution of responsibilities. Caregiver support is not secondary. If the caregiver is the main pillar of the current arrangement, strengthening or relieving that pillar is part of protecting the whole structure. Ignoring the caregiver until they collapse is a poor form of planning.

There are moments when escalation is urgent. If immediate safety is in question, if the person receiving care is at serious risk, if the caregiver feels unable to continue safely, or if essential needs are not being met, delay can be dangerous. In such cases, the caregiver may need to contact appropriate local services, medical professionals, emergency routes, or trusted support immediately. The specific route depends on the situation and location, but the principle is clear: some thresholds are not matters for slow family debate.

Other thresholds are less urgent but still serious. The caregiver may notice that the current setup works only because they are sacrificing sleep, income, health, or family life. The person receiving care may be just safe enough for now, but only with constant informal monitoring. Helpers may be present but unreliable. Paperwork may be repeatedly late. Meals may be inconsistent. Emotional distress may be increasing. These are not necessarily immediate emergencies, but they are signs that the arrangement is weakening. Acting at this stage is far better than waiting for a forced crisis.

Escalation may require tolerating an imperfect next step. Caregivers sometimes delay because they want the perfect solution: the right helper, the right timing, the right agreement, the right service, the right emotional readiness. Meanwhile, the current arrangement deteriorates. A next step does not have to solve everything to be worth taking. It may simply reduce one risk, create one backup, bring one professional perspective, or secure one regular break. The care system does not need a perfect rescue before it is allowed to improve.

However, escalation should not be used to avoid specific boundaries that are still needed. More support may be necessary, but the caregiver may still need to say no to late calls, stop being the only driver, refuse abusive conversations, or ask relatives for defined tasks. Escalation and boundaries work together. More help without boundaries can still leave the caregiver overexposed. Boundaries without more help may not be enough if the need has outgrown the support available. The balance depends on the situation.

The caregiver should beware of the phrase "just a bit longer." Sometimes a short extension is reasonable: a temporary crisis, a waiting period, a planned transition. But "just a bit longer" can also become a way of avoiding reality indefinitely. If the same phrase has been used for weeks or months while the caregiver's condition worsens, it is no longer a temporary bridge. It is denial. A true temporary arrangement has an end point, a review date, and a backup. Without those, it becomes permanent by stealth.

Escalation also involves the courage to let others see the gap. If the caregiver keeps filling every failure silently, no one else can see how serious the situation is. This does not mean allowing harm. It means stopping the habit of hiding the system's weakness through personal sacrifice. If transport is not covered, name it. If no one is available for evening support, name it. If the caregiver cannot continue daily checks, name it. A visible gap can be uncomfortable, but invisibility keeps the burden trapped.

When discussing escalation, the caregiver should focus on concrete thresholds rather than emotional persuasion. "I am exhausted" may invite sympathy, but it may also be minimised. "I have had to leave work three times this month for preventable care issues, and I cannot continue being the only emergency contact" gives a clearer picture, if such details are accurate. If the caregiver does not have exact figures, they can still be specific without inventing them: "This is happening repeatedly." "The evening calls are affecting my sleep." "The medication routine is no longer reliable." Specificity gives the conversation weight.

It is also important to consider the person receiving care's dignity during escalation. More support should not be presented as punishment for being difficult or as proof that they are a burden. It can be framed as a way to make care steadier, reduce last-minute stress, protect the caregiver's capacity, and keep essential needs covered. The person may still dislike it, but the language should not shame them for needing more than the old arrangement can provide.

Caregivers should not confuse dignity with avoidance. Sometimes families avoid necessary support because they say they want to preserve dignity, when in truth they are avoiding discomfort, cost, family conflict, or the reality of decline. Dignity is not protected by unsafe or chaotic care. It is protected by honest arrangements that meet needs as respectfully as possible. A person's pride matters, but pride cannot be the sole care plan.

Escalating support may uncover difficult truths about the relationship. Perhaps the caregiver has been over-functioning for years. Perhaps other relatives will not help. Perhaps the person receiving care refuses reasonable options. Perhaps paid help is more limited than hoped. Perhaps the caregiver's own body has been signalling distress for a long time. These truths can be painful, but they are less dangerous than the fantasy that one more effort will make the old setup work.

A decision signal worth taking seriously is when the caregiver starts fearing their own reactions. If they worry they may snap, withdraw, make mistakes, drive while exhausted, forget important details, or speak in ways they later regret, support should be escalated. This is not a confession of being unsafe as a person. It is a responsible acknowledgement that strain is affecting behaviour. Acting before harm occurs is mature caregiving.

Another signal is when care has begun to crowd out the caregiver's essential life. Not merely leisure, but essentials: sleep, income, health care, parenting, partnership, basic household functioning, and emotional stability. If these are repeatedly sacrificed, the arrangement is borrowing from places it should not borrow. A care plan that protects one person by steadily damaging another is not balanced. It may be understandable. It is not sustainable.

The caregiver may need a phrase to hold steady: "The current level of support no longer matches the level of need." This sentence avoids blame and exaggeration. It is calm. It is hard to dismiss. It can be repeated to relatives, helpers, professionals, and oneself. It does not demand a specific solution before naming the problem. It simply states the reality from which solutions must begin.

Escalating support before collapse is one of the most compassionate acts a caregiver can take. It protects the care recipient from crisis-driven decisions. It protects the caregiver from being used beyond their limits. It protects relationships from the bitterness that grows when everyone waits too long. It allows change to happen with more thought, more dignity, and more choice than a forced emergency usually permits.

The question is not whether the caregiver has tried hard enough.

The question is whether the current arrangement is still safe, viable, and humane for everyone inside it.

When the answer begins to shift, the next act of care is not to push harder. It is to tell the truth sooner.

Chapter 9
Resentment Repair and Relationship Care

How can care given from love begin to feel like a debt no one is paying back? The question is painful because resentment rarely appears in a caregiver all at once. It gathers in small, ordinary moments: the call answered while dinner goes cold, the appointment managed without thanks, the sibling who sends advice but not availability, the boundary crossed again because it was easier for everyone else to pretend it was flexible. The caregiver may keep smiling, keep doing, keep showing up. Yet something inside begins keeping score.

Resentment is often treated as an ugly emotion, something a decent caregiver should rise above. But resentment is not always a sign of selfishness or lack of love. More often, it is a sign that a cost has gone unnamed for too long. Effort has been unseen. Choices have felt forced. Promises have been vague. Limits have been crossed and then politely ignored. The heart does not become bitter in a vacuum. It hardens around repeated imbalance.

The central tension is that resentment can damage a relationship, yet it can also reveal what the relationship now needs. If ignored, it leaks into tone, timing, patience, and presence. A harmless request sounds like an accusation. A repeated question becomes unbearable. A visit becomes something to survive. But if resentment is examined rather than denied, it can point towards the real fracture: not merely the person receiving care, but the broken arrangement around them.

This distinction matters because caregivers often aim their anger at the nearest person. That person may be ill, frightened, dependent, confused, grieving, or simply present when everyone else is absent. They become the face of the burden. Yet the caregiver may not only be angry at them. They may be angry at the workload, the invisibility, the lack of backup, the old family role, the lost freedom, the unfairness of decline, or the silence of people who should have helped sooner. Separating the person from the system does not excuse harmful behaviour, but it prevents resentment from turning the care recipient into the enemy.

The stakes are relational. Care can continue long after warmth has gone underground. Tasks may still be completed, meals arranged, medicines checked, and appointments attended, while the relationship itself becomes thin and functional. The caregiver is there, but not fully there. The person receiving care may sense the withdrawal and respond with more need, complaint, guilt, or fear. The caregiver then feels more trapped. Without repair, both people can become locked in a painful exchange: one reaching for reassurance, the other silently resenting being reached for.

Conflict is almost inevitable in this terrain. Tired people snap. Frightened people accuse. Overloaded people speak sharply. Dependent people resist. Relatives disappoint. A relationship under care pressure will not remain untouched by strain. The question is not whether every conversation can be kept gentle, but whether rupture can be repaired without erasing the limits that were needed in the first place. An apology that gives away the boundary is not repair; it is fear wearing a softer voice. Real repair acknowledges impact while still telling the truth about what must change.

There is also a quieter danger: the caregiver can disappear into usefulness. Hobbies stop first, then friendships, then future plans, then the small private habits that once made life feel like their own. Their name becomes attached to tasks rather than desires. They are the driver, organiser, caller, form-reader, comforter, problem-solver, emergency contact. A person can be needed so constantly that they begin to feel less like a person and more like a function. Resentment grows quickly in the space where identity has been neglected.

The work begins by listening to resentment with precision, asking what it is really protesting rather than condemning it as moral failure. From there, damaged moments need repair that is honest enough to rebuild trust and firm enough to preserve necessary limits. Beyond the conflict itself, the caregiver's identity has to be protected through small anchors of life that are not organised around care: a relationship, an activity, a goal, a private thread of continuity that says, *I still exist here too.*

The difficult question is not whether resentment should be allowed to run the relationship. It should not. The sharper question is what resentment has been trying to say because no calmer signal was taken seriously. What, exactly, are you angry about: the person, the task, the loneliness, the disrespect, the grief, or the system that keeps asking you to absorb what no one has agreed to carry?

Understanding Resentment Patterns

Resentment is one of the emotions caregivers are most likely to hide and least able to outrun. It may not appear at the beginning, when the need is new, the adrenaline is strong, and the desire to help feels uncomplicated. It grows later, in the repeated moments: the errand no one counts, the late call that breaks sleep, the sibling who says "you are amazing" but does not take a task, the person receiving care who criticises the meal you made while you are already tired. The feeling may be small at first, a flicker of irritation quickly swallowed. Then it returns.

Caregivers often feel ashamed of resentment because it seems to contradict love. They may think, "How can I resent someone who is ill?" or "What kind of person gets angry about helping?" These questions are understandable, but they are too blunt. Resentment does not always mean the caregiver lacks compassion. Often it means that compassion has been forced to operate inside an unfair, unspoken, or unsustainable arrangement. Love may still be present. The conditions around love may be broken.

Resentment is not the same as ordinary anger. Anger can flare quickly in response to a particular moment: a harsh comment, a missed task, a broken promise. Resentment is slower. It gathers around repeated imbalance. It remembers what was not noticed, not shared, not respected, not repaired. It carries the history of swallowed noes and reluctant yeses. It is what happens when the caregiver's effort becomes expected rather than recognised, when their choices feel forced rather than freely made, and when their limits are crossed so often that the crossing begins to feel normal to everyone except the person paying the cost.

This is why resentment should not be dismissed as ugliness. It should be examined as information. The question is not, "How do I stop feeling this so I can be a better person?" The better question is, "What is this resentment pointing towards?" It may be pointing towards workload. It may be pointing towards disrespect. It may be pointing towards grief. It may be pointing towards isolation. It may be pointing towards the fact that the caregiver has become the silent solution to a care system that no one has properly designed.

Workload resentment is among the most common. It grows when the caregiver is carrying too many tasks, especially tasks that remain invisible. They may not resent the person receiving care directly; they resent being the person who notices everything, remembers everything, and fills every gap. They resent that a simple visit is not simple because it includes planning, travel, emotional regulation, food checks, medication reminders, paperwork, and recovery afterwards. They resent that other people judge the visible task without seeing the hidden labour around it.

This kind of resentment often sounds like, "Why is this always mine?" That sentence is worth taking seriously. It is not necessarily a complaint about one task. It may be a complaint about the entire pattern of ownership. The caregiver may have become responsible because they were nearby, competent, emotionally available, unmarried, childless, retired, female, eldest, youngest, trusted, or simply the one who acted first. Whatever the reason, responsibility may have drifted towards them without conscious consent. Resentment then becomes the emotional record of a role that expanded without agreement.

Disrespect resentment has a different texture. It grows when the caregiver's time, boundaries, judgement, or effort are treated as less important than the needs or opinions of others. A person receiving care may speak sharply, dismiss the caregiver's limits, or act as though help is owed rather than given. Relatives may criticise from a distance, offer advice without labour, or question decisions they did not help make. Professionals may suggest tasks without asking whether the caregiver has capacity. The caregiver begins to feel not merely tired, but used.

This form of resentment often contains anger at being taken for granted. The caregiver may not need applause, but they do need the care system to respect that their life has edges. When those edges are ignored, resentment becomes a boundary trying to speak through the body. It says, "I am not a limitless service." It says, "My time is not automatically available." It says, "You do not get to benefit from my reliability and then treat my limits as inconvenience."

Grief resentment is more complex because it can feel cruel to name. The caregiver may resent the situation itself: the illness, the decline, the lost freedom, the changed relationship, the future that has narrowed. They may resent the fact that a parent now needs parenting, a spouse now needs nursing, a sibling bond now revolves around tasks, or a friendship has become one-directional. This resentment is often braided with sorrow. The caregiver is not only angry about what they must do. They are grieving what has been taken from both people.

When grief is not recognised, it can disguise itself as irritation. The caregiver snaps about a small task because the deeper loss is too painful to touch. They become angry about a repeated question because each repetition confirms a change they do not want to accept. They resent another appointment because it symbolises the life that has been replaced by medical time, waiting rooms, forms, and vigilance. The surface anger may look petty. The root may be heartbreak.

Isolation resentment appears when the caregiver feels alone inside a role that others discuss but do not truly share. This can happen even when people are physically around. A relative may visit occasionally but not understand the daily mental load. Friends may ask how things are and then retreat when the answer is complicated. The person receiving care may be the centre of concern, while the caregiver becomes the background mechanism that keeps everything running. The caregiver may feel surrounded by people and still fundamentally unseen.

Isolation is particularly corrosive because it removes the caregiver's sense of witness. Human beings can bear a great deal when someone sees the weight honestly. Resentment intensifies when no one does.

Praise can even make it worse if it replaces practical support. "You are wonderful" may sound kind, but if it is not followed by relief, it can feel like a decorative label placed on an unfair arrangement. The caregiver may begin to hear admiration as a way of keeping them in position.

To understand resentment, the caregiver must separate the trigger from the source. The trigger may be a comment, a phone call, a request, a late arrival, an unwashed dish, or a repeated question. The source is the deeper pattern that gives the trigger its force. A caregiver may feel rage when asked to pick up one more item from the shop, but the source may be months of unshared errands. They may feel cold after a parent complains about dinner, but the source may be years of feeling nothing is good enough. They may resent a sibling's casual message because the source is unequal labour.

This distinction matters because reacting only to the trigger often creates confusion. The caregiver may explode over a small thing and then feel ashamed because the reaction seems disproportionate. But the reaction may be proportionate to the pattern, not the moment. The task is to identify the pattern before it bursts out through the wrong doorway. Resentment asks to be decoded. What keeps happening? What keeps being ignored? What keeps being expected? What keeps being paid for by one person?

A useful private sentence is: "I am angry about more than this moment." That sentence slows the reaction. It helps the caregiver look beneath the immediate irritation and find the real grievance. Perhaps the real grievance is not that the person asked for help, but that the request came at a time the caregiver had already marked as unavailable. Perhaps it is not that a sibling forgot once, but that their unreliability has become part of the caregiver's workload. Perhaps it is not that the care recipient is distressed, but that the caregiver has become the only container for that distress.

The next task is to separate the person from the broken system. This does not mean excusing every behaviour. Some people do behave badly. Some care recipients may be demanding, dismissive, manipulative, or hurtful. Some relatives may be selfish, absent, or critical. A caregiver is not required to pretend otherwise. But even when individual behaviour is difficult, resentment becomes more workable when the caregiver can see the system around the person: the missing backup, the unclear roles, the lack of routines, the unspoken expectations, the emotional pressure, the absence of recovery.

Without this separation, the person receiving care can become the symbol of everything the caregiver has lost. They become the reason the caregiver is tired, trapped, unseen, lonely, and interrupted. That may feel emotionally true in a hard moment, but it is usually incomplete. The person may be the immediate source of need, but the resentment may belong partly to the way that need has been organised. A broken system makes relationships carry weight they were never meant to carry alone.

For example, a caregiver may resent a parent for calling every evening in distress. But the deeper problem may be that no evening routine, emotional support plan, phone boundary, or backup contact exists. A caregiver may resent a spouse for needing help with meals, but the deeper problem may be that all meal planning, shopping, preparation, and cleaning have become one person's responsibility. A caregiver may resent a sibling for not visiting, but the deeper problem may be the absence of specific task agreements and the caregiver's pattern of covering gaps silently.

Separating person from system creates more options. If the person is the whole problem, the caregiver can only blame, withdraw, or endure. If the system is part of the problem, the caregiver can redesign, delegate, document, set boundaries, ask for support, simplify tasks, or escalate help. This does not remove the emotional difficulty, but it prevents resentment from hardening into contempt. Contempt says, "They are the problem." Clarity says, "This arrangement is producing harm."

The caregiver should also distinguish resentment from hatred. Resentment can feel frighteningly intense, especially when the caregiver has been suppressing it. They may fear that feeling resentment means they no longer love the person. Often, that is not true. Resentment may exist precisely because love is still trying to survive under pressure. The caregiver may want to be kind, but the load has become too heavy. They may want to be present, but the interruptions never stop. They may want connection, but every interaction has become functional.

Love can coexist with resentment. That coexistence is painful, but it is not hypocrisy. It is evidence that caregiving is morally and emotionally complex. A caregiver can feel tenderness during one moment and anger in the next. They can want the person safe and still resent the cost of providing that safety. They can feel grateful for a relationship and resent what the role has taken. Emotional contradiction does not make the caregiver false. It makes the situation real.

However, resentment should not be allowed to run unchecked. If it remains unnamed, it often leaks out indirectly. The caregiver may become sarcastic, curt, avoidant, passive-aggressive, or emotionally absent. They may do the task but with a coldness that both people feel. They may keep saying yes while secretly punishing the person with tone. They may appear helpful but withdraw affection. This is why understanding resentment is not indulgence. It is relationship care.

The caregiver needs to ask where resentment is already shaping behaviour. Do they delay responding because they feel used? Do they speak sharply because they feel unseen? Do they avoid visits because they dread criticism? Do they over-explain to relatives because they want them to finally understand? Do they say yes and then silently resent the person for accepting the yes? These questions are not meant to shame. They are meant to show where the emotion has begun making decisions from underground.

There is a particular pattern in which caregivers give from resentment and then expect the other person to notice the sacrifice. They say yes, but the yes is not free. It carries an unspoken invoice: recognise this, appreciate this, understand what it cost, do not ask again. The person receiving care may not see the invoice, especially if they are frightened, unwell, or focused on their own distress. The caregiver then feels even more unseen. The solution is not to become less generous. It is to stop offering yeses that are secretly noes.

A clean no is often kinder than a resentful yes. This can feel harsh to caregivers who equate love with availability. Yet a resentful yes may preserve short-term comfort while damaging the emotional climate. It teaches others that the caregiver is available, while teaching the caregiver that their own limits do not matter. Over time, the relationship becomes dishonest. The mouth says yes. The body says no. Resentment is the body remembering the truth.

Understanding resentment patterns also requires looking at old roles. Caregiving does not create every pattern from nothing. It often intensifies what was already present. The responsible child becomes more responsible. The avoidant sibling becomes more avoidant. The critical parent remains critical. The family mediator is once again expected to keep peace. The person who has always minimised their own needs continues to do so, now with higher stakes. Resentment may be old anger wearing a new caregiving uniform.

This does not mean the caregiver should blame the past for everything. It means old roles should be named so they do not operate invisibly. A caregiver may not only be angry about today's task. They may be angry that the same family dynamic has returned: they adjust, others take, someone criticises, no one thanks, and the caregiver is expected to remain steady. Naming the pattern helps the caregiver respond to the current reality without being wholly captured by old pain.

Resentment can also grow from lack of choice. Caregiving may technically involve decisions, but many caregivers feel there was never a real choice. The need appeared, the family system looked around, and the caregiver stepped in because someone had to. Later, people may speak as though the caregiver chose the whole role freely. This can create deep anger. A person can love someone and still resent being drafted into a life they did not consent to in any meaningful way.

Restoring choice, even in small ways, reduces resentment. The caregiver may not be able to choose whether care is needed. They may be able to choose which tasks they do, when they are available, what they refuse, who else is asked, what routines are created, and what support is escalated. Resentment often softens when the caregiver can say, "This is the part I choose, and this is the part I will no longer carry." Choice does not make caregiving easy, but it restores dignity.

Another resentment pattern appears when the caregiver's identity has been narrowed to usefulness. They are needed, but not necessarily known. They are contacted for tasks, updates, emergencies, and decisions, but not asked about their own life. Their hobbies, friendships, ambitions, rest, and ordinary pleasures shrink. They become the reliable person rather than the full person. Resentment then grows not only towards care tasks, but towards the role itself. The caregiver begins to resent being useful because usefulness has replaced being seen.

This form of resentment cannot be repaired only through better task division. It also requires identity protection. The caregiver needs spaces where they are not the organiser, not the fixer, not the emotional container, not the responsible one. Without these spaces, even a reduced workload may still feel consuming because care remains the central definition of the self. Resentment asks not only, "Who will help me?" but also, "Where did I go?"

The caregiver should pay attention to bodily resentment signals. A tightening jaw when a certain person calls. A sinking feeling before a visit. A rush of heat when a relative says "just". A heavy silence after agreeing to another task. A desire to disappear when the next message arrives. The body often identifies the resentment pattern before the mind has language for it. These reactions are not orders, but they are data.

A simple resentment record can help: What happened? What did I feel? What did I think I was angry about? What might I actually be angry about? Was this about workload, disrespect, grief, isolation, old roles, lack of choice, or identity loss? What boundary or change would address the real source? This process turns resentment from a general fog into a more precise signal. Precision matters because different sources require different responses.

Workload resentment may require delegation, simplification, routines, or escalation. Disrespect resentment may require boundaries around tone, time, or access. Grief resentment may require emotional support, mourning, or gentler expectations of oneself. Isolation resentment may require truthful conversation, support outside the care relationship, or more visible sharing of tasks. Old-role resentment may require refusing inherited family assignments. Identity resentment may require rebuilding parts of life that are not about care. The feeling may be one word, but the remedies differ.

Caregivers sometimes worry that examining resentment will make it stronger. In reality, denial often strengthens resentment because the feeling has to shout to be heard. Naming it calmly can reduce its power. "I resent being the only one who handles evenings" is easier to work with than a sudden explosion after another late call. "I am angry that my time is assumed" is clearer than months of cold compliance. Language gives resentment a route other than leakage.

The caregiver should choose carefully where and how to speak resentment aloud. Not every raw feeling belongs in every conversation. Telling the person receiving care, "I resent you," may wound without creating change, especially if the resentment is really about the system. A more useful sentence might be, "The evening calls are becoming too much for me, and we need a new plan." Or, with a sibling, "I am carrying transport and appointments, and that is not sustainable." The emotional truth informs the boundary, but the spoken request focuses on change.

There may be moments when a more direct emotional conversation is appropriate, especially in close relationships where repair is possible. But even then, the caregiver should aim for accuracy rather than accusation. "I have been feeling resentful because I am doing tasks I never agreed to carry alone" is different from "You have ruined my life." The first opens a path to negotiation. The second may express pain but is likely to deepen harm. Resentment deserves honesty, not cruelty.

Repair begins when resentment is understood before it becomes contempt. Contempt is more corrosive because it stops looking for change. It labels the other person as selfish, helpless, useless, impossible, or unworthy of effort. Once contempt settles, repair becomes harder because the caregiver no longer sees a strained human relationship; they see a fixed character flaw. The earlier resentment is decoded, the more chance there is to restore respect, even if the care arrangement itself must change significantly.

Understanding resentment patterns does not mean the caregiver must excuse everyone. Some grievances are valid. Some relatives have failed to help. Some boundaries have been ignored. Some care recipients have behaved hurtfully. Some systems have left too much to unpaid labour. But resentment that remains only a grievance will continue to burn. Resentment that becomes information can lead to boundary, repair, redistribution, recovery, or escalation.

The caregiver does not need to be free of resentment before making changes. They need to be honest enough not to let resentment choose the harshest path. They can say no before bitterness speaks for them. They can repair after snapping without giving up the limit. They can ask for help before contempt replaces connection. They can protect identity before usefulness becomes a cage. They can separate the person they care about from the arrangement that has injured them.

The question is not whether resentment is allowed. It is already present when the pattern exists.

The real question is whether the caregiver will treat resentment as shameful evidence of failure, or as a message from the part of them that still knows the difference between loving care and self-erasure.

Repairing After Conflict

Conflict in caregiving can feel uniquely painful because it often happens between people who are already carrying too much. The caregiver may be tired, frightened, overstretched, or resentful. The person receiving care may be anxious, ashamed, dependent, confused, grieving, or struggling with the loss of control. A sibling may be defensive because they know they have not done enough. A spouse may be wounded because the relationship has become crowded with tasks. The argument is rarely only about the sentence that was spoken. It is about the pressure that had nowhere else to go.

A caregiver snaps after the third late-night call. A parent says something cutting after being reminded about medication. A sibling offers advice and is met with a sharp reply. A partner asks for attention and hears, “I do not have anything left.” The words may be brief, but the impact can linger. The next call feels awkward. The next visit carries a chill. The caregiver replays the moment and feels guilty, then defensive, then guilty again. The person on the other side may feel hurt, rejected, misunderstood, or afraid that the relationship has changed permanently.

Repair matters because caregiving relationships cannot survive on task completion alone. Meals may be prepared, appointments attended, medicines organised, and paperwork filed, while trust slowly thins. When conflict is ignored, it does not disappear. It moves into tone, distance, hesitation, sarcasm, avoidance, and the quiet habit of expecting the worst from one another. Repair is the work of bringing the relationship back into honesty before resentment becomes its default language.

But repair is often misunderstood. It is not the same as taking blame for everything. It is not the same as withdrawing every boundary because someone was hurt. It is not grovelling, self-punishment, emotional performance, or a promise never to feel angry again. Repair is the act of acknowledging harm, clarifying truth, and making a better next step possible. It should restore connection without returning the caregiver to the very conditions that caused the rupture.

This distinction is essential. Many caregivers apologise in a way that cancels their own limits. They say, “I am sorry I snapped; I should always be there for you.” Or, “I am sorry I upset you; call whenever you need me.” Or, “I am sorry I complained; forget I said anything.” These apologies may soothe the immediate discomfort, but they quietly rebuild the old trap. The caregiver repairs the moment by sacrificing the boundary. Then the same pressure returns, and the next conflict becomes more likely.

A better repair separates tone from truth. The caregiver can apologise for how something was said without apologising for the limit itself. "I snapped yesterday. I am sorry for speaking sharply. I am still not available after 9 p.m., and we need a new plan for evenings." This kind of sentence is powerful because it holds two realities at once. It says, "My behaviour had an impact, and I take responsibility for that." It also says, "The need for change remains."

Many caregiving conflicts become worse because people collapse these two realities into one. If the caregiver spoke harshly, the other person may assume the boundary is invalid. If the person receiving care became upset, the caregiver may assume the limit was cruel. If a sibling reacted defensively, the caregiver may abandon the request to avoid further conflict. Repair must resist this confusion. A poor delivery does not automatically make the message wrong. A painful reaction does not automatically mean the limit was unnecessary.

The first step in repair is to identify what actually needs repairing. Was the problem the content, the tone, the timing, the assumption, the broken promise, the lack of clarity, or the absence of follow-through? A caregiver may feel a large wave of guilt after conflict and assume everything is their fault. That is not useful. The repair should fit the injury. If the caregiver shouted, repair the shouting. If they failed to communicate a change, repair the communication. If they agreed to something they could not do and then withdrew, repair the unreliable promise. If they set a necessary boundary and someone disliked it, that may require reassurance, not apology.

This is where precision protects everyone. "I am sorry for everything" sounds humble, but it is often vague and unstable. What is everything? Does it include the boundary? The request for help? The refusal to continue late calls? The anger that came after weeks of being ignored? A broad apology may briefly calm the other person, but it gives no clear path forward. It may also invite the other person to place more blame on the caregiver than belongs there.

A precise repair sounds different. "I am sorry I raised my voice." "I should not have called you selfish." "I was wrong to agree to drive and then cancel without enough notice." "I should have told you earlier that I could not manage the form." "I spoke from exhaustion rather than clarity." These statements are accountable because they name the behaviour. They do not collapse into self-condemnation. They do not ask the other person to comfort the caregiver. They simply own the part that is true.

The next step is to acknowledge impact. This does not mean agreeing with every interpretation the other person has made. Someone may say, "You made me feel abandoned," when the caregiver set a boundary. The caregiver may not agree that the boundary was abandonment. But they can still acknowledge the impact: "I understand that it felt frightening when I said I could not come over." Or, "I can see that my tone hurt you." Or, "I know the sudden change unsettled you." Acknowledging impact says, "I recognise that this affected you." It does not have to say, "Your entire conclusion is correct."

This matters because many apologies fail by defending too quickly. The caregiver says, "I am sorry I snapped, but you kept calling and I was exhausted and no one helps me." The explanation may be true, but the other person may hear only the defence. The repair becomes another argument. A stronger sequence is to acknowledge first, then explain only if useful. "I am sorry I snapped. That was not how I wanted to speak to you. I was exhausted, and that tells me we need a different evening plan." The explanation becomes part of redesign, not an excuse.

Repair also needs a future-facing element. An apology that does not change anything can become another loop in the conflict pattern. The caregiver snaps, apologises, carries on, becomes overloaded again, snaps again, apologises again. Trust does not rebuild through apology alone; it rebuilds through a different arrangement. After conflict, the question should be: what needs to change so this is less likely to happen again?

Sometimes the change is practical. A call time needs to move. A task needs to be shared. A helper needs clearer instructions. A boundary needs to be stated earlier. A recovery period needs to be protected after visits. A family update needs to be batched rather than scattered across the week. Sometimes the change is relational. The caregiver and care recipient need to avoid certain topics late at night. A sibling needs to stop giving advice unless they are also taking responsibility. A difficult conversation needs to happen with another person present.

Repair without renegotiation can become empty. Renegotiation does not mean reopening every boundary for debate. It means adjusting the care arrangement where the conflict has revealed a weak point. If the caregiver snapped after repeated calls after 9 p.m., the answer is not only, "I am sorry I snapped." It is also, "We need a new plan for evenings." If a sibling was hurt by being asked for help sharply, the answer is not only, "I am sorry I sounded angry." It may also be, "The task still needs an owner." If the person receiving care felt frightened by a new routine, the answer may include explaining it more calmly while still keeping the routine.

A strong repair therefore has four parts: acknowledgement, ownership, limit, and next step. The caregiver might say, "I can see yesterday upset you. I am sorry I spoke sharply. I am not able to take calls after 9 p.m., so let us agree what counts as urgent and what can wait until morning." This is not a formula to be recited mechanically, but a structure that keeps repair balanced. It prevents the caregiver from becoming either defensive or self-erasing.

The same structure applies when the person receiving care has caused harm. Caregivers sometimes avoid naming this because the person is vulnerable. But vulnerability does not make hurtful behaviour harmless. If the person receiving care shouted, insulted, manipulated, or dismissed the caregiver's limits, repair may need to move in the other direction. The caregiver can say, "Yesterday's conversation hurt me. I want us to keep talking, but I will not stay in calls where I am insulted. If that happens again, I will end the call and try later." This is not punishment. It is relationship protection.

It may be tempting to wait for the other person to apologise first. Sometimes they should. Sometimes they will not. The caregiver has to decide what kind of repair is within their control. They can repair their own tone, clarify their boundary, and name the next step. They cannot force another person to show insight. They cannot make a sibling admit unfairness. They cannot make a parent understand the emotional cost. Repair is not always mutual at the start. Sometimes it begins with one person refusing to let the conflict define the next interaction.

However, the caregiver should not use repair as a way to absorb everyone else's responsibility. If a conflict involved several people, each person has a part. The caregiver may need to apologise for snapping, while a sibling still needs to address their absence. The caregiver may need to soften their delivery, while the person receiving care still needs to respect the evening boundary. The caregiver may need to repair a missed commitment, while the wider system still needs to stop relying on them alone. Repair should clarify responsibility, not gather all responsibility into the caregiver's lap.

There is a difference between guilt-driven repair and values-driven repair. Guilt-driven repair says, "I feel terrible, so I will give more, explain more, apologise more, and remove the discomfort." Values-driven repair says, "I care about this relationship, so I will address the harm honestly and protect what is necessary." The first may feel urgent and emotional. The second may feel steadier, even if uncomfortable. Caregivers need values-driven repair because guilt-driven repair often feeds the exact patterns that create future resentment.

Timing matters. Repair should happen soon enough that distance does not harden, but not so quickly that the caregiver speaks while still flooded. A rushed apology may be more about escaping discomfort than restoring trust. It may promise too much, blame too much, or reopen the argument. A short pause can help the caregiver identify what they actually regret and what they still need to hold. "I want to talk about yesterday, but I need a little time to think clearly" can be a responsible bridge.

The caregiver should also choose the right medium. Some repairs need a conversation. Others may begin better in writing, especially if spoken conversations become circular or emotionally intense. A written message can be brief and calm: "I have been thinking about yesterday. I am sorry I snapped. I was overwhelmed, but I should not have spoken like that. I am still not able to take late calls, so we need to agree a clearer evening plan." Writing can prevent over-explaining and gives the other person time to absorb the message. It also creates a record of the boundary and next step.

In closer relationships, repair may need more warmth. A spouse, parent, or long-standing friend may need reassurance that the relationship matters beyond the task. “I love you, and I do not want us to speak to each other like that.” “I care about you, and I also need us to change how evenings work.” “I want to stay close, but I cannot stay close if every conversation becomes a demand.” These sentences are emotionally honest without surrendering the practical reality.

Repair becomes more difficult when old patterns are involved. A parent who has always criticised may hear any boundary as rejection. A sibling who has always avoided responsibility may treat a request as accusation. A caregiver who has always been the peacemaker may feel almost physically unable to leave conflict unresolved. The present rupture may sit on top of years of habit. In such cases, repair should not try to heal the whole family history in one conversation. It should address the current behaviour and the current next step.

This is especially important for caregivers who tend to over-apologise. Over-apology can look generous, but it often comes from fear. The caregiver apologises for having needs, for causing disappointment, for being tired, for setting limits, for asking others to help, for not being endlessly patient. Over time, this teaches others that the caregiver’s boundaries are regrettable rather than legitimate. A healthy apology is specific. It does not apologise for existing with limits.

A useful test is: am I apologising for my behaviour or for my boundary? “I am sorry I shouted” repairs behaviour. “I am sorry I cannot answer late calls” may imply the boundary is a wrongdoing. A better version is, “I know the evening boundary is hard, and I am sorry my tone was sharp when I explained it.” The caregiver remains compassionate without framing the limit itself as an offence.

There will also be moments when no apology is needed, only clarification. If the caregiver calmly set a boundary and the other person became upset, the caregiver may feel guilty but not necessarily responsible for harm. They can say, "I know this is difficult to hear. I care about you, and the arrangement still needs to change." That is not an apology. It is reassurance. Caregivers often blur the two because they feel bad whenever someone else feels bad. But another person's disappointment is not always evidence that the caregiver has done wrong.

Repair after conflict should include self-repair. Caregivers often focus only on the other person's feelings and ignore the impact on themselves. After a difficult exchange, they may feel shaken, ashamed, angry, or drained. They may need to write down what happened, speak to someone safe, rest, take a walk, or remind themselves of the larger context. Without self-repair, the caregiver may enter the next conversation still flooded. They may overcorrect, withdraw, or become defensive.

Self-repair also means refusing to turn one mistake into an identity. "I snapped" is a behaviour. "I am a terrible caregiver" is a global verdict. The global verdict is unhelpful and often false. It leads to shame, and shame tends to produce either collapse or defensiveness. A more useful response is, "I snapped because the current pressure exceeded my capacity in that moment. I need to repair the impact and change the pressure." This keeps accountability linked to practical change.

Some conflicts require a reset rather than a long discussion. A reset is a deliberate return to a workable tone after a rupture. It might sound like, "Yesterday was difficult. I do not want us to carry that tone into today. Let us start again with the practical plan." Or, "We were both upset. I want to speak calmly now." A reset is not avoidance if the core issue is still addressed. It is a way of preventing yesterday's emotional weather from governing every future interaction.

A reset can be especially useful when the person receiving care is easily overwhelmed by prolonged emotional processing. Some people cannot tolerate long repair conversations. They may become anxious, confused, defensive, or distressed. In those cases, the caregiver may need to keep repair simple: acknowledge, reassure, state the next step, and return to routine. The aim is not to force emotional depth. The aim is to restore enough trust and clarity for care to continue without hidden hostility.

Renegotiation is necessary when conflict reveals that the current arrangement is not working. This may mean changing availability, redistributing tasks, adjusting routines, defining emergencies, involving another helper, or escalating support. Renegotiation should be practical. What exactly will change? Who will do what? What happens if the old pattern returns? What boundary will be held? What support is needed? Repair that does not reach this level may soothe feelings temporarily while leaving the structure untouched.

For example, after a conflict about repeated evening distress, the caregiver might say, "I am sorry I was abrupt last night. Evenings are becoming too difficult in the current form. From now on, I will call at 7 p.m. for a short check-in, and non-urgent calls after that will wait until morning. If you feel unsafe, use the emergency plan." This repair is kind, clear, and structural. It does not rely on the caregiver becoming infinitely more patient.

After conflict with a sibling, the caregiver might say, "I was angry when I spoke to you, and I am sorry for the way I said it. The issue remains that I am doing all appointment transport. I need you to take one appointment a month or tell me clearly that you cannot, so I can make another plan." Again, the apology does not erase the request. It cleans the delivery so the real issue can be addressed.

After conflict with the person receiving care, the caregiver might say, "I know yesterday's visit ended badly. I am sorry I left so abruptly. I was overwhelmed. I will not stay when I am being shouted at, but I do want us to have better visits. If things get heated, I will take a short break and come back if we can speak calmly." This type of repair protects dignity on both sides. It acknowledges harm, names a limit, and offers a path forward.

Repair can also include making amends. If the caregiver missed a task, they may need to complete it or arrange a replacement. If they caused confusion, they may need to clarify. If they spoke unfairly, they may need to name what was unfair. But amends should remain proportionate. The caregiver does not need to repay one harsh sentence with weeks of over-availability. They do not need to compensate for guilt by taking on tasks they cannot sustain. Proportion is what keeps repair from becoming self-punishment.

The other person may not accept the repair immediately. They may remain hurt, angry, defensive, or sceptical. This can be hard for caregivers who want emotional closure. But repair is an offering, not a command. The caregiver can apologise sincerely and still allow the other person time. They can clarify the plan and still tolerate discomfort. They can hold a boundary and still remain open to future conversation. The measure of repair is not whether the other person instantly feels better. It is whether the caregiver has acted with honesty, responsibility, and steadiness.

There are also conflicts where repair is not safe or not possible in the usual way. If conversations involve repeated verbal harm, coercion, threats, intimidation, or severe manipulation, the caregiver may need stronger boundaries, third-party support, or a changed contact pattern. Repair should not become a reason to keep entering harmful exchanges. A caregiver can wish for a better relationship and still protect themselves from repeated damage. Sometimes the repair is not a tender conversation; it is a safer structure.

When conflict keeps repeating, the caregiver should look for the pattern beneath the rupture. Are arguments happening at the same time of day? Around the same task? With the same person? After the caregiver has had no rest? When a boundary is unclear? When a helper cancels? When the person receiving care feels embarrassed or afraid? Repeated conflict is rarely random. It is often a signal that the care design needs attention. Repair after each individual argument will not be enough if the same structure keeps producing the same injury.

The caregiver should also notice whether they are using conflict to express what they have not been able to say calmly. Sometimes a snap contains a truth that should have been spoken earlier in a steadier voice. "I cannot do everything." "You cannot keep calling this late." "I need help." "I am tired of being criticised." "This is not fair." The fact that the truth came out badly does not mean the truth should be buried again. Repair the delivery. Then return to the truth.

This is one of the most important disciplines in caregiving repair: do not let guilt erase the message. After a blow-up, the caregiver may feel so ashamed that they abandon the necessary conversation entirely. They apologise and retreat. The old pattern resumes. Pressure builds again. Another blow-up follows. To break the cycle, the caregiver must learn to say, "I am sorry for how I said it. I still need us to talk about what I said." This is not stubbornness. It is the only way repair becomes real.

Trust is rebuilt through repeated evidence. If the caregiver says they will pause before speaking harshly, they need to practise that pause. If the person receiving care agrees not to shout, that limit needs to be respected. If a sibling agrees to take a task, they need to do it or communicate early. If a new evening routine is agreed, it needs to be followed consistently. Words begin repair; behaviour confirms it. Without changed behaviour, apology becomes theatre.

Repair also requires remembering the relationship beyond the conflict. Caregiving can shrink interactions until they are only about problems. After rupture, it may help to restore one ordinary human contact: a cup of tea without discussing care tasks, a brief gentle call, a shared memory, a practical kindness, a moment of humour, a familiar ritual. This does not replace structural change, but it reminds both people that the relationship is not only the argument. The person receiving care is not only a source of demand. The caregiver is not only a worker under strain.

This kind of relational care must be protected from being swallowed by tasks. If every visit becomes a checklist, repair has little space to breathe. If every call becomes administration, warmth has nowhere to return. A repaired relationship needs at least small moments where both people can exist outside the immediate problem. That may be modest, especially in difficult care situations, but modest does not mean meaningless.

Caregivers should not expect repair to feel neat. Some apologies will feel awkward. Some resets will be imperfect. Some boundaries will need repeating. Some relationships will remain complicated. Repair does not require a perfectly healed emotional field. It requires willingness to return with truth, take responsibility where appropriate, refuse false responsibility where necessary, and build a better next step.

The caregiver who learns this becomes less afraid of conflict. Not because conflict becomes pleasant, but because it no longer means the relationship is doomed or the boundary must disappear. A rupture can be addressed. A harsh tone can be repaired. A limit can be restated. A pattern can be renegotiated. The relationship can be cared for without pretending the old arrangement was working.

Repair is not weakness. It is maintenance.

It is the tightening of the loose screw before the chair breaks.

The question after conflict is not, "How do I make everyone feel comfortable again as quickly as possible?" The better question is, "What part of this rupture belongs to my behaviour, what part belongs to the care arrangement, and what must change so we are not standing in this same painful place again?"

Keeping Your Identity Intact

Caregiving can shrink a life without announcing that it is doing so. At first, the changes look temporary and reasonable. A weekly class is missed because there is an appointment. A friend's message waits because there is paperwork. A walk is skipped because the visit ran late. A personal goal is postponed because the care situation is unsettled. None of these choices looks like a tragedy on its own. Each one can be explained. Each one may even feel necessary.

The problem is accumulation. The things that made the caregiver feel like a person begin to disappear in small, defensible pieces. Hobbies become "not now". Friendships become "when things calm down". Future plans become "after we get through this stage". The caregiver remains busy, useful, responsible, and needed, but gradually less connected to the self that existed before the role expanded. They may still recognise their name, but not the shape of their days.

This loss of identity is often mistaken for maturity or devotion. The caregiver may be praised for being selfless, reliable, or strong. They may be told that others could not manage without them. Praise can feel comforting, but it can also become a polished cage. If the only version of the caregiver that receives approval is the version that sacrifices without protest, then personhood becomes conditional. They are valued most when they are most useful.

Caregiving asks for generosity, but it should not require disappearance. There is a profound difference between adapting your life around care and surrendering your life to care. Adaptation says, "This responsibility matters, and I will make room for it." Disappearance says, "Only this responsibility matters now." The first is difficult but human. The second is dangerous because it turns the caregiver into a function: driver, organiser, caller, form-reader, emotional container, emergency contact, and silent backup plan.

When identity narrows, resentment often deepens. The caregiver may begin to resent not only the tasks, but the way every task confirms their reduced role in their own life. A phone call interrupts more than an evening; it interrupts the fragile attempt to have one. A request for help feels larger than the request itself because it lands on top of all the abandoned plans, unanswered messages, unread books, cancelled exercise, lost privacy, and postponed ambition that care has already consumed. The anger is not only about what is being asked. It is about what keeps being taken without being named.

Protecting identity is therefore not a decorative act of self-care. It is relationship protection. A caregiver who has no life outside care eventually brings that deprivation back into the care relationship. They may become sharper, colder, more controlling, more easily wounded, or more desperate for gratitude. They may expect the person receiving care to recognise sacrifices that were never spoken aloud. They may give help while secretly blaming the recipient for the life they no longer have. Identity loss does not stay private. It changes the emotional atmosphere of care.

Keeping your identity intact begins with refusing the idea that only large freedoms count. Many caregivers cannot immediately reclaim whole weekends, regular holidays, long social evenings, or ambitious personal projects. Waiting for that level of freedom may become another way of postponing personhood. Identity can be protected through small but deliberate anchors: one relationship that is not organised around care, one activity that belongs to the caregiver's own pleasure or growth, one goal that points beyond the next appointment or crisis.

An identity anchor is not an escape from responsibility. It is a fixed point that reminds the caregiver they are more than the role. It might be a weekly walk with a friend where care is not the only topic. It might be a creative practice, a garden, a book group, a language lesson, a fitness habit, a faith gathering, a quiet morning ritual, a professional ambition, or a private project that has no practical value to anyone else. Its value lies precisely there. Not everything in the caregiver's life should have to justify itself by being useful.

This can feel surprisingly uncomfortable. Caregivers who have spent months or years responding to need may feel guilty doing something that is simply theirs. They may hear an internal voice saying, "How can you spend time on this when there is so much to do?" That voice sounds responsible, but it is not always wise. There will always be more to do. If the caregiver must wait until no task remains, the self will remain on hold indefinitely.

A relationship anchor is often the most urgent place to begin. Caregiving can isolate a person even when they are constantly interacting with others. Many conversations become practical: updates, appointments, concerns, arrangements, symptoms, supplies, money, transport, medication, family messages. The caregiver may be speaking all day and still not feel known. They need at least one relationship where they are allowed to be a whole person, not merely the person with responsibilities.

This does not mean every conversation must avoid care. Sometimes the caregiver needs to speak honestly about what is happening. But a relationship anchor should also make room for ordinary life: humour, memory, shared interests, silence, mutual concern, and topics that do not revolve around the care recipient. The caregiver should not become interesting to others only through the drama or difficulty of caregiving. They deserve contact that remembers their wider self.

An activity anchor gives the body and mind a route out of constant duty. The activity does not need to be impressive. In fact, it is often better if it is ordinary and repeatable. A regular swim, a half-hour of reading, a weekly craft session, a music practice, a walk in the same park, a small cooking ritual, or a class attended imperfectly can all become reminders that the caregiver still has preferences, sensations, curiosity, and pleasure. The activity says, quietly, "I am still here."

A goal anchor is different. It points forward. Caregiving often traps the mind in short horizons: this call, this appointment, this week, this form, this new concern. A goal restores a line into the future that is not entirely determined by care. It may be small: completing a course, saving for something, returning to a neglected skill, improving health, developing a professional plan, writing regularly, learning something new, rebuilding a room, or planning a modest trip. The point is not speed. The point is direction.

Future plans can feel disloyal when the person receiving care has a shrinking future or uncertain health. This guilt is understandable, but it should be challenged. The caregiver does not honour another person's limits by abandoning their own possibility. A future is not a betrayal. It is part of being alive. Care may change the pace, shape, or timing of personal goals, but it should not erase the right to have them.

Identity anchors must be protected with boundaries, or they will be swallowed. A friend's evening will disappear under a non-urgent call. A class will be missed because someone forgot to arrange transport. A walk will be interrupted by family messages. A goal will be postponed because guilt makes every care task feel more deserving. The caregiver must decide, in advance, what kind of care issue is serious enough to interrupt the anchor and what can wait. Without this decision, the anchor is only a wish.

This is where previous boundary work becomes practical. "I do not answer routine messages during this hour." "I am unavailable on Wednesday evenings unless there is a true emergency." "I will return calls after my walk." "This appointment is mine, and I do not cancel it for routine care tasks." These sentences may feel firm, but they protect more than time. They protect the caregiver's continuity as a person.

The caregiver should expect some pushback, especially if others are accustomed to total access. A relative may imply that personal time is indulgent. The person receiving care may feel hurt that the caregiver is choosing something else for an hour. The caregiver's own guilt may be louder than anyone's objection. The answer is not to turn identity into another argument that must be won. The answer is to make the anchor part of the care plan. "I am not available then. I will call afterwards." "That time is already committed." "This is not an emergency, so it can wait."

Language matters. The caregiver should avoid presenting identity anchors as fragile treats that can be cancelled at the first sign of discomfort. "I was hoping to go, but I can skip it if you need me" invites the old pattern. "I am at my class tonight and will respond tomorrow" teaches a different one. This does not mean the caregiver never makes exceptions. It means exceptions are chosen consciously and named clearly, not extracted by guilt.

Keeping identity intact also requires reducing the mental dominance of care. A caregiver may be physically away from tasks but mentally still inside them, replaying conversations, anticipating problems, or composing messages. Identity anchors work best when there is a transition into them. Writing down the next care action before leaving. Setting a response window. Turning off non-urgent notifications. Naming what can wait. The mind needs a handover as much as the calendar does.

There is also a private identity that does not depend on anyone else's recognition. The caregiver may need to ask themselves questions that have nothing to do with care: What do I enjoy? What do I miss? What do I want to learn? What kind of conversation restores me? What kind of movement makes me feel alive? What did I used to do before every spare hour became available to need? These questions can feel strange at first. A self that has been neglected may answer slowly.

The answers should be treated gently. A caregiver may discover grief for the life that has narrowed. They may realise they have lost friendships, confidence, ambition, or simple habits of pleasure. They may feel anger at how much has been given away. This grief is not self-pity. It is the mind recognising loss. Identity repair begins by allowing that recognition without immediately turning it into another task to optimise.

Small restoration is enough to begin. Send one message to a friend. Reclaim one walk. Return to one book. Cook one meal because you like it. Spend one hour on a goal that belongs to your future. Put one personal appointment in the calendar and treat it as real. These acts may look insignificant beside the size of the care load, but they are not insignificant. They are evidence. They prove that the caregiver's life has not been wholly absorbed.

The caregiver should be careful not to turn identity anchors into performance. The aim is not to become a perfectly balanced person with a photogenic self-care routine. That kind of pressure only adds another layer of failure. The aim is to preserve contact with life outside usefulness. Some weeks the anchor will be small. Some weeks it may be missed and resumed. The measure is not perfection. The measure is whether the caregiver keeps returning to the fact that they are still someone beyond the care role.

This is especially important when caregiving is long-term. Short-term sacrifice can be painful but survivable when there is a clear end. Long-term caregiving requires a different ethic. A person cannot live indefinitely as an emergency resource without damage. The longer the role lasts, the more deliberately identity must be maintained. Otherwise the caregiver may wake up months or years later and realise that the only part of life still receiving regular attention is the part organised around someone else's need.

Identity anchors can also improve the quality of care. A caregiver who has contact with their own life may return with more patience, more perspective, and less hidden demand for gratitude. They are less likely to expect the person receiving care to compensate emotionally for everything care has cost them. They are less likely to make the relationship carry the full weight of their deprivation. This is not because they care less. It is because care is no longer the only place where their personhood is being spent.

There will be situations where identity protection requires larger decisions. If no anchor can survive because the care needs are too intense, too unpredictable, or too unsupported, the issue may not be poor discipline. The issue may be that the arrangement needs more support or a different structure. A caregiver who cannot maintain even one relationship, one activity, or one goal outside care is receiving an important signal. The care role may have become too consuming to remain unchanged.

This signal should not be minimised. It is easy to say, "This is just how it is." Sometimes care is indeed demanding. But "demanding" and "totalising" are different. A demanding role takes effort. A totalising role consumes identity. When the caregiver's life has no protected space beyond care, resentment, burnout, and emotional collapse become more likely. Identity loss is not a sentimental concern. It is a stability issue.

The caregiver may need to renegotiate with relatives, helpers, or the person receiving care to protect identity anchors. This conversation can be simple and firm: "I need Tuesday evenings to remain free." "I am rebuilding one activity outside care, and it is not available for routine tasks." "I need someone else to cover that time." The caregiver does not need to prove that the activity is important enough. Its importance lies in the fact that it belongs to their life.

There may also be a need to renegotiate internally. Some caregivers are more willing to disappoint others than to disappoint the internal image of the perfect caregiver. They may believe that a good caregiver does not need much, does not complain, does not pursue personal goals, and does not protect joy while another person suffers. That image is not noble. It is brittle. It leaves no room for a human being to provide care over time without disappearing.

A more truthful image is needed: a caregiver with edges, commitments, private needs, and a future. A caregiver who can love deeply without becoming only useful. A caregiver who can turn up for another person while still belonging to themselves. A caregiver who understands that identity is not selfish decoration, but part of the foundation that keeps resentment from becoming the dominant emotional climate.

Keeping identity intact also means refusing to let caregiving become the only story other people know about you. When someone asks how you are, it may be tempting to give only a care update because that is what feels most available. Sometimes that is necessary. But where possible, include yourself in the answer. "Care has been heavy, and I have started walking again." "There is a lot going on, and I am trying to get back to reading." "I am managing appointments, but I am also working on something for myself." These statements may seem small, but they reintroduce the caregiver into their own narrative.

The person receiving care may also benefit from seeing the caregiver as a full person. Depending on the relationship and capacity, it can be healthy for them to know that the caregiver has commitments, friendships, rest, and goals. This may initially cause anxiety if they are used to constant availability, but over time it can support a more balanced relationship. The caregiver is not merely a service entering the room. They are a person who comes, helps, leaves, returns, and has a life in between.

Of course, some care recipients may not be able to hold this perspective well. They may be too anxious, ill, dependent, or emotionally fixed in old patterns. In those cases, the caregiver may need to protect identity without expecting understanding. This is hard. It is painful to maintain a boundary that someone else interprets as rejection. But the caregiver's personhood does not require full approval from the person who benefits from their availability.

Identity also needs protection from constant care talk among relatives. Family conversations can become entirely practical or crisis-driven. If every interaction with siblings or extended family revolves around care logistics, old relationships narrow. Where possible, some contact should exist outside the care agenda, or the caregiver should seek other relationships that do not require them to be the family coordinator. No one can remain emotionally well if every relational pathway leads back to responsibility.

A caregiver may need to rebuild slowly because identity can feel distant after long neglect. They may not know what they like anymore. They may feel restless during free time. They may feel guilty when not productive. They may start an activity and find their attention pulled back to care. This is normal. The self does not always return immediately when given space. It may need repetition, patience, and low expectations. The first goal is not joy. It may simply be presence.

There is a practical exercise hidden in this work: choose one relationship, one activity, and one goal. The relationship is someone with whom the caregiver can be more than useful. The activity is something that restores a sense of aliveness, even modestly. The goal is a thread into the future. These anchors should be small enough to begin and important enough to protect. They are not meant to fix the entire life. They are meant to keep the life from vanishing.

The caregiver should write them down. Not as a sentimental list, but as a commitment to continuity. Which relationship will I tend this month? Which activity will I protect this week? Which goal will receive one small action? Written anchors make identity visible. They remind the caregiver that care is not the only claim on the calendar.

These anchors should be reviewed when care intensifies. During difficult periods, the caregiver may need to scale them down rather than abandon them. A weekly class may become a fifteen-minute practice at home. A long visit with a friend may become a voice note exchange. A large goal may become one small step. Scaling down preserves the thread. Abandoning everything teaches the care role that it may consume the whole life whenever pressure rises.

The caregiver should also celebrate returns. Returning to a friend after silence. Returning to a walk after missed weeks. Returning to a goal after interruption. These returns matter because caregiving often breaks continuity. The ability to resume is more important than never stopping. An identity anchor does not fail because care interrupted it. It fails only when the caregiver begins to believe it no longer matters.

Keeping identity intact may bring sorrow because it reveals how much has already been lost. But it can also bring steadiness. The caregiver begins to feel less like they are being erased by responsibility. They remember preferences. They speak to people who know them outside tasks. They make plans that are not entirely dependent on the next crisis. They become less available for resentment because their whole life is no longer silently sacrificed at the altar of care.

The care role may remain demanding. Love may still ask much. Duty may still carry weight. There may be seasons of restriction, grief, and compromise. But even then, the caregiver needs at least a small part of life that answers to their own name.

The question is not, "How do I get my old life back exactly as it was?"

The question is, "What part of me must remain alive so that care does not turn me into a function and call it love?"

Chapter 10
Long-Term Care Plans That Adapt

How can a care plan be both firm enough to rely on and flexible enough to survive real life? This is the question that separates temporary coping from long-term stability. Caregiving often begins with immediate needs: a lift to an appointment, a call to check medication, a meal delivered, a form completed, a worrying moment handled before it grows. At first, the plan may live in the caregiver's head because the situation seems manageable enough, or too urgent to organise properly. The caregiver knows who to call, what to watch, what usually works, and what must never be forgotten.

But care does not stay still. A routine that once worked can become too light for the need it now carries. A person who once needed reminders may begin needing supervision. A short visit may no longer be enough. A caregiver who once had spare evenings may now have work demands, health concerns, children, fatigue, or limits that cannot be ignored. The danger is not simply that needs change. The danger is that the care plan does not change with them, and everyone keeps behaving as though last season's arrangement should still be enough.

The paradox is that caregivers often resist planning because care feels uncertain, yet uncertainty is exactly why planning matters. A plan does not remove the unknown. It does not promise that ageing, illness, family life, or human emotion will behave neatly. Its value is humbler and more practical: it reduces the number of decisions that have to be made in panic. It turns scattered knowledge into a shared picture. It gives other people a way to understand the arrangement without needing the main caregiver to translate everything at the worst possible moment.

The central tension is between a care system built around one person's private memory and a care system that can be understood, reviewed, and adapted by more than one person. When everything lives in the caregiver's head, the arrangement may look smooth for a while. In truth, it is fragile. If the caregiver is ill, unreachable, overwhelmed, or simply tired, the plan becomes harder for anyone else to operate. The question is not whether the caregiver is competent. The question is whether competence has become the only structure holding the arrangement together.

The stakes rise over time because long-term care punishes assumptions. An unspoken role becomes a permanent burden. A vague backup becomes no backup at all. A risk that was tolerable months ago becomes unsafe when the person's needs increase. A helper who was useful for errands may not be suitable for more sensitive tasks. A boundary that protected the caregiver in one season may need to be firmer in another. Without review, care arrangements drift. They do not usually fail because no one cared; they fail because no one updated the design.

There is also an emotional cost when plans do not adapt. The caregiver may feel trapped by promises made under different conditions. The person receiving care may feel frightened by sudden changes that could have been introduced more gradually. Relatives may argue from outdated impressions of what is happening. Helpers may step in without enough information and create more confusion than relief. Guilt then fills the gaps where planning should have been. People begin asking who is to blame, when the more useful question is what no longer fits.

The work now gathers the book's earlier disciplines into one usable view: roles, routines, risks, contacts, boundaries, recovery, and support must be visible enough that care is not held together by memory alone. From there, predictable changes need honest anticipation, not fearful avoidance, so that possible shifts in supervision, mobility, cognition, and caregiver availability have at least a rough response path before they become emergencies. The final movement is review without guilt: returning regularly to what is working, what is breaking, and what must be renegotiated as an act of maintenance rather than a confession of failure.

A long-term care plan should not be impressive. It should be usable. If it is too complicated for a tired person to understand, it will fail when it is most needed. If it depends on perfect cooperation, it will fail under ordinary stress. If it requires the caregiver to update, remind, chase, explain, and rescue every part of it, it is not truly a plan; it is a more organised version of the same overload. The best plan is clear enough to guide action, simple enough to maintain, and honest enough to show when the current arrangement has reached its limit.

The unresolved question at the end of this work is not, "How do I create a perfect care plan?" Perfection would be too brittle for real caregiving. The sharper question is this: if someone had to understand the care arrangement quickly, without relying on everything you remember, what would they need to see, and what would that reveal about the parts of care that are still depending too heavily on you?

Creating a Care Plan Overview

A long-term care plan begins to matter most when the usual caregiver is not available to explain everything. That is the test. Not whether the plan looks impressive, not whether it contains every possible detail, not whether it would satisfy an outsider's idea of organisation. The real test is whether another capable person could look at it and understand, quickly and accurately, how care is currently working.

Many caregiving arrangements are held together by one person's memory. The main caregiver knows the routines, the risks, the passwords, the preferred foods, the difficult times of day, the professional contacts, the medication changes, the family politics, the emotional triggers, the transport habits, the paperwork deadlines, and the small signs that something is not right. This knowledge is valuable, but when it lives only inside one person, it becomes fragile. If that person is ill, exhausted, at work, away, emotionally overwhelmed, or simply unreachable, the care system suddenly loses its map.

A care plan overview is that map. It is a simple, usable view of the care arrangement as it stands now. It does not need to be perfect. It does not need to predict every possible development. It does not need to become a heavy administrative project. Its purpose is more practical: to bring the main moving parts of care into one place so that roles, routines, risks, and contacts are visible. Visibility reduces panic. It also reduces the quiet resentment of being the only person who knows how everything works.

The first principle is simplicity. Caregivers are often tempted to overbuild the plan because the care situation feels complicated. They imagine a large folder, detailed forms, colour-coded pages, long explanations, and exhaustive histories. There may be situations where detailed records are necessary, but the overview itself should be short enough to use when someone is tired. A care plan that only works for a calm person with an uninterrupted afternoon is not a practical care plan. The overview should be understandable under pressure.

The second principle is currency. An elegant plan that is out of date can be worse than a messy plan that is accurate. Care changes. Medication changes. Helpers change. Mobility changes. Communication needs change. A relative who used to drive may no longer be available. A routine that worked months ago may now create conflict. A professional contact may have changed. A risk that used to be minor may now matter more. The overview should show the current reality, not the version of care everyone wishes were still true.

The third principle is usefulness. The care plan overview should answer the questions people actually ask when care becomes urgent or uncertain. Who is involved? What does the person receiving care need each day? What routines keep things stable? What risks require attention? Who should be contacted for what? What does the caregiver do, and what do others do? What information must be known before stepping in? What should not be disturbed because it creates distress? These are not abstract questions. They are the questions that decide whether help is genuinely helpful.

A useful overview begins with the person at the centre of care, but it should do so with dignity. The person is not a case file. They are a human being with preferences, fears, habits, history, and ways of feeling safe. The overview might include their preferred name, communication needs, important routines, food preferences, mobility concerns, emotional triggers, and what helps when they become anxious or resistant. The tone matters. "Becomes anxious if rushed" is more humane and useful than "difficult in the morning". A good plan guides care without reducing the person to their problems.

The next part is roles. Who does what? This may sound obvious until it is written down and the gaps become visible. One person books appointments. Another collects prescriptions. Another handles family updates. Someone visits on a particular day. Someone manages bills. Someone is the emergency contact. Someone provides respite. Or perhaps, after writing it down, the caregiver discovers that their name appears beside almost everything. That discovery may be uncomfortable, but it is also valuable. A care plan overview does not only organise care; it reveals imbalance.

Roles should be specific. "Family helps" is not a role. "Sam collects prescriptions on Fridays and confirms in the group message" is a role. "Rina calls on Sunday evenings" is a role. "I coordinate appointments but do not provide regular transport" is a role with a boundary. Specific roles prevent tasks from drifting back to the main caregiver through vagueness. They also make it easier to see when someone has agreed to a real responsibility rather than offering general goodwill.

Routines are the next essential layer. These are the repeated patterns that keep daily and weekly life from becoming crisis-driven. The morning check-in. The medication cue. The meal defaults. The weekly supply check. The communication window. The paperwork review. The evening boundary. These routines should be written plainly, not as ideal instructions but as the minimum reliable rhythm that actually works. A routine that only happens when everyone is calm is not yet a routine. The overview should show what usually happens, who is responsible, and what to do if the routine is disrupted.

This is especially important for handoffs. If another person needs to step in, they should not have to ask the main caregiver twenty questions before doing a simple task. The overview should make the ordinary pattern visible enough for someone else to follow. If breakfast usually needs to happen before medication, say so. If the person becomes distressed when appointments are discussed too early, say so. If evening calls should be brief because they otherwise spiral into anxiety, say so. These details are not fussy. They are the practical intelligence of care.

Risks must be included, but they should be described clearly rather than dramatically. A risk is not every possible thing that could go wrong. It is a known area that needs attention because delay, confusion, or neglect could create harm or serious strain. Medication uncertainty. Falls risk. Missed meals. Night-time distress. Financial vulnerability. Confusion around appointments. Unsafe driving. Emotional escalation during certain conversations. Lack of backup if the caregiver is unavailable. The overview should identify the risks that actually shape decisions.

For each risk, the plan should offer a response path. Not a complicated procedure, but a clear first step. If medication is missed, who is contacted? If the person does not answer the check-in call, what happens next? If transport falls through, who is the backup? If a letter arrives with a deadline, where does it go? If the caregiver is unavailable, who should be contacted first for non-urgent concerns? These response paths reduce panic because they prevent people from inventing the next step while anxious.

Contact points are another foundation. A care plan overview should include relevant contacts in one place: relatives, regular helpers, neighbours if appropriate, pharmacy, transport contacts, professional services involved in care, and any agreed emergency route. The list should be practical, not excessive. Too many contacts can create confusion. The question is: who would someone realistically need to reach in order to keep care functioning?

The overview should also make boundaries visible. This is often missed because people think of care plans as describing tasks, not limits. But boundaries are part of the operating system of care. If the main caregiver does not answer non-urgent calls after a certain time, that belongs in the plan. If they coordinate appointments but do not provide regular transport, that belongs in the plan. If family updates are sent once a week rather than through scattered messages, that belongs in the plan. A boundary that is not written down can easily be treated as a mood, preference, or temporary inconvenience.

Including boundaries in the overview protects both the caregiver and the care arrangement. It tells others how access works. It reduces repeated negotiation. It makes it harder for tasks to creep back into old patterns. It also helps the caregiver hold the line because the boundary is no longer only a private decision; it is part of the shared structure. This does not remove the need for firmness, but it gives firmness a place to stand.

The care plan should include recovery and backup arrangements for the caregiver. This may feel unusual, but it is essential. A long-term care plan that contains no protection for the caregiver is incomplete. Who covers care during the caregiver's protected time? What counts as urgent enough to interrupt them? What regular recovery blocks exist? What happens if the caregiver is ill? If the answer is "the caregiver just manages", the plan is not honest. The caregiver is not a spare battery hidden inside the system. They are a person whose stability affects the quality and safety of care.

The overview should be accessible to those who need it, but not carelessly shared. Privacy matters. Not every helper needs every detail. A driver needs appointment and mobility information; they do not necessarily need financial records. A neighbour checking in may need emergency contact details; they do not need private medical history beyond what is relevant. The care plan overview can have a main version and smaller task-specific extracts where needed. The principle is simple: enough information to help well, not so much that privacy is lost.

The format should serve the people using it. A printed sheet may work better than a digital file if helpers are not comfortable with shared documents. A shared note may work well for relatives who communicate by phone. A folder in the home may be best for current paperwork and emergency information. A calendar may carry appointments and task ownership. The tool is not the point. The point is that the overview can be found, understood, and updated without requiring the main caregiver to act as translator every time.

The caregiver should beware of making the overview so detailed that no one uses it. A care plan overview is not the complete archive. It is the front page of the system. It points to where more detail can be found. The medication list may be attached or kept in a known location. Paperwork may be in the current folder. Financial documents may have a separate secure place. The overview should tell people where to look, not reproduce every document in full. A map is useful because it simplifies the territory.

Creating the overview may bring emotional discomfort. It may reveal that no one else knows enough to step in. It may show that tasks are badly distributed. It may expose that the caregiver has been relying on memory, improvisation, and constant availability rather than a shared system. This can feel like failure. It is not failure. It is information. A hidden weakness cannot be strengthened. A visible weakness can be addressed.

The overview may also change family conversations. Instead of vague debates about who is "doing enough", the plan shows the actual arrangement. It becomes clear who owns transport, who handles prescriptions, who sends updates, who provides companionship, who holds paperwork, and where the gaps are. Some people may not like this clarity. Clarity can disturb comfortable vagueness. But comfortable vagueness is often what keeps the main caregiver overloaded.

There is a strong case for building the overview gradually. Trying to assemble everything in one sitting can overwhelm even the most organised caregiver. Start with the essentials: key contacts, medication information, daily routines, known risks, current roles, and what to do if the main caregiver is unavailable. Then add details as pressure points reveal themselves. A care plan overview does not need to be born complete. It needs to become useful quickly, then improve with use.

Once created, the overview must be reviewed. A care plan that is not reviewed becomes a snapshot of the past. A monthly reset can be enough for many situations, though some care arrangements may need more frequent attention. The review should ask whether roles still fit, routines still work, risks have changed, contacts are current, boundaries are holding, and the caregiver's capacity still matches the load. Review is not bureaucracy. It is maintenance.

Maintenance is a mature caregiving habit. It refuses the fantasy that one plan can solve a changing situation permanently. It also refuses the opposite fantasy, that because care is unpredictable, planning is pointless. The truth sits between those extremes. Care is unpredictable, so the plan must be simple and adaptable. Care changes, so the plan must change without guilt. People forget, so the plan must be visible. Helpers step in, so the plan must be shareable. Caregivers tire, so the plan must not depend entirely on them.

A care plan overview also gives the caregiver psychological relief. When everything lives in the head, the mind cannot fully rest. It keeps scanning for missed details. It rehearses instructions no one else knows. It worries about what would happen if the caregiver could not answer. Writing the overview does not remove every concern, but it transfers some of the burden from private memory to shared structure. That transfer matters. It is one way a caregiver stops being the only container for the whole arrangement.

The plan should remain honest about uncertainty. It cannot guarantee that nothing will go wrong. It cannot force people to be reliable. It cannot prevent illness from changing. It cannot make every helper competent. What it can do is reduce confusion, expose gaps, support handoffs, clarify boundaries, and give the care system a better chance of adapting before pressure turns into crisis. That is enough to make it worth doing.

The most useful care plan overview is the one that someone can open on a hard day and understand the basics without needing a speech. Who is cared for. What matters. What happens daily. Who does what. What risks need watching. Who to contact. What boundaries protect the caregiver. Where more information lives. What to do if something changes.

It is not a monument to perfect organisation.

It is a working document for imperfect humans under real strain.

The question that should guide every line is simple: would this make care easier to understand if I were not standing there to explain it?

Planning for Predictable Changes

A care plan that never changes is not a sign of stability. It is usually a sign that reality is being ignored. Caregiving is shaped by movement: bodies tire, memory shifts, mobility changes, confidence rises and falls, family availability alters, and tasks that once seemed small begin to carry more consequence. The plan that worked in one season may become too thin for the next. Not because anyone failed, but because care is alive to circumstance.

Many caregivers resist planning for change because it feels like inviting bad news. To speak about increased supervision, mobility decline, confusion, reduced independence, or the caregiver's own future unavailability can feel disloyal, pessimistic, or frightening. The person receiving care may not want to discuss it. Relatives may prefer reassurance. The caregiver may secretly hope that if they keep managing well enough, the next difficult transition can be postponed. Silence then becomes a form of emotional shelter.

But silence is a poor shelter. Predictable changes do not become less likely because they are unnamed. They simply arrive into a system that has not prepared for them. A missed step becomes a panic. A change in memory becomes an argument. A sudden increase in appointments becomes a scheduling crisis. The caregiver's work deadline, illness, or family responsibility becomes a threat to the whole arrangement because no one has asked what happens when the main caregiver cannot keep stretching. The issue is not whether uncertainty can be removed. It cannot. The issue is whether uncertainty is allowed to become chaos.

Planning for predictable changes is not the same as assuming the worst. It is the practice of looking at the care situation with enough courage to ask, "What is likely to become harder, and what would we do if it did?" This question is not dramatic. It is practical. It allows the caregiver to prepare response paths before emotion is high and decisions are urgent. A plan made in calm conditions will almost always be kinder than a plan invented at the edge of crisis.

One of the most important areas to anticipate is increased supervision. A person who once needed occasional reminders may begin needing more regular checks. A person who was safe alone for long stretches may begin feeling anxious, confused, or physically less steady. A person who could manage meals, medicines, or household tasks may start missing steps. This change can be subtle at first, and caregivers often compensate quietly. They call more often, visit more frequently, double-check tasks, and fill gaps without naming the shift. That quiet compensation can hide the fact that the care need has changed.

The danger is that supervision can expand invisibly until the caregiver is on duty in all but name. They are not living with the person receiving care, perhaps, but they are mentally monitoring them throughout the day. They wonder whether food has been eaten, whether the medicine was taken, whether the person is safe, whether a call should be made, whether a silence means rest or trouble. Once supervision becomes constant in the caregiver's mind, the care plan must be reviewed. A private state of vigilance is not a sustainable supervision system.

An adaptable plan asks what signs would mean more supervision is needed. Repeated missed medication. Regular confusion about time or place. Meals left uneaten. Increased distress when alone. Unsafe use of appliances. Frequent calls that suggest anxiety or disorientation. Mobility incidents or near misses. These signs should not be treated as accusations against the person receiving care. They are signals that the level of support may no longer match the level of need.

A simple "if this, then that" response can reduce panic. If missed medication happens more than once, then the medication routine is reviewed and another person or system becomes involved. If evening distress becomes frequent, then the evening plan is changed rather than handled as a fresh emotional emergency every night. If the person is no longer safe for long periods alone, then supervision options are discussed before the next incident forces the conversation. The language is plain because the purpose is clarity, not drama.

Mobility changes also need early planning. A person may begin moving more slowly, avoiding stairs, struggling to get in and out of chairs, losing confidence outdoors, or becoming unsteady during ordinary routines. Families often adapt informally at first. Someone offers an arm. Furniture is moved. Appointments are scheduled with more travel time. The caregiver gives more physical help than before. These adjustments may be appropriate, but they should not remain invisible. Increased physical support changes the risk and the workload.

The caregiver should be honest about what physical help they can safely provide. Love does not protect a person's back, balance, sleep, or reaction time. A caregiver who begins lifting, steadying, guiding, or rushing to prevent falls may be taking on more physical responsibility than the plan recognises. If mobility is changing, the question is not merely, "Can we manage?" The question is, "Can this be managed safely and repeatedly by the people currently involved?"

Again, an adaptable plan uses thresholds. If stairs become difficult, then the home routine or room use is reviewed. If getting to appointments becomes physically stressful, then transport support is reconsidered. If the caregiver is providing physical help that feels unsafe, then more suitable support must be discussed. If the person refuses a mobility aid, then the consequences and alternatives need calm attention rather than repeated arguments in the moment. Planning turns a frightening change into a sequence of decisions.

Cognitive shifts require particular tenderness because they touch identity, pride, independence, and fear. Forgetfulness, repeated questions, confusion about appointments, difficulty following instructions, misplaced items, poor judgement, or increased suspicion can unsettle everyone involved. The person receiving care may feel embarrassed or defensive. The caregiver may feel grief, irritation, worry, or denial. Relatives may minimise because they do not see the pattern every day. Without a plan, cognitive change becomes a source of conflict: "You already asked me that," "You said you would remember," "You are not listening," "You are treating me like a child."

A better approach is to reduce reliance on memory before memory becomes the battleground. Written cues, visible routines, shared calendars, simplified choices, repeated scripts, and clearer handoffs can protect dignity by lowering the number of moments where the person is exposed to failure. The aim is not to label or diminish them. The aim is to make the environment more supportive as needs change. When cognitive shifts are anticipated, the caregiver can respond with design rather than exasperation.

An "if this, then that" plan might say: if appointment details are forgotten repeatedly, then the calendar becomes visible and one person is responsible for reminders. If repeated questions increase anxiety for both people, then key information is written in a familiar place. If financial or administrative confusion appears, then paperwork support is increased. If safety judgement becomes unreliable, then the level of supervision is reviewed. These responses do not settle every emotional difficulty, but they prevent the caregiver from treating each incident as an isolated frustration.

Caregiver availability is another predictable change that families often avoid discussing. The main caregiver may become ill, face heavier work responsibilities, need surgery, have children who require more attention, move house, experience burnout, or simply reach a point where the current level of availability can no longer continue. Yet many care arrangements behave as though the caregiver's capacity is fixed. It is not. A plan that depends on one person remaining constantly available is not adaptable. It is brittle.

The caregiver should name availability changes before they become emergencies. "From next month, I cannot do weekday transport." "I will be unavailable during these work hours." "I need someone else to cover evenings after difficult appointments." "If I am ill, this is who should be contacted." These statements may feel uncomfortable, but they are kinder than sudden collapse. The caregiver's life is not an unpredictable inconvenience to the care plan. It is part of the reality the plan must include.

Planning for caregiver unavailability should include backups. Who can step in for urgent tasks? Who knows the routine? Who has essential contact information? Who can provide transport? Who can make a call, check supplies, or sit with the person receiving care? If the answer is always the main caregiver, the plan is exposing everyone to risk. Backup planning is not selfish. It is responsible. It acknowledges that no care system should require one person to be permanently capable.

Some predictable changes involve family dynamics rather than health. A helper may become unreliable. A sibling may promise more than they deliver. A relative may begin interfering with routines. A paid or informal support arrangement may no longer fit. A previously calm communication pattern may become crowded with opinions. These changes also deserve planning because they affect the emotional safety and practical stability of care. If a helper repeatedly cancels, then their role must be reviewed. If family messages become disruptive, then communication moves to a set window. If advice arrives without responsibility, then requests become more specific.

The key is to treat repeated patterns as decision signals. A single failure may need patience. A repeated failure needs redesign. A difficult day may require flexibility. A recurring difficulty requires a plan. A one-off emotional reaction may be absorbed. A regular pattern of distress, risk, or overload must not be normalised. Adaptable care depends on the caregiver's willingness to see repetition as evidence.

Planning should be specific enough to guide action, but not so elaborate that no one uses it. "If mobility worsens, we will reassess" is too vague. "If getting to appointments becomes unsafe or requires physical support I cannot provide, transport and support arrangements will be reviewed before the next appointment" is clearer. "If memory gets worse, we will help more" is kind but weak. "If appointments are forgotten or medicines are missed repeatedly, reminders and responsibility will move from memory to a written and shared system" gives direction. The plan does not have to answer every future question. It needs to reduce the panic of not knowing where to begin.

The person receiving care should be involved where possible and appropriate. Predictable changes touch their autonomy, privacy, and dignity. They may have preferences about who helps, what support feels acceptable, what routines feel intrusive, and what they fear most. Those preferences should be heard. However, involvement does not mean every difficult reality can be avoided. If safety or caregiver viability is at stake, the plan must hold more than preference. A humane plan balances dignity with reality.

Relatives may need to hear that planning is not criticism. Discussing mobility support is not saying the person is helpless. Discussing memory support is not humiliating them. Discussing caregiver backup is not threatening abandonment. Discussing increased supervision is not an act of pessimism. The language should remain calm and practical: "This may never happen soon, but if it does, we need a response." Or: "We are not deciding everything now. We are reducing panic later." This tone helps keep the conversation from becoming a referendum on fear.

The caregiver should beware of promises that leave no room for adaptation. "I will always manage this myself." "We will never need outside help." "Nothing will change." "I will always be available." Such promises may be made from love, fear, guilt, or pressure. They may comfort people briefly, but they can become traps when circumstances shift. A wiser promise is more truthful: "I will do what I can to keep care safe and humane, and we will review the plan as needs change." This kind of promise does not abandon commitment. It protects it from becoming impossible.

Anticipating change also reduces resentment. When changes are not planned, the caregiver often absorbs them first. More calls. More reminders. More visits. More emotional labour. More physical help. More paperwork. More worry. Because no formal decision was made, no one else sees the expansion. The caregiver may then resent the person receiving care, when the deeper issue is that the care plan failed to update. Planning makes change visible before it becomes private burden.

There is an emotional skill in saying, "This is a threshold." A threshold is a point at which the old arrangement must be reviewed.

It is not a punishment. It is not a threat. It is a marker. If the person cannot manage nights safely, that is a threshold. If the caregiver cannot sleep because of repeated calls, that is a threshold. If medication cannot be managed reliably through reminders, that is a threshold. If transport requires unsafe physical support, that is a threshold. Naming thresholds helps everyone understand that change is not based on mood; it is based on signals.

A threshold should lead to a review, not necessarily an immediate drastic decision. This distinction can reduce fear. A caregiver might say, "If this happens again, we need to review the level of support." That does not mean a final answer has already been chosen. It means the signal will not be ignored. Review creates space for judgement. Denial creates emergencies.

Planning for predictable changes should be written into the care plan overview. Not in pages of anxious speculation, but as a few clear response paths. If supervision needs increase, who is involved in deciding the next step? If mobility changes, what support is considered? If cognitive concerns become more frequent, how will information and safety be managed? If the caregiver becomes unavailable, who is contacted and what tasks must be covered? These statements turn future fear into practical readiness.

The plan should also say when it will be reviewed. Predictable changes are easier to manage when there is already a rhythm for looking at what has shifted. Without review, the caregiver may wait until something feels bad enough to force attention. With review, the question becomes ordinary: what has changed, what no longer fits, and what needs adjusting? This reduces guilt because change is treated as maintenance, not failure.

Planning does not remove grief. It may even bring grief closer because it asks everyone to admit that things may become harder. But grief faced early can be gentler than grief faced during crisis. When families avoid predictable changes, they often meet them later with fear, blame, and rushed decisions. When they prepare, they may still feel sadness, but they have more room to choose carefully.

The caregiver should not confuse calm planning with emotional distance. It is possible to speak practically because the matter is tender, not because it is cold. In fact, practical planning can be one of the most compassionate responses to vulnerability. It says, "Your needs matter enough that we should not wait until everyone is panicking." It says, "My limits matter enough that care should not depend on my collapse." It says, "This relationship matters enough to protect it from preventable crisis."

Predictable changes will not arrive exactly as imagined. That is fine. The point is not to script the future. The point is to build muscles of adaptation. When the care system is used to asking "if this, then that", it becomes less shocked by change. It can adjust sooner. It can share decisions more clearly. It can keep the caregiver from becoming the automatic answer to every new pressure.

The question is not whether care will change.

It will.

The question is whether the plan will change early enough to preserve safety, dignity, and the caregiver's capacity before the old arrangement breaks under the weight of a new reality.

Reviewing and Resetting Without Guilt

A care plan is not a promise that nothing will change. It is a working agreement with reality, and reality keeps moving. Needs shift. Energy changes. Helpers become more or less available. The person receiving care may become more anxious, more physically limited, more forgetful, more resistant, or more dependent on routines that used to be optional. The caregiver may become more tired, less available, more aware of their limits, or simply less able to keep carrying what once seemed manageable.

This is why review is not failure. It is maintenance. A plan that needs adjusting has not been proved worthless; it has proved that it is being used in real life. The guilt often begins because caregivers treat every change as evidence that they did not plan well enough, love enough, prepare enough, or endure enough. They think, "We already discussed this," or "I should be able to keep going," or "Changing the arrangement will upset everyone." But a plan that cannot be reviewed becomes a trap. It stops serving care and starts serving the comfort of not having another difficult conversation.

Guilt thrives when review is delayed. The longer the caregiver waits, the more the evidence piles up: missed tasks, strained conversations, poor sleep, emotional distance, resentment, frantic errands, repeated warnings from the body. By the time the plan is finally questioned, the caregiver may feel as though they are causing a crisis by naming it. In truth, the crisis has often been building quietly for some time. Review does not create the problem. It brings the problem into the light while there is still a chance to respond with thought rather than panic.

A regular reset changes the emotional meaning of adjustment. Instead of waiting until someone is exhausted enough to demand change, the care arrangement has an ordinary rhythm for asking what still fits and what does not. That rhythm removes some of the drama. It allows the caregiver to say, "This needs reviewing," without sounding as though everything is collapsing. It allows relatives to hear concerns before they arrive as anger. It allows the person receiving care, where appropriate, to experience change as part of ongoing support rather than sudden withdrawal.

The reset should begin with what is working. This is not sentimental. It prevents the review from becoming only a list of failures. What routine is reducing stress? Which helper is reliable? What boundary has held? What task has become easier? What part of the week feels calmer than before? Caregivers often overlook what is working because the unfinished and difficult parts shout louder. Naming what works protects useful structures from being accidentally discarded during frustration. It also reminds everyone that progress may be modest and still real.

Then comes the harder question: what is breaking? Not what is mildly imperfect, not what someone dislikes, but what is repeatedly causing strain, risk, confusion, conflict, or depletion. Perhaps evening calls are stretching again. Perhaps transport has quietly returned to the main caregiver. Perhaps medication reminders are no longer enough. Perhaps paperwork is piling up. Perhaps a helper is unreliable. Perhaps the caregiver's recovery time is being treated as optional. A reset should be honest enough to name the pattern, not merely the most recent incident.

The most useful reset questions are plain. What keeps returning as a problem? What is taking more energy than expected? Which task has no clear owner? Which boundary is being tested? What has changed in the person receiving care? What has changed in the caregiver's capacity? What support has become too thin? What needs to stop, move, shrink, or be shared? These questions move the conversation away from blame and towards design. They ask how the system is functioning, not who is morally superior.

A reset also needs to identify what must be renegotiated. Some problems do not need a new emotional discussion; they need a new agreement. If a sibling promised to visit but rarely does, the arrangement needs reality, not hope. If the caregiver said they could manage appointments but now cannot, the role needs to change. If the person receiving care needs more supervision, the old routine must be updated. If a boundary is being crossed, the next consequence or clarification must be stated. Renegotiation is the moment where review becomes action.

This is where guilt often returns with force. The caregiver may worry that changing a role means letting someone down. They may feel that reducing availability is abandonment. They may feel ashamed that they need more help or that a routine no longer works. But guilt is not the measure of whether a reset is necessary. The better measure is fit. Does the current arrangement still fit the need, the risks, the available support, and the caregiver's real capacity? If not, the plan needs adjustment whether or not guilt approves.

A reset should not be used to punish people. It should not become a courtroom where every failure is read aloud with bitterness. That may be tempting, especially when the caregiver has felt unseen for a long time. But the purpose of review is to make care more workable, not to build a case for resentment. The tone can be firm without becoming cruel. "This task is not being completed reliably" is more useful than "You never do what you say." "I cannot keep covering transport at short notice" is clearer than "Everyone takes advantage of me." Precision protects the conversation from becoming a family trial.

At the same time, avoiding blame does not mean avoiding truth. Some people are unreliable. Some tasks have drifted back to the caregiver. Some boundaries have been ignored. Some needs have increased. Some arrangements are no longer safe. A reset that protects everyone's feelings at the expense of accuracy will not change much. The aim is not softness for its own sake. The aim is truthful practicality. Care cannot be made humane through denial.

The reset should include the caregiver's condition as part of the care data. This is essential. Many reviews focus only on the person receiving care: their appointments, meals, medicines, moods, mobility, and risks. But the caregiver's sleep, health, emotional steadiness, work, family life, and recovery are also part of the system. If the caregiver is becoming irritable, numb, forgetful, resentful, or constantly tired, that is not a private inconvenience. It is information about whether the care arrangement is sustainable.

A useful reset statement might be, "The person receiving care is safer with the current routine, but I am not recovering enough after visits." Or, "The appointment system is working, but transport depends too much on me." Or, "The daily check-ins help, but evening contact is becoming unmanageable." These statements are balanced. They do not deny what is working. They do not exaggerate what is wrong. They identify where the plan needs refinement.

Monthly resets can be especially helpful because they make review ordinary. A monthly rhythm is long enough for patterns to appear and short enough to prevent problems from hiding for too long. The exact timing matters less than the regularity. It may be a conversation, a written update, a private review followed by requests, or a brief meeting with involved helpers. The point is that care is not allowed to drift indefinitely on assumptions that may no longer be true.

The reset does not need to be long. In fact, if it becomes too elaborate, it may be avoided. A short review can ask what is working, what is breaking, what has changed, what needs reassignment, what boundaries need reinforcement, and what recovery must be protected. The caregiver should leave with fewer open loops, not more. A reset that produces a long list of worries without decisions has become another burden. Its purpose is clarity.

Documentation helps. After a reset, the agreed changes should be written down. Who is taking which task? What routine has changed? What boundary is being reinforced? What will be reviewed next time? What remains unresolved? Writing prevents the conversation from dissolving into memory and mood. It also protects the caregiver from becoming the sole keeper of the new plan. If the reset is real, it must exist somewhere outside the caregiver's head.

There will be times when a reset reveals that small adjustments are not enough. The caregiver may notice that the same risks keep returning despite routines. The person receiving care may need more help than the current network can provide. The caregiver may be too depleted for another round of minor changes. In that case, the reset has done its job. It has shown that the issue is not poor organisation, but a mismatch between need and support. That mismatch may require escalation, professional input, paid help where possible, respite, or a more serious family conversation.

This is where courage is needed. Caregivers sometimes use small resets to avoid larger truths. They rearrange the calendar, rewrite the list, adjust the call time, and add another reminder, while the fundamental problem remains untouched. If the care need has outgrown the current arrangement, no amount of neat planning will make the old structure humane. Reviewing without guilt means being willing to see when the next step must be bigger than another small fix.

A reset should also allow tasks to be removed, not only added or reassigned. Care plans often expand but rarely contract. Every concern becomes another check. Every past problem becomes another precaution. Every relative's anxiety becomes another message. Over time, the plan can become cluttered with tasks that no longer serve care well. Reviewing should ask what can stop, what can be simplified, what can be batched, and what can be allowed to be good enough. Sustainable care is not built by adding endlessly. It is built by choosing wisely.

The caregiver must be especially alert to guilt around stopping. Stopping a task can feel harsher than starting one, even when the task is no longer useful. The caregiver may feel that if they stop doing something, they are withdrawing love. But not every task is care. Some tasks are habit. Some are anxiety. Some are attempts to prevent other people's judgement. Some are old promises that no longer fit. A reset gives the caregiver permission to ask whether an action still serves safety, dignity, connection, or stability. If it does not, it may need to end.

Reviewing also protects relationships because it prevents resentment from becoming the only messenger. When care arrangements are not reviewed, the caregiver may eventually communicate through anger, coldness, avoidance, or sudden refusal. Regular resets give the relationship a calmer path. They make it possible to say, "This is not working," before the sentence becomes, "I cannot stand this anymore." They create opportunities for repair, clarification, and redistribution before bitterness hardens.

The person receiving care may not always welcome resets. They may experience them as unsettling, especially if changes touch independence, routines, or access to the caregiver. Their feelings should be handled with respect. But the caregiver should not confuse discomfort with harm. Some discomfort belongs to adjustment. If a plan needs to change in order to remain safe and humane, the aim is to make the change as dignified as possible, not to avoid change altogether.

Relatives may also resist review, particularly if the current arrangement benefits them. A reset can make invisible labour visible. It can reveal that one person is doing far more than others. It can turn vague sympathy into specific requests. It can expose gaps that people preferred not to see. The caregiver should expect some defensiveness and keep returning to the practical centre: what is working, what is breaking, what must change, and who owns the next step.

Review without guilt also requires the caregiver to release the fantasy of a final settled plan. Caregiving is not a puzzle solved once. It is a living arrangement with human beings inside it. Bodies change. Emotions change. Families change. Capacity changes. A plan that adapts is not weaker than a plan that stays fixed. It is stronger because it can respond before strain becomes crisis.

This does not mean living in constant review. The caregiver should not be endlessly analysing every small variation. That would be exhausting. The purpose of a regular reset is partly to *stop* constant mental review. When there is a known time to look at the plan, the caregiver can place non-urgent concerns there instead of carrying them all day. The reset becomes a container for decision-making.

A good reset leaves behind three things: clearer reality, clearer responsibility, and clearer next action. Clearer reality means naming what is actually happening, not what everyone hoped would happen. Clearer responsibility means knowing who owns what, including what does not belong to the main caregiver. Clearer next action means the review produces movement, however modest. Without those, review becomes conversation without consequence.

The caregiver should include a small act of self-recognition in the reset. What have I carried this month? What did I handle well? What cost me more than I expected? What do I need to protect next month? This is not indulgence. It counters the invisibility that so often fuels resentment. Caregivers need evidence that their work exists, even if no one else names it fully. Self-recognition is not applause. It is accuracy.

A reset can also mark recovery. After reviewing difficult realities, the caregiver may need a pause, a walk, a quiet evening, or a conversation with someone safe. Planning can stir grief, anger, fear, and guilt. The act of looking honestly at care is emotional work. If the caregiver moves straight from review into another task, they may carry that emotional charge forward. A care plan that includes review should also include recovery from review.

There will be months when the reset feels discouraging. The same problems may return. Helpers may disappoint. The person receiving care may resist change. The caregiver may feel tired of renegotiating. This does not mean the practice is useless. Repeated review may reveal that the current support network cannot carry the situation. That knowledge is painful but important. A reset is not only for small improvements. It is also for recognising when the level of help must change.

The caregiver should not interpret the need for repeated adjustment as proof that they are failing. A garden is not failing because it needs tending again. A home is not failing because repairs recur. A body is not failing because it needs rest repeatedly. Care is the same. Maintenance is not an interruption of caregiving. Maintenance is caregiving. It keeps the arrangement from decaying under the pressure of real life.

The language of reset matters because it shapes emotion. "We failed" creates shame. "This no longer fits" creates room for action. "I cannot cope" may be true in a moment of distress, but "The current plan is exceeding my capacity" is more useful. "They are getting worse" may be frightening, while "The level of need has changed" is clearer. Good language does not soften reality into denial. It gives reality a shape that can be worked with.

As the final rhythm of sustainable care, review asks the caregiver to replace heroic endurance with honest adjustment. Heroic endurance may be admired, but admiration does not refill a person. It does not update medication routines, redistribute transport, protect sleep, repair conflict, or make helpers reliable. Honest adjustment is less glamorous. It is also more humane. It says care is allowed to change before the caregiver breaks.

The long-term aim is not to create a care plan that never needs attention. It is to create a rhythm in which attention is regular enough that crisis is not the only force that produces change. The caregiver does not have to wait for collapse, resentment, or a frightening incident before asking whether the plan still works. They can review because reviewing is what responsible systems do.

The question at each reset is simple and demanding: what are we pretending still works, and what would become more humane if we told the truth now?

About the Author

Kaia Solander writes for people who keep going even when they are running on fumes - the dependable ones who quietly hold families together. Her work focuses on the everyday mechanics of resilience: how boundaries become kinder when they are clear, how routines can reduce fear, and how asking for help can be designed so it actually helps. She is especially interested in the emotional knots caregivers face - guilt, resentment, and the feeling that any choice will hurt someone - and in turning those knots into practical decisions you can live with.

Kaia approaches caregiving as both love and logistics. She believes care should protect dignity on both sides: the person receiving support and the person giving it. That viewpoint is shaped by listening to caregivers describe the same dilemma in different settings - across kitchen tables, hospital corridors, and late-night phone calls where everything feels urgent. A recurring thread in her writing is the long tradition of mutual aid found in many communities, where neighbours once shared tasks as a matter of course, and where private struggle was softened by public responsibility. Kaia brings that spirit into modern life with tools that fit real schedules, imperfect families, and limited energy.

She lives by a simple principle: sustainable caregiving is not a personality trait. It is a set of choices and systems you can learn, practise, and revisit as life changes.